]

This bo
self s

1

Environmental Sustainability

With globalisation fast becoming an irreversible process, it is necessary to pay increased attention to the implications for environmental sustainability. Some commentators have uncritically assumed that globalisation would result in all-round prosperity, whereas the opposing view holds that in order to sustain growth and consumption, a certain threshold level of per capita income (PCI) should be attained – the so-called Environmental Kuznets Curve (EKC) argument. This argument implies that rapid economic growth in many developing countries should be environmentally unsustainable.

Environmental Sustainability addresses this dichotomy and articulates a notion of consumption sustainability that is both universal and pertains to the indefinite future. Additionally, it emphasises the importance of addressing a broad spectrum of sources of environmental degradation and relates this measure to an index of economic achievement more complete than PCI. The EKC conclusion is examined and is demonstrated to be untenable, it is argued that there is scope to permit developing countries to target high rates of economic growth and that lowering rich countries' consumption would be consistent with environmental sustainability.

Jha and Murthy critique the environmental sustainability index (ESI), which has been proposed as a measure of the overall state of the environment, and advance an alternative methodology for computing environmental sustainability. The authors empirically substantiate the proposition that a certain type of development in the presently high-income countries is primarily responsible for global environmental degradation. Several policy conclusions for global environmental management are also advanced.

Raghbendra Jha is Rajiv Gandhi Chair Professor and Executive Director, Australia South Research Centre, Division of Economics at the Australian National University.

K.V. Bhanu Murthy is Professor, Department of Commerce, Delhi School of Economics, University of Delhi.

Routledge Explorations in Environmental Economics
Edited by Nick Hanley
University of Glasgow

Environmental Sustainability

A consumption approach

**Raghbendra Jha and
K.V. Bhanu Murthy**

Routledge
Taylor & Francis Group

LONDON AND NEW YORK

Dedicated to Saibaba

Contents

Figures

Tables

Preface

With globalisation becoming an irreversible process, our prime concern can no longer be limited to whether peoples and regions of the world would develop concurrently. It must include very vital concerns about the implications of such a 'type of development' for environmental sustainability, interpreted as a universal phenomenon and one that applies to the very long run. This definition of sustainability has been insufficiently articulated in the literature.

A principal and related concern is whether global environmental sustainability, so defined, is consistent with rising consumption levels in the developing countries. The skeptics of the process of globalisation dismiss the possibility and scope for global economic development through uncontrolled globalisation. Global structural inequalities are seen as a deterrent to such development, while the institutions of global management are seen, by them, as iniquitous tools.

Some adherents of the process of globalisation uncritically assume that such globalisation would result in unmitigated growth, development and all-round prosperity. Thus, a certain inevitability is assumed in the process of development. They believe that developed economies have already laid out a path of development for developing countries to emulate. Global development hence is only a question of time. However, the more environmentally nuanced argument is that, in order to ensure environmental sustainability of this seemingly endless vista of economic growth and consumption, one has to cross a certain threshold level of income – the so-called Environmental Kuznets Curve (EKC) argument. Once this threshold level of income is crossed every country would become environmentally sustainable since the income elasticity of demand for the environment is (assumed to be) greater than 1. If this logic were to be accepted then developing countries would find themselves in the predicament that their further rapid economic growth would be environmentally unsustainable. Indeed some authors have argued that developing countries should eschew strategies for rapid economic growth. Sometimes this argument is dressed up in terms of developing countries using better technology or being more restrained in their use of fossil fuels, but the basic advice remains that they should forego much needed growth and even more necessary consumption, even in the face of extreme poverty and poor consumption levels, for the sake of global environmental sustainability. If this position is correct then prospects for developing countries indeed appear grim.

Both approaches would then deny developing countries the possibility of raising living standards and lowering poverty through sustained high economic growth. The former approach denies the possibility of global economic development and virtually condemns developing countries to their present state. The EKC approach links environmental sustainability to restraint in consumption (and hence economic growth) from the developing countries although these countries are already stressed with low per capita incomes (PCIs) and high levels of poverty. Ironically, the presently developed countries did not face any environmental restrictions on their economic growth plans during their long phase of sustained economic growth.

Clearly, there is a need to review these approaches towards environmental sustainability and global economic development and, if possible, to advance a strategy that will ensure global environmental sustainability even as it permits developing countries to grow rapidly and reduce their high levels of poverty. In this book we attempt to develop such an approach.

The building blocks of our analysis are as follows: Chapter 1 entitled 'Global disparity and environmental sustainability' provides some evidence on critical inequalities across the world in resource endowments and environmental outcomes. Chapter 2 entitled 'Consumption and sustainable development: an overview' develops the argument behind viewing consumption as the prime vehicle of environmental degradation. This is viewed as an externality and this chapter reviews some reasons why such externalities are not fully internalised. Chapter 3 discusses methodological issues relating to the links between environmental degradation and economic development, whereas Chapter 4 entitled 'Global environmental degradation: concept and methodology of measurement' surveys the literature on the links between the twin issues of environmental degradation and economic development. Chapter 5 entitled 'Sustainability: behaviour, property rights and economic growth' articulates the notion of environmental sustainability put forward in this book. Environmental sustainability is viewed as pertaining to the indefinite long run and being universal. Chapter 6 entitled 'An inverse Global Environmental Kuznets Curve' articulates and quantifies the relation between global environmental degradation, viewed broadly, and a composite index of human development. We thus address the issue of the EKC and emphasise the role of the level of environmental degradation and its link with an index of economic achievement more complete than PCI. We discover that the EKC conclusion is untenable and there is indeed scope to permit developing countries to target high rates of economic growth. Indeed, we find that lowering rich countries' consumption is consistent with environmental sustainability. Chapter 7 is entitled 'A critique of the environmental sustainability index'. This index has been developed by collaboration of the World Economic Forum, Geneva, Center for International Earth Science Information Network, Columbia University, and Yale Center for Environmental Law and Policy, New Haven and is a measure of the overall progress towards environmental sustainability developed for 142 countries. This chapter points out that this index is deeply flawed. We argue that the basic design of the ESI has conceptual problems in its visualisation of environmental degradation and sustainability. The choice of variables as well as the statistical methodology of compiling the index are also found to be wanting. We then propose an alternative methodology for computing environmental sustainability. In Chapter 8 entitled 'A consumption-based human development index and the Global Environmental Kuznets Curve' we identify 'excessive' consumption and the percolation of such consumption patterns as an important contributor to global environmental degradation (GED). We thus shift the focus in the growth–environment debate towards consumption as a part of a complete model that explains the relationship between development and GED. Chapter 9 entitled 'Political economy of global environmental governance' considers the contours of a meaningful response to environmental degradation that can be taken at the global level, in particular the role of an organisation such as the World Environmental Organization. Chapter 10 entitled 'Issues in global environmental management' concerns itself with the basic principles, the functions and the priorities of global environmental management. Chapter 11 offers a summary and some concluding remarks.

In writing this book we have run up a long list of debts of gratitude. The work on this book was funded in part by a grant from the John D. and Catherine T. MacArthur Foundation, Chicago. We are grateful to the Foundation for supporting this work. For their intellectual support and comments on various chapters of the book we are grateful to J. Whalley and D. Rukmini. We are also grateful to the editors and anonymous referees of the *Journal of Comparative Economics* for their comments on Chapter 6, which was originally published in this journal and to Elsevier Science for permission to reprint the article in this book. Chapter 5 was published in the *Proceedings of the World Congress on Managing and Measuring Sustainable Development*, held in August 2000 in Ontario, Canada. We are grateful to Germain Dufour for his permission to reprint this chapter in this volume. Some of this work was presented in two conferences (GTAP Conference, Washington, DC, 2004; and Frontiers 2 Conference: European Applications in Ecological Economics at Tenerife, Canary Islands, Spain, February 2003) and at seminars at The Australian National University and The University of Warwick. We are grateful to the participants of these conferences and seminars for their comments and encouragement. Of course, all organisations and individuals mentioned earlier are absolved of the responsibility for the opinions expressed in this volume as well as for any errors that may have crept in.

The editorial staff at Routledge has worked with exemplary speed and affability on this manuscript. In particular, we are grateful to Robert Langham and Taiba Batool for overseeing the work of publication of the book. We are also grateful to an anonymous referee of Routledge for incisive comments on the book proposal as well as to Gerald Epstein of University of Massachusetts for his comments and encouragement. At Australia South Asia Research Centre in the ANU Stephanie Hancock provided critical editorial assistance. To all these people and organisations we express our sincere gratitude for their unflinching support and encouragement through, sometimes, trying times. Our families have borne the burden of this book at least as much as us not just because much of our time spent in writing this book rightfully belonged to them. We thank them for it – although we realise that it would be presumptuous to do so.

Raghbendra Jha,   K.V. Bhanu Murthy,
Canberra, Australia   New Delhi, India
June 2005   June 2005

1 Global disparity and environmental sustainability

Introduction

The global economy has embarked on a new phase of growth and development in the new millennium. The current phase of globalisation has had recent beginnings but already signs of its impact have become visible. These are apparent from the trends in income distribution, trade, environmental pollution, and so on. But what is most noticeable about these trends, particularly in relation to environmental degradation, is the extreme disparity on a global scale. We shall discuss these trends in disparity shortly and relate them to the crux of the matter, that is, environmental sustainability.

In a state of such upheaval although all intellectual inquiry has great responsibility, environmental studies have a particularly important onus to understand and anticipate global challenges rather than merely reacting to them. Any serious attempt to study the process of globalisation and its implications for environmental sustainability has to necessarily follow a truly global approach. While such a position might sound tautological, there is grave paradigmatic problem with this fundamental position. A truly global approach has three dimensions to it. It should be global in the sense of including all factors responsible for global environmental degradation (GED). Second, it must transcend space to include all countries of the world. Finally, it should also be truly global in the sense of being concerned with the global interests from the point of view of global environmental management and not just be based on certain sectional interests. To be global in all senses of the term, the first and foremost requirement is to be able to understand the global environmental issues and concerns, in the spirit in which it has been outlined above.

In this context, the paradigmatic problem, referred above, is rather complex. One approach to environmental sustainability decries any method that involves valuation and value judgement in the realm of environmental studies. Further, this approach eschews aggregation across factors of environmental degradation and across countries.[1] An alternative approach is based on valuation, value judgement and measurement, but deems the tools of analysis to be inadequate for global studies. Hitherto, the approach has been to study questions of environmental sustainability from the point of view of a region within a country, a country or a group of countries that are similar. More often than not studies have been centred on OECD countries. More often than not this approach equates global environmental concerns with transboundary pollution and ignores other factors such as, water consumption, paper consumption and so on. As a result extant studies have been based on single pollutants, such as, carbon dioxide (CO_2) or sulfur dioxide (SO_2). With regards to aggregation, this approach considers methods such as forming composite indices to be the preserve of a few.[2]

Even a casual look at the trends, which we briefly discuss below, would make it clear that it is urgent to overcome such polemics and evolve an overall approach to environmental sustainability. Our 'Consumption Approach to Environmental Sustainability' is one such attempt to evolve such a global approach that is all-inclusive in terms of factors as well as countries of the world.

Our study is based on cross-sectional data. The reasons we advance in support of this are as follows. First, it is difficult to get sufficiently long-term data so as to be able to appreciate changes in the global economy. Second, the data sources need to be consistent. These two conditions are not satisfied in practice so, in this study, we have mostly used cross-sectional data from UNDP's Human Development Report.[3] Third, whereas consistent long-term data is available for different groups of countries, like the OECD, such a data source may result in one-sided results since the countries involved are all in a similar phase of development and the necessary global flavour would be lacking. Further, even if such data were available these may conceal global disparities.[4] We propose to make it apparent that at the hub of these problems lies global disparity and conflict of interest. For any attempt at global environmental management (GEM) to succeed *ab initio* it has to reconcile with this given *datum*. Our intention is not to say that any such attempt at global management is not welcome. Nor is it to say that it would be doomed to failure. On the other hand, we wish to emphasise the urgent need for such a thrust.[5]

Global trends in development and environment – the carbon sink

Several issues are pertinent to an understanding of global trends in environmental indicators; however, we wish to confine ourselves to some of the most pertinent issues. Many of the factors that affect the global environment are interconnected. Therefore, in the following analysis we shall study these interrelationships from the point of view of understanding the problems in GED and GEM.

In what follows we provide a basic analysis of global trends in three related aspects – forest cover, CO_2 emission and paper consumption. While the relationship between them may be amply clear to the aware reader, we would like to reiterate the relationship. Paper of any kind is made from wood pulp. Essentially the demand for paper arises from rich countries and is largely for fine quality paper:[6] the finer the paper the higher the grade of wood required and hence the more superior the tree that is to be felled. We may presume that the wood of such trees is much more expensive than ordinary wood and hence its role in nature is much greater. For instance, while local handmade paper is made from bamboo, high-quality paper is made from pinewood.[7] The choice that developing countries face is to earn by exporting such superior wood and augmenting growth and incomes domestically or preserving the forests and remaining poor. Needless to say this is apparently an individual choice being exercised by some poor countries but has a global implication for environmental sustainability. Pine trees have a great capacity to absorb CO_2 and act as a 'carbon sink' than bamboo trees. Such carbon sinks are the only insurance against global warming being caused by 'green-house gases (GHGs)', like CO_2, that destroy the ozone layer. By felling such forests these countries benefit themselves and by retaining forests the world benefits, at large, and they lose.

From a global point of view the question is: who owns the 'carbon sink'? Who is responsible for CO_2 emission and who really needs these forests? The global trends in CO_2 emission, paper consumption and forest cover may answer this question.

Table 1.1 shows the status of global forest cover in 1999. Since the data relates to Human Development Report we have also indicated the HDI[8] Ranks. It is

Table 1.1 Countries whose share is more than 1 per cent of global forest cover (1999)

Rank in global forest cover	Country	HDI rank	Percentage of forest cover	Forest area in '000 sq. km.	Percentage share in global forest cover
1	Russian Federation	55	50.41	8513.92	22.55
2	Brazil	69	62.97	5324.81	14.10
3	Canada	3	26.52	2445.71	6.47
4	United States	6	24.67	2259.93	5.98
5	China	87	17.04	1589.00	4.20
6	Australia	2	20.58	1580.80	4.18
7	Congo	126	59.64	1352.07	3.58
8	Indonesia	102	57.95	1049.86	2.78
9	Angola	146	55.95	697.56	1.84
10	India	115	21.56	641.13	1.69
11	Sudan	138	25.94	616.27	1.63
12	Mexico	51	28.92	552.05	1.46
13	Bolivia	104	48.94	530.68	1.40
14	Colombia	62	47.75	496.01	1.31
15	Venezuela	61	56.13	495.06	1.31
16	Tanzania	140	43.92	388.11	1.02

Summary Statistics	*Developed countries*	*Developing countries*
Weighted average of percentage forest cover	24.36	81.00
Simple average of percentage forest cover	23.92	43.89
Share of countries having more than 1% global forest cover	16.65	58.93
Percentage of countries (out of 162 countries)	1.85	8.02
Forest area in '000 sq. km.	6286.44	22,246.97

Source: Based on *Human Development Report* 1999 and 2000, UNDP, New York.

interesting to note that this index conceals the fact that high-ranking (highly developed) countries do not contribute much to green cover. So the index takes into account economic and social criteria but not environmental criteria. The top 48 countries, that is, 30 per cent of per cent of all countries possess only 23 per cent of the cover. Out of these three countries – USA, Canada and Australia, that is 1.85 per cent of the total number of countries – have 16.65 per cent and the rest of the 28 per cent have less than 13 per cent of the global cover. In the case of medium development countries (48 per cent of all countries) they have 67 per cent of the forest cover, in the world. The low development countries form 22 per cent of all countries and have only 10 per cent of the cover. But they are also not yet gainers from development and globalisation.

Sixteen countries possess significant forest cover. (We define any country that contributes more than one per cent to the total forest cover in the world as having 'significant cover'.) Of theses only three countries USA, Canada and Australia are developed countries. The rest 13 are all developing countries. The greatest single contributor is the Russian Federation, which has a 22.55 per cent share in global, forest cover. The smallest is Tanzania with around 1 per cent share. The three rich countries have an average forest cover (out of their total land area) of less than 24 per cent. The same proportion when calculated as a weighted average[9] goes up by a few points. On the other hand, the 13 developing countries have simple average cover (within their country) of about 44 per cent and as a weighted average their cover is 81 per cent! The share of these 13 developing countries in the global cover is almost 59 per cent! Hence, the major carbon sink is possessed by developing countries. Devoid of this cover the globe would be at the brink of disaster (Figure 1.1).

The forest cover in many of the developed countries has evolved out of reforestation efforts. This raises the question of the quality of forests. First, the new varieties of trees are often not suitable to the habitat.[10] Second, it has been established that tree plantations host about 90 per cent fewer species than the forests that preceded them. (Allen Hershkowitz, *Bronx Ecology*, 2002 p. 75), thus reducing biodiversity. Moreover, such monoculture makes the breed of the vegetation more susceptible to disease.

The counterparts of forest cover are paper consumption and CO_2 emission. Of the total paper consumed annually, in the world, in per capita terms, 86.75 per cent is consumed by 45 rich countries, which is just 25 per cent of all the countries in the world. On the other hand, 20 per cent of the world's countries or 35 poorest countries consume only 0.25 per cent of paper. Ninety-four developing countries amounting to 55 per cent of all countries consume the rest, that is, 13 per cent. The per capita paper consumption in developed countries is nearly 60 kilograms. In medium development countries it is around 4 kilograms and in the case of poor countries it is just 0.22 kilograms.

The maximum consumption could go up to 240 kilos in the rich countries! The modal consumption level in rich countries is 115 kilos. The mode in poor countries is 0.1 kilo. These trends are further laid out in Table 1.2 and Figure 1.2.

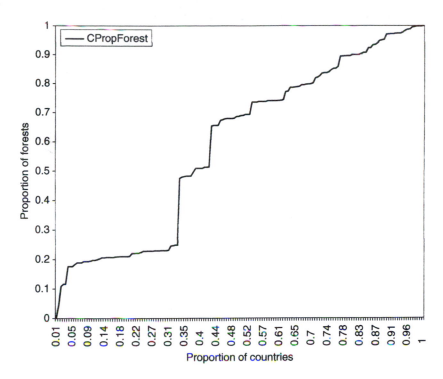

Figure 1.1 Global distribution of forest cover.

Source: Based on *Human Development Report* 1999 and 2000, UNDP, New York.

Table 1.2 Snapshot: paper and the environment

- Of the global wood harvest for 'industrial uses' (everything but fuel wood) 42% goes to paper production. (Abromovitz and Mattoon, *Worldwatch Paper: Paper Cuts*, p. 20, 1999)
- Of the 42% of the world's industrial wood harvest going to paper, almost two-thirds comes from wood harvested specifically for pulp, while the rest derives from mill residues such as wood scraps and sawdust. (Abromovitz and Mattoon 1999, *Worldwatch Paper: Paper Cuts*, p. 20)
- Global production in the pulp, paper and publishing sector is expected to increase by 77 per cent from 1995 to 2020. (OECD Environmental Outlook. Paris: OECD, 2001, p. 215)
- The pulp and paper industry is the single largest consumer of water used in industrial activities in OECD countries and is the third greatest industrial GHG emitter, after the chemical and steel industries (OECD *Environmental Outlook*, p. 218)
- Paper pulp exports from Latin America from forests converted into plantations and from the harvesting and conversion of tropical and subtropical forests are expected to grow 70% between 2000 and 2010. (Mark Payne, 'Latin America Aims High for the Next Century', Pulp and Paper International 1999)
- Most of the world's paper supply, about 71%, is not made from timber harvested at tree farms but from forest-harvested timber, from regions with ecologically valuable, biologically diverse habitat. (*Toward a Sustainable Paper Cycle: An Independent Study on the Sustainability of the Pulp and Paper Industry, 1996*)

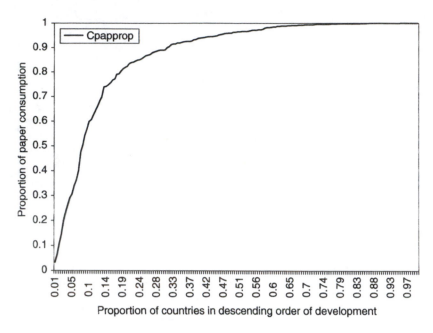

Figure 1.2 Global distribution of paper consumption.

Source: Based on *Human Development Report* 1999, UNDP, New York.

The third component of the environmental trinity we study is CO_2 emission. To study this aspect we consider three measures based on Human Development Report 1999:

1   Per capita CO_2 emission, in metric tons, per annum (Figure 1.3).
2   Share of global CO_2 emission, in percentage terms (Figure 1.4).
3   Frequency Distribution of Countries by their percentage contribution to global CO_2 (Figure 1.5).

The most popular argument in this regard is that since poor countries are populous they are the most significant sources of pollution. The data presented here goes a considerable way in exploding this myth.[11] The per capita measure takes into account the population factor. In per capita terms rich countries contribute 61.87 per cent and their overall share is 52.72. In per capita terms their contribution is about 20 per cent more. Just 45 rich countries are responsible for between half to two-thirds of the world's CO_2 emission. The contribution of 20 per cent of the poor countries is 2.43 in per capita terms and 0.65 in overall terms. Also, about the last 30 per cent of the countries contribute only 5 per cent by either count. Ninety-four developing countries contribute 36 per cent in per capita terms and 46 per cent in overall terms. Therefore, in per capita terms their

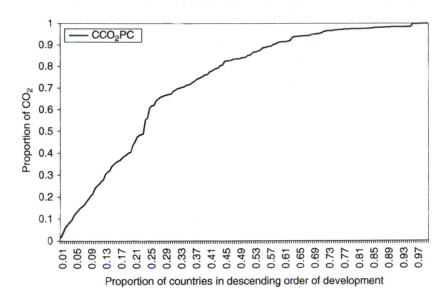

Figure 1.3 Global distribution of CO₂ per capita.

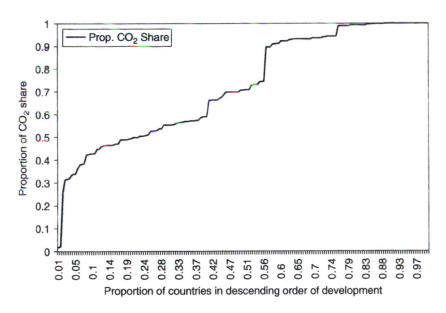

Figure 1.4 Global distribution of CO₂ share.

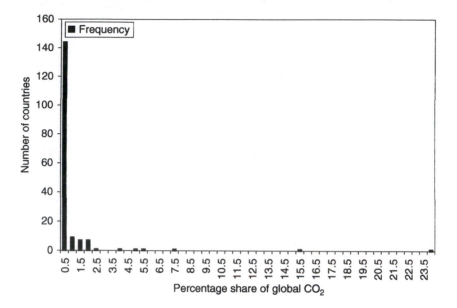

Figure 1.5 Frequency distribution of countries by their percentage contribution to global CO_2.

contribution is even less. On an average the per capita contribution of rich countries is over 11.87 metric tons while that of developing countries is 3.03 and poor countries is just 0.56. The maximum per capita CO_2 contribution from a rich country is 52.3 tons. Similarly, on an average the share of each rich country is more than 1 per cent, that of developing countries is less than half that magnitude and that of poor countries is less than 0.02 per cent. To further analyse these trends we look at the frequency distribution of all countries in terms of their contributions in Figure 1.5.

The frequency distribution is based on class intervals of 0.5 per cent contribution each. The range of contribution is from 0 to 23.38 (for USA). Out of 174 countries 144 contribute less than 0.5 per cent and 168 countries contribute less than 2.5 per cent, on an individual basis. The last 20 countries or the poorest countries as a class do not contribute anything to global CO_2 emission! Half the countries in the world contribute less than 0.05 per cent, individually. In other words the median of all countries' contributions is 0.05 and the average contribution of all countries is just 0.57. Finally, just six countries contribute about 61 per cent of all the CO_2 in the world!

Global trends in development and environment – the elixir of life

The single feature of our planet that distinguishes it from other planets is water – 'The Elixir of Life'. It is obvious that this unique resource of our planet is not distributed uniformly in the world. Table 1.3 gives details of the overall distribution of water. As has been stressed earlier, while understanding the core issues in global environmental sustainability it is important to understand the interconnection amongst factors. Three such factors can be identified – water, fertiliser and population. The relationship between them is as follows. Land is the next most important natural resource after water. The exploitation of land is essential for food, which in turn is essential for survival of the population. Such exploitation is justified if it is done at a sustainable rate, that is, at a rate that gives nature the time to recoup. Hence, there must be a balance between these three factors. If on the other hand, modern farming methods are used to accelerate land exploitation this will require the use of chemical fertilisers. These fertilisers require huge amounts of water. Therefore, there must be a consonance and a balance between the use of fertiliser and water, and the population.

Hence, the foremost question is: which countries possess this elixir? Latin America and Caribbean, Medium Income, South East Asia and the Pacific, Eastern Europe and the CIS and High Income, are all the groups of countries that possess the maximum water resources, in declining amounts. Latin America and the Caribbean region have, on a per capita basis, around 27,000 cubic meters of water, Medium Income countries have half as much, while South East Asia and the Pacific, Eastern Europe and the CIS countries have around 12,000 cubic meters. High-income countries have just 2000 cubic metres more than the average, which is around 7000, and OECD countries are almost at the average. The categories of countries that have below-average water resources are Least Developed Countries, Developing Countries in general, Sub-Saharan Africa, Low-Income

Table 1.3 Annual internal renewable water resources in 2000 (cubic meters per capita)

All developing countries	**6235**
Least developed countries	6976
Arab States	522
East Asia	2194
East Asia (excl. China)	2013
Latin America and Caribbean	27,328
South Asia	1361
South Asia (excluding India)	1660
South East Asia and the Pacific	12,478
Sub-Saharan Africa	6202
Eastern Europe and the CIS	12,470
OECD	**7928**
High human development	9374
Medium human development	6890
Low human development	5162
High income	9458
Medium income	14,360
Low income	3578
World	**7122**

Source: Based on *Human Development Report* 2000, UNDP, New York.

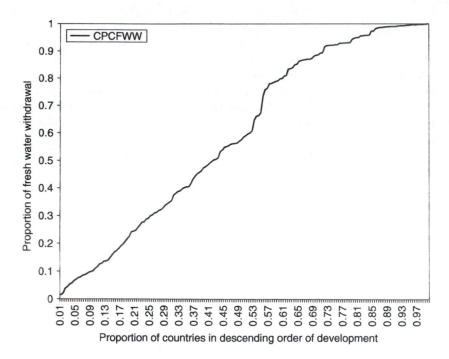

Figure 1.6 Global distribution of per capita fresh water withdrawal.

Source: Based on *Human Development Report* 1999, UNDP, New York.

Countries, South Asia and Arab States, in that order. While High-Income Countries have 30 per cent more than the world average, Developing countries have 20 per cent less than the same. Needless to say Arab States possess the least. Figure 1.6 shows the global distribution of water resources.

The water resources consumption patterns are as follows. The rich or high-development countries (25 per cent of all countries), 45 in number, consume 30 per cent of all water, on a per capita basis. The medium development countries (55 per cent of all countries) consume 64 per cent of the water. The low development countries (20 per cent of all) consume only 6 per cent. In terms of percentage of their fresh water resources high development countries draw 108 per cent, medium development countries draw 80 per cent and low development countries draw only 15 per cent. A more interesting feature is that the standard deviation of low development countries is the lowest amongst the three classes of countries. Thus, they are consistently drawing only a fifth of the world average level of drawls. This is despite the fact that their possession is barely 10 per cent less than the world average. This clearly points to sustainable use. While medium development countries have a possession that is almost equal to the world average they draw 20 per cent less than their endowment. Therefore, only high development countries are displaying over-consumption. This is in spite of having a lower population, which we now discuss.

These trends need to be contrasted with both the trends in population and fertiliser use. The population patterns are reflected in Figure 1.7 below and fertiliser consumption patterns in Figure 1.8. The top 30 per cent countries have only 18 per cent of the population. The developing countries (48 per cent) have 68.4 per cent of the population and the poor countries (22 per cent) have 23.6 per cent. The average population in each country was 36.18 million in 1999, while high development countries had a mean population of 22 million. The average for medium development countries was 51 million and that of low development countries was 19.5 million. The total populations of high, medium and low development countries were 1054 million, 3990 million and 680 million, respectively. If medium development countries were to consume more they would have a legitimate reason. But it is the high development countries that have a fourth of the population of medium development countries and still make heavy drawls of resources and indulge in over-consumption.

Fertiliser is essential for agriculture and food, which are, in turn, essential for the sustenance of the population. There is a justification for developing and poor countries to accelerate food production for feeding their ever-growing and malnourished populations. But the use of fertiliser accelerates the use of water. However, we find that developed countries, which have much lower population but consume much more fertiliser. These countries consume 72 per cent of the global fertiliser while they are just 30 per cent countries. Developing countries consume only 26 per cent although they are 48 per cent of all countries. The

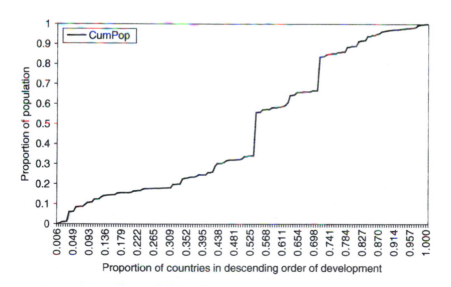

Figure 1.7 Distribution of global population.

Source: Based on *Human Development Report* 2000, UNDP, New York.

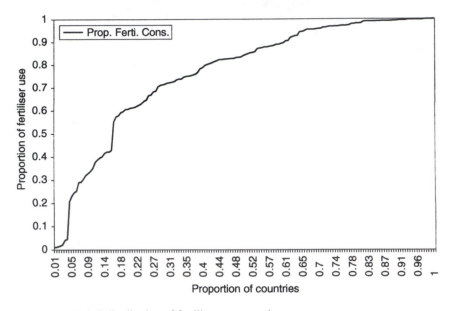

Figure 1.8 Global distribution of fertiliser consumption.

Source: Based on *Human Development Report* 2000, UNDP, New York.

low development countries are 22 per cent of all countries but consume only 2 per cent although their state of poverty is such that they need to augment their domestic food supplies urgently.

Development patterns and the environment

So far we have been studying various factors that relate to the environment and have examined their interrelationship. The picture that emerges is that developed countries have the lowest population but, even on a per capita basis, have displayed highly unsustainable consumption levels. This has resulted in gross global environmental degradation. The complex web of factors that are responsible for this state cannot be seen in isolation of each other. Our analysis above has shown that a comparative study of these patterns of consumption across levels of development and classes of countries reveals that consumption, level of development and environmental degradation are intricately related.

Consumption is however, enabled by income. Therefore, the question is as to what is the kind of income generation process that has evolved and what are the implications of such a process for environmental sustainability. We shall now examine the global distribution GDP per capita (in real terms – PPP $) and its relationship with three related factors in this regard, namely, Trade, Urbanisation and Energy. This is shown in Figures 1.9 to 1.12.

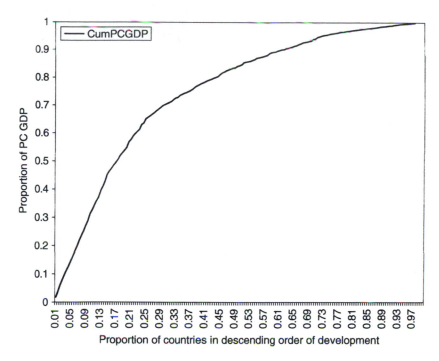

Figure 1.9 Global distribution of per capita GDP.

Source: Based on *Human Development Report* 2000, UNDP, New York.

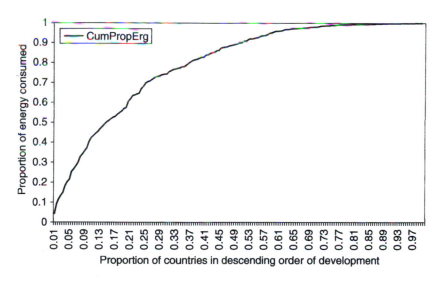

Figure 1.10 Global distribution of energy.

Source: Based on *Human Development Report* 2000, UNDP, New York.

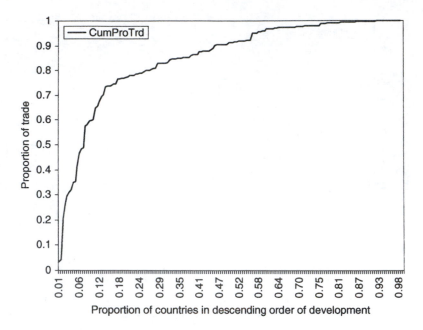

Figure 1.11 Global distribution of trade.

Source: Based on *Human Development Report* 2000, UNDP, New York.

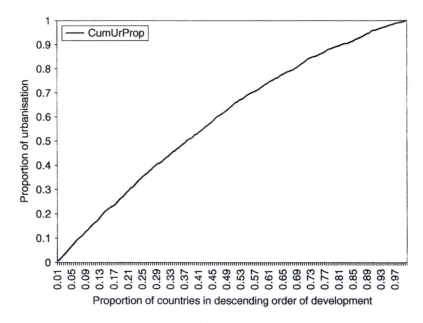

Figure 1.12 Global distribution of urbanisation.

Source: Based on *Human Development Report* 2000, UNDP, New York.

The relative shares in each of theses aspect is extremely illuminating. In the case of GDP per capita (expressed in real PPP $ terms) the high development countries (30 per cent in all) corner 70.22 per cent, followed by medium development countries (48 per cent of the countries) whose share is 26.28 per cent and lastly, low development countries (22 per cent of all countries) who have only 3.5 per cent. In terms of trade the distribution for the three development classes is as follows: high development, 83 per cent, medium development, 16.04 per cent and low development, just 0.96 per cent! For energy the corresponding shares are 74.28 per cent, 24.92 per cent and 0.80 per cent. Finally, with the relative distribution of urbanisation the distribution is 42 per cent, 46 per cent and 12 per cent, respectively across the three groups of countries. While urbanisation has the least disparity in comparison to other factors, the shares of both developing and poor countries are less than proportionate. The high development class still has a share which is one and a half times its proportion.

This analysis points to the lop-sided pattern of development. Thus, the income generation process consists of high energy use, openness of the economy and a high degree of urbanisation. These spell out a pattern or 'type of development' being adopted by developed countries. In actual terms the GDP per capita varies from a low of $410 to $30,860. In the case of energy the range is from 14 to 23,816. Trade volume varies from 0.02 to 2107. The rate of urbanisation varies from 5.8 per cent of the total area to 100 per cent. The extreme variation in energy use is the single largest indicator of the 'type of development'.

The high energy consumption by developed countries is extremely distressing for the environment. Ordinarily, extant literature views the question of energy by emphasising the relatively efficient technologies and efficiency of energy use by developed countries. Such a relative notion ignores the absolute level of energy use. Therefore, it is a misnomer that developed countries are much more efficient in energy use than developing countries. The growth and industrialisation of developed countries has been based on extremely high energy use which, in turn, causes environmental damage. Further, this is done at the cost of using environmentally degrading development inputs. The developed world is capable of producing and exporting industrial goods by using large quantities of energy. Further they use large quantities of fertiliser and water to support their population, as well as agriculture and export primary products on a large scale, as well. Therefore, their trade volumes are much larger. Thus, they actually leave no space for poor countries to use their comparative advantage in cheap labour. The developing countries can neither compete in industrial exports through their cheap labour nor can they compete in agricultural exports. Even more alarming than all this, is the fact that the pattern of development and more so the patterns of consumption are converging globally (see Chapter 8 of this book).

Conclusions

The trends in development and the environment discussed in this chapter reveal great disparities that are inherent in the process of globalisation. A prime question is as to why it is important to study such disparities. At one level the response to such a question is to look into the issues arising from the equity angle that relate to inequality and poverty. An approach that caters to a broad view of social and human development has often been emphasised in the literature. In fact, the human development approach has been formalised in the form of Human Development Indicators (HDIs) and the corresponding index along with the ranks given to countries and these are published periodically. The intention of HDI is to evaluate human development and reward such progress through periodic ranking.

Our approach is however different in many ways. First, while we may be concerned about the equity angle, and the human dimension of development, our primary purpose of delving into disparity in the process of globalisation is analytical. Our understanding is that global disparities lie at the root of aggravating global environmental degradation. Second, while we use the HDI and HD ranks in our analysis and modelling, in the process we are able to expose how the HDI conceals the level of environmental performance of different countries and more so, different developmental classes. Our methodology relates global environmental degradation to global disparities through the use of human development ranks. Third, our approach is to illuminate how globalisation has brought about a process by which patterns of development as well as consumption are converging and are likely to set-in a process of environmental degradation in the indefinite future. Finally, an essential part of our approach is not merely to study the cause and analytical framework of GED, but to point out that there is an urgent need for GEM, whose central theme would be to address these disparities as the basis of environmental degradation. An institution like the World Environment Organization (WEO) has to evolve and come to terms with this reality. Mere tinkering with treaties, conventions and permits would not be a solution.

2 Consumption and sustainable development

An overview

Introduction

Sustainable development was defined by the World Commission on Environment and Development (1987), widely known as the Brundtland Commission (after its chairperson) as 'Development that meets the needs of the present without compromising the ability of future generations to meet their own needs'. Such a definition rightly emphasises the temporal dimension of sustainability but ignores the spatial dimension and the implications of integration and globalisation for sustainability. It thus ignores the spatial and historical inequalities.

An apparently appealing argument is that population growth is the most potent cause of environmental damage. It is true that there is considerable pressure on the earth's resources through high population growth, which spells danger for future generations. More than 81 million people are added to the planet each year and more than 1 billion people are added to the world every decade. The world's population has grown because of a combination of positive changes such as improved sanitation, nutrition, and health care, which enable people to live longer, more productive lives. Population momentum implies that as more people are born in the world, there is a larger pool of people entering their childbearing years at the same time, which creates a 'population bulge'. Thus nearly 3 billion young people (equal to the whole population of the world in 1960) will enter their childbearing years in the next generation and even if each couple chose to have only one child, the sheer number of people bearing children in the same time period will put enormous strain on the earth's resources. Such unprecedented population growth results in the requirement of unprecedented natural resources, environmental services, and ambience. The problem then is the extremely rapid pace at which change is taking place, in particular the pace and scale of exploitation of nature and the degradation of the environment.

The impact of such population growth is dual. On the one hand it exacerbates resource use and on the other hand it leads to environmental pollution both of which are a fall-out of consumption. It could be argued that production is as important a dimension as consumption and that we need not consider consumption separately. However, it would suffice to state that there can be no justification for production without consumption demand but there can be consumption demand even without production. Hence, consumption is primary and production is secondary. The demand for production is derived from consumption, in which it exists. Moreover, population can continue to be the cause for environmental degradation only if the population can be sustained on the basis of consumption. Otherwise it would perish. Even the dual impact of population growth, that is, resource use and pollution, can be seen in two ways: (i) population growth amplifies resource use and pollution on account of the absolute increase in numbers; and (ii) it intensifies the same on account of the concentration of population growth in urban areas. Since poor countries are not so urbanised, the former is true of populous developing countries and the latter is more likely to be true for underpopulated developed countries. These surmises are confirmed by the fact that there are large differences between the levels of consumption per head of developed vis-à-vis developing countries. Per capita consumption in developed countries is higher than that in poor countries by a factor of several multiples. Hence, in both cases there is an equal case for claiming that population growth causes environmental degradation. However, on closer examination it is clear that population growth is not by itself the prime driver of environmental degradation but consumption is since population growth only follows consumption. It can be seen that the argument based on population constitutes only a part of the picture and a wrong picture at that because of two reasons: (i) population growth is not uniform across the globe; and (ii) all populations do not possess the same endowments.

What the naïve population argument ignores is that consumption is enabled only by income. We are no longer in an era of consuming free goods of nature. Most of these free goods are now priced resources, for example, water, fruits, trees and the ambience of a seaside resort, are all priced. How can such highly populated countries with low per capita incomes (PCIs) generate such high levels of income so as to step-up the consumption unprecedentedly? After all, they are poor countries. Even if total income increases, their PCI would virtually be unchanged or record only marginal growth on account of population growth. Further, production occurs primarily for addressing consumption demand and hence production cannot be said to be a driver of such degradation.

Some poor countries are richly endowed with natural resources. However, some of them also experience high population growth. The present day developed countries enjoy a long head start over the developing countries in the process of industrialisation. Hence the developed countries have much higher levels of per capita incomes (PCIs) and, therefore, consumption. Correspondingly poor countries are endowed with lower levels of income and hence of consumption. This points to the need to distinguish between two types of consumption: (i) economic consumption for attaining a standard of living; and (ii) consumption or degradation of nature and the environment. The former is the cause and the latter is the effect. The anomaly is that while the former consumption is local the latter could be global. With globalisation continuing apace at least since the mid-nineteenth century (with some breaks during the Great Depression and the immediate post-Second World War years), through trade, investment and technology, consumption that takes place anywhere on the globe could result in resources being harnessed from anywhere else on the globe and thus pollution effects can be felt anywhere in the world.

Even among wealthy nations the US is an outlier – it constitutes only 20 per cent of the world's population, yet uses more than 70 per cent of its resources. Many of these resources are extracted from low-income countries with accelerating environmental degradation if such extraction is not well regulated. This often destroys the very resources (trees, land, etc.) that low-income people depend upon to meet their basic needs. This creates a vicious circle of underdevelopment and environmental degradation in many of these countries (Jha and Whalley 2001). Hence, if consumption were regarded as impacting on environmental degradation then one would have to ascribe responsibility for this largely to developed countries.

The facts about increases in consumption and related aspects around the globe are compelling. During the twentieth century global population quadrupled to 6 billion whereas industrial output increased by a factor of 40. During the same period energy use increased by a factor of 16, annual fish harvesting by a factor of 35 and carbon and SO_2 emissions by a factor of 10 (McNeill 2000). In terms of specific resources such as water, the atmosphere as a carbon sink and a wide variety of ecosystem services, Vitousek *et al.* (1986, 1997) and Postel *et al.* (1996) indicate that the growth rates for such services are unsustainable. Further evidence along these lines is presented in Chapters 7 and 8. There is a staggering international inequality in consumption. This is evident from Table 2.1.

A competing point of view argues that just as earlier generations invested in capital goods, research and education and enabled the present generation to reach high levels of consumption, the present generation would be willing to make the same investments to enable continuing high, even rising, consumption in the future. *Here, it must be pointed out that the central issue of sustainability is not whether it is possible to achieve or satisfy rising consumption levels, or, in other*

Table 2.1 Consumption levels: industrialised and developing countries

	North	*South*	*North/South ratio*
Meat consumption (kg/cap)	77.1	26.9	2.87
Safe water access (%)	100	29	3.45
Televisions (per 1000)	524	145	3.61
Years to live at 60	9.15	2.2	4.16
Ecological footprint (Ha/cap)	7.4	1.7	4.35
Calories over 2400 (kcal)	757	172	4.40
Income (USD)	16337	3068	5.32
Telephones (per 1000)	414	39	10.62
Residential electricity (KWH/cap)	2024	182	11.12
Writing or printing paper (kg/cap)	78.2	5.2	15.04
Computers (per 1000)	156.3	6.5	24.05
Cars (per 1000)	405	16	25.31

Sources: Ecological footprints: Wackernagel (2000). Meat consumption: FAO STAT (2002). Electricity consumption: IEA (1997). Other data: UNDP (1998).

words, the sustenance of consumption for growing populations, but about what level of consumption is environmentally sustainable – across space, across the globe and temporally.

The underlying understanding is that consumption is a socio-psychological phenomenon that has a necessary economic basis in purchasing power or income. In approaches that owe allegiance to ecological economics consumption is treated as a physical state (Reisch and Ropke 2004). Such an approach does not help in understanding the socio-economic, the historical and the policy bearings of consumption, which is the hub of environmental degradation, globally.

Conceptual issues in the links between consumption and the environment

Princen (1999) clarifies the precise role of consumption in affecting the environment. The extant literature seems to suggest that over-consumption ranks with population growth and technology as a major driver of global environmental change. However, Princen argues that in many cases the literature does not distinguish between consumption as such on the one hand and production or economic activity on the other. Thus, Myers (1997) defines consumption as 'human transformation of material and energy'. This becomes a problem when 'it makes materials or energy less available for future use, and . . . threatens human health, welfare or other things that people value' (p. 54). Other authors have opted for even broader definitions, namely, consumption is defined as spanning the full range of goods and services that contribute to human well-being. But one could easily substitute production or economic activity for consumption.

The *American Heritage Dictionary* describes consumption as expending or using up, degrading or destroying.

> Thermodynamically it is to increase entropy. Biologically, it is capturing useable material and energy to enhance survival and reproduction and, ultimately to pass on one's genes. Socially it is using up material and energy to enhance personal standing, group identity and autonomy.
>
> (Princen 1999, p. 355)

Princen then defines three notions of consumption. The first is background consumption, which is needed for normal biological functioning of all organisms, humans included. Over and above that we have over-consumption and misconsumption.

Over-consumption is an aggregate concept and refers to the level and quality of consumption that undermines a species' own life support system. Individual behaviour may be perfectly rational; indeed even group behaviour may be rational. For example, increasing consumption to stimulate employment may be in the best interests of a country – yet the aggregate outcome may indicate a threat (e.g. excessive deforestation) to the species' own existence. If a household is subject to time constraint it may be individually rational for it to use more cars to maximise its utility although this leads to greater GHG emission. Thus, over-consumption in the aggregate may be perfectly rational at the level of individual decision makers.

In addition there is the problem of misconsumption. This may be individually irrational – say the taking of drugs – as well as collectively so. Misconsumption, therefore, refers to consumption – individual or aggregate – that leads to a net loss in utility.

In this book we are concerned primarily with the level and distribution of existing consumption and their relation to environmental degradation broadly conceived. We argue that there is excessive consumption in the rich countries, specifically countries with high values in UNDP's Human Development Index and, further, that this amounts to *over-consumption* since such consumption is responsible for the existing high level of environmental degradation. Further, since this trend may be unsustainable a redistribution of consumption would help alleviate environmental degradation.

Formal analyses of consumption and sustainable development

Against this background Arrow *et al.* (2004) consider two notions of sustainability of consumption and, therefore, of the underlying development process. In the first they define the value of intertemporal social welfare V_t as the present discounted value (a constant discount rate is used) of the flow of utility from consumption from the present to infinity. This notion focuses on intertemporal equity issues and abstracts from intra-temporal equity, which is of significant concern to us. They define an optimal consumption path as one that maximises the present value of this stream of utility and consider aggregate consumption at any point in time to be excessive if current consumption is higher than that prescribed by this maximised present value criterion.

An alternative notion of sustainability – the sustainability criterion – does not maximise net present value of the stream of utility from aggregate consumption but requires that V_t never declines at any point in time, that is, $(\mathrm{d}V_t/\mathrm{d}t) \geq 0$ *for all t.*

At such broad levels, estimates – particularly point estimates – can hardly be said to be conclusive. However, Arrow *et al.* (2004) find that, in the aggregate, consumption's share of output is higher than that required by the maximum present value criterion. Several individual countries fail the sustainability criterion. Since consumption across countries is modelled as being interdependent, the satisfaction of this criterion by some countries is the result of the failure of other countries to meet it.

From the viewpoint of the present study an important lacuna in the Arrow *et al.* (2004) study is that they concentrate almost exclusively on natural resource depletion – defined to include damage from CO_2 emission, energy depletion, mineral depletion and net forest depletion – and not on environmental degradation more broadly conceived. Further the effect of these depletions – at least insofar as reducing total investment is concerned – is taken as additive, without any system of weighting for respective influences. In addition this approach does not consider the important question of the atemporal distribution (alternatively equity) of consumption. Finally the notion of sustainability for individual countries needs to be replaced, in view of increasing international interdependence, by that of global environmental sustainability. We address some of these issues in this book.

An important reason why environmental and natural resources receive relatively little attention in the literature is that their contribution to economic growth is not easy to quantify. In this context Dasgupta (2003) argues that models of economic growth embed a rather simplistic notion of the contribution of natural and environmental resources to economic growth. These models assume a positive link between the creation of ideas (technological progress) and population growth with natural resources constituting a fixed and indestructible factor of production. However, in reality this assumption is wrong and environmental and natural degradation, along with population growth, could be important constituents of an explanation for continued stagnation in poverty in the poorest countries of the world. These factors are often ignored in growth models, at least in explanations for inadequate growth and poverty reduction performances. Instead, standard explanations for such inadequate performance include factors such as 'institutional quality' or 'governance' factors that are hard to quantify on a consistent basis at the international level.

Consumption and sustainability – our notion

We now sketch our understanding of the link between environmental degradation and consumption.[1] In our view, the problematic of environmental degradation cannot be approached, let alone be understood, without enunciating certain concepts or principles. We elucidate some of these now.

As a backdrop consider the assertion of the extant literature that all problems, except global warming, are local or at best, trans-boundary environmental issues. For understanding the link between consumption and GED two points need to be understood. First, with a globalising world economy virtually no environmental effect is local. Even if this assumption seems to be far-fetched in the present day, our analysis, it must be understood, is prognostic and this assumption has every possibility of being valid in the near future. Second, pollution is not the only relevant environmental issue, although it may be the most pressing in some circles. Even other issues such as water use, land degradation, paper consumption, etc., are equally important environmental issues. We now enunciate three welfare principles taken as axiomatic in this book.

Welfare principles

1   The first principle that we wish to propose is that without any moral or ethical grounding any notion or construct of environmental sustainability, or degradation, that results from lack of sustainable development ('unsustainability') is trivial.

2   The second principle is that consumption and production (including extraction and acquisition) done in pursuance of mere subsistence is local by nature and is environmentally neutral, in the sense that it justifies the nature and extent of resource use and environmental degradation thereof.

3   The third principle is that any consumption (in excess of the aforementioned minimum) and hence, production (including extraction and acquisition) done in pursuance of the market diktats is global in nature and ought to be justifiable by the yardstick of global environmental sustainability.

Macroeconomics of sustainability and the micro-foundation of global consumption

On the assumption that markets are globalised, let us reconsider the ordinary notions of consumption and production in macroeconomics from the point of view of sustainability.

In the standard national accounting framework it is assumed that the market equilibrates consumption with production, in such a way that individuals maximise satisfaction and minimise resource use simultaneously and automatically, while the optimal level of global consumption is reached by a summation of their decisions.

This notion of the micro-foundation of consumption ignores the following factors:

1   that optimisation of individual consumption is not environmentally neutral;
2   that if our concern is global consumption, income inequalities create multiple optima in consumption;
3   that even if a single optimum of consumption were reached globally, the market optimisation process does not ensure a global optimisation (minimisation) of environmental degradation, since the market cannot eliminate net environmental cost, which is an absolute positive quantum and also price inelastic;
4   that relative prices can lead to efficient choice with the given budget constraint but they cannot lower the level of absolute consumption to desirable levels, since absolute consumption levels depend on socio-psychological behaviour;
5   that even if the global optimum in consumption is reached, historic inequalities in endowment of consumption can always justify a redistribution because of differences in marginal utility of consumption.

It is sometimes claimed that the income elasticity for a better environment is greater than one at high levels of income (as argued in the Environmental Kuznets Curve (EKC) literature). Although this notion in itself can and is being questioned in this book (and elsewhere), it does not address the question of whether the price elasticity of consumption of environmentally unfriendly goods is at least negative, whether greater or less than one. Consider, for instance, products such as mobile phones, cars, plastics, etc. In a global economy, such products are cheaper in poorer countries but their demand and consumption is greater in rich countries. If it is purported that the greater demand is due to higher income levels and higher income elasticities, then such an argument is a clear repudiation of the position taken in the EKC literature that the income elasticity is high and positive for a better environment. Neither price elasticity nor income elasticity favour the argument that rich countries are more environmentally conscious or friendly. Where economic arguments clearly fail there is a definite possibility that social psychology could promote the over-consumption of environmentally unfriendly goods; see Michaels (1988).

The macroeconomic conception of consumption

Now consider the view that equilibrium national income is reached with consumption and production equalised. In such a situation it is typically assumed that producer profits are maximised; hence, resources are optimally utilised. If production is less than this magnitude at any point in time there would be dissaving in a closed economy or there would be imports in an open economy.

Organisation of production

In a *subsistence economy* the equilibration of production and consumption is ensured not through price adjustment but through socio-psychological behaviour. The objective is to produce just enough for subsistence. There cannot possibly be any *over-consumption*. Sustainability is a natural consequence of pursuing normal rational behaviour within these parameters. Neither price elasticity nor income elasticity plays any role. However, such subsistence economies are rare (although not non-existent) in the modern world, as these cannot constitute the basis of normal economic activity. The essential point is that even today there are such societies where the income and consumption level is very low but these societies are quite sustainable. Although it may be politically incorrect to make such comparisons but in such an economy the moral question is whether it is right to expect people to survive *ad infinitum* in such lowly conditions.

In such a primitive economy there is no *over-consumption*. Since consumption is minimal (needs based), there is equilibrium between acquisition (production) and consumption. There is no waste. In the primitive economy if, on account of lack of production possibilities, production falls short of consumption the species perishes, in the long run. So the long-term adjustment of production and consumption is disastrous – slow and traumatic – in such economies. It however, holds lessons for more affluent societies because if such societies do not learn to curb *over-consumption* there is the possibility of perishing. The choice is between learning lessons early enough and suffering a temporary loss of consumption (or redistribution) or of ignoring warnings and finding equilibrium through a torturous route.

The problem is that in the case of a *market economy* we cannot expect people to continue to exist at this level of development. Typically consumption in a market economy is more than that in a subsistence economy. It is necessary that people enjoy the fruits of development and increase their level of consumption.

On the other hand, once economic development transcends this stage, there is no natural mechanism that can ensure equilibrium at sustainable levels.

Closed global economy

Now let us consider the global economy as a closed economy. This implies that resources cannot come from elsewhere and pollutants cannot be moved to the outside of the system. Thus if

$$Ac > Sc \text{ then } Ns < 0$$

where Ac = Actual (global) consumption; Sc = Global Sustainable Consumption, Ns = Net resource saving.

This leads to either (i) using up past savings, that is, existing environmental resources or (ii) drawing on future resources. Neither belongs to the present generation. Thus, even a present day, intragenerational equity question gets integrally linked to the intergenerational question. Only appropriate property rights can resolve such questions. We discuss these issues in Chapter 5.

The moral question here is whether we leave it to the market to decide how much the global consumption per capita should be. If it were to be low, it would work against the poor countries since they would have to bear the brunt of the curtailment, although already having a low level of consumption. The rich countries would always have an advantage. If it were too high it would work against global sustainability.

The economic models that deal with the problem of sustainability in such market economies have only taken care of intergenerational issues. But they have ignored spatial issues. As stated earlier, any production that is not for subsistence is potentially global. This is because the raw material used in production could originate anywhere and be used anywhere. Similarly, goods could be sold anywhere and most of all pollution (degradation) could emanate anywhere, while consumption could be undertaken somewhere else. The ethical question is not answered by simple principles like 'polluter pays' and is very serious. If historically poor countries already have very low levels of consumption they should not be expected to bear the brunt of moderating consumption (and income). If the EKC argument that rich countries are more efficient in production than developing countries were true then global welfare would be higher if rich countries produced and re-distributed the consumption such that poor countries with a higher marginal utility of consumption gain more than the loss of utility of rich countries. *There would then be a net gain in welfare.* This would, however, need intervention beyond the market of any single country. This brings us to global environmental management and the need for an international agency to oversee such internalisation efforts. We discuss this later in this chapter.

Open global economy

The excess of consumption over production or *over-consumption* is resolved through the international flows of goods and services in the global economy.

Therefore, if one economy is not attempting to moderate its consumption it is being facilitated at the cost of other economies that are displaying desirable (sustainable) consumption levels. Ideally, the market mechanism should work on incentives and reward such countries that economise on resource use. In the context of globalisation it can be shown that such an incentive mechanism is regressive. Economies that indulge in over-consumption continue to maintain their unduly high levels of economic consumption and degradation, and the economies that are already paying a cost of curtailing present consumption (not preferring present consumption) contrary to normal satisficing economic behaviour, are penalised in two ways: (i) their current utility is lowered; and (ii) they suffer from excessive environmental degradation for which they are not responsible.

Thus, in a state of *laissez faire* without any intervention the market economy cannot provide an overall solution that is optimal by standards of efficiency, equity and sustainability. There is every possibility that this inter-spatial problem could become intergenerational and perpetuate existing inequities in responsibility for environmental degradation. This calls for two policy responses: (i) the proper articulation and assignment of property rights; and (ii) steps to ensure appropriate global environmental management. Our perspective on the former issue is discussed in Chapter 5. Later in the present chapter we examine the reasons why internalisation (appropriate global environment management) is difficult to achieve in the global economy.

Open global economy and mesoeconomic structures

Global products and international production organization, both of which have long-term implications for sustainability, characterise the global economy. The following features are clearly discernable and are becoming increasingly established.

1   The flow of foreign direct investment (FDI) and the proliferation and growth of multinational corporations (MNCs). The size of MNCs is so overwhelming that they encompass the productive capacities and GNPs of several poor countries. So the dominant mode of the production organisation is not just market-oriented but can be labelled as 'international or global production'.[2]
2   As a result of the above tendencies there is an increasing trend towards global products and their consumption across the globe, as well as global technologies.
3   Many of these products, such as mobile phones, computers, consumer electronics, cars, etc., are highly technology-based. They are not biodegradable; draw on resources and energy, as well as cause pollution.
4   Cost is not a constraint, first because resources can be acquired from anywhere in the world, hence, the supply is perfectly elastic, and second, because business processes can be outsourced to other countries, wherever they are the cheapest. MNCs have a reach that can obtain the most critical resource (technical manpower) at the most competitive cost.
5   Further global products enable mass production and economies of scale.

6   The indivisibilities in the cost of innovation and product development are overcome easily due to the global nature of products. Intellectual property rights and patents that allow monopoly production arising out of innovation and product development further buttress this tendency. This results in long-run cost (virtually devoid of fixed cost) being based on marginal cost.

The above distinctive features lead to certain structures in consumption and production and are increasingly becoming intricately enmeshed with technology change. Consumption patterns are percolating from rich countries to poor countries at an increasing pace as technologies become cheaper and more mobile. For example, digital technologies are enabling technology transfer at a speed and scale to poor countries in an unprecedented manner. Such technologies are cheap and enable mass production and consumption. They are easy to maintain and service in a globally networked environment.

The pricing of products, in the case of MNCs is based on transfer pricing, which, in turn is based on marginal cost. Further MNCs are able to keep down the marginal cost, in the long run, to the minimum, by virtue of supply chain management.[3] As a result the entire production process, decision-making and technology change are becoming demand determined.[4]

In order to be able to trace the effects of macroeconomic factors or policies on individuals and households, the relevant linkages between the macro- and the micro-spheres need to be detailed. Both are linked through what is called the mesoeconomy, composed of markets, technology and infrastructure as critical elements. Economic parameter changes on the macro level are passed through the mesoeconomy down to the micro level, where they manifest themselves as supply and demand factors. These macroeconomic changes in the global economy are linked to the microeconomic price structure and consumption through certain mesoeconomic structures. The two tools we use for understanding these structures are:

1   The Price Consumption Curve (PCC) – this shows the relationship between price and consumption (Figure 2.1).
2   The Technology Consumption Curve (TCC) – this shows the relationship between the long-term changes in relative price and the structure of consumption, caused by technology change (Figure 2.2).

While the former is a well-established tool the latter has been developed on the basis of the above analysis and is intricately related to the PCC. Both the real business cycle theory and growth theory, which explain long-term changes in macroeconomic terms, emphasise that the long-run drivers of exogenous change are government expenditure and technological progress. In global analysis, government expenditure is difficult to generalise. But the effect of technology and its relation to demand and structure of consumption can be generalised.

The PCC measures consumption of two commodities X and Y, through the budget lines $X1Y1$, $X1Y2$, and so on. The only modification to the PCC (above) is that the budget lines, including the quantities and prices have been defined with a time

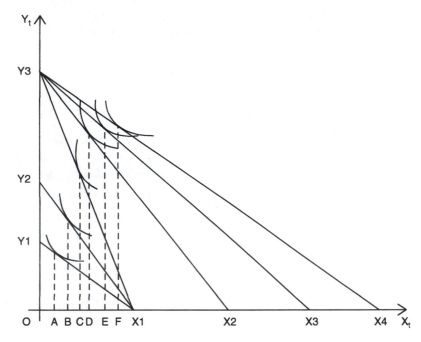

Figure 2.1 Price consumption curve.

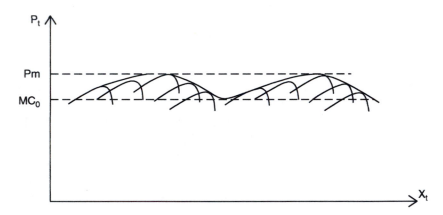

Figure 2.2 Technology consumption curve.

dimension – denoted by subscript 't'. Usually, the budget line is defined during a single time period. This implies that the consumption (demand) for X_t – main global product that is environmentally unfriendly, is defined per unit of time (say annually). The essential filtrate of the concept of sustainable consumption is that there is a maximum level of consumption that is affordable, not by price standards but by environmental standards. As long as production and consumption are restricted to that level there is no threat to the environment. Let us assume that the sustainable level of annual consumption is OA, of X_t, per unit of time.

Let us assume that product X_t is being demanded and produced at the minimum marginal cost MC_0. International production of a global product, by MNCs ensures that the marginal cost remains MC_0, in spite of cost innovation and development of new products, new technologies and new models.

We also assume that, as per the extant EKC literature, rich countries have cleaner technologies, and further that the private marginal cost is equal to the social marginal cost (PMC = SMC). By conventional theory of production the production process is optimal. But it shall be seen that this does not ensure that output is restricted to OA, which is the level of sustainable consumption. From the following analysis it can be seen that price cannot ensure that sustainable consumption is achieved and that demand and consumption structures are so vitally linked to the technology cycle that in spite of having minimum MC and efficient production (and resource allocation) total demand far outstrips the sustainable level of consumption – OA. For understanding the demand structures it is necessary to examine the PCC.

The PCC shows that initially consumers are prepared to pay a very high price. This is represented by the rise in the budget line, in Figure 2.1, from $X1Y1$ to $X1Y3$. In the beginning it may be the case that the price of a new product (based on new technology) may be effectively lowered by giving incentives, so that the product is accepted. But very soon the consumers experience a 'hype' and the demand increases. They are prepared to pay more. Price goes up to (the slope of) $X1Y3$. But it can be seen that the distance BC is lower than AB because the initial hype is wearing out. The consumer becomes 'blasé'. The highest price is equal to Pm. This is the maximum that 'the traffic will bear'. Beyond $X1Y1$ price any increase in the price (up to $X1Y3$) has the effect of increasing demand. This is because consumers want new technologies, new 'features' and new 'models'. Therefore, any increase in price due to a public policy (tax) shall not have any effect of restricting consumers. At this price producers drop the price and the demand rises. This is because they may not be interested beyond the point where basic needs are met (Figure 2.3). A price effect has to be induced by lowering the price. The attempt to restrict the consumption at OA fails because the consumers are 'willing to pay (WTP)' up to $X1Y3$. Hence, price elasticity cannot be relied upon to contain consumption up to OA. Also the income elasticity is positive so demand increases from C to D, D to E and E to F. Thus, AF indicates *over-consumption*. This increase, is however, at a decreasing rate.

To the above PCC based on technology we can add the concept of obsolescence. Beyond the peak in any cycle there is a decline. Therefore, there is a rise and fall pattern of technology, consumption and profits. We can add to the above analysis the possibilities that declining technologies may not result from product failure but from obsolescence. New 'models' appear before the old have been 'phased-out'. Thus, the individual PCCs intersect, in Figure 2.2, while the TCC is an envelope curve (not a single PCC). Strictly speaking it is not a demand curve

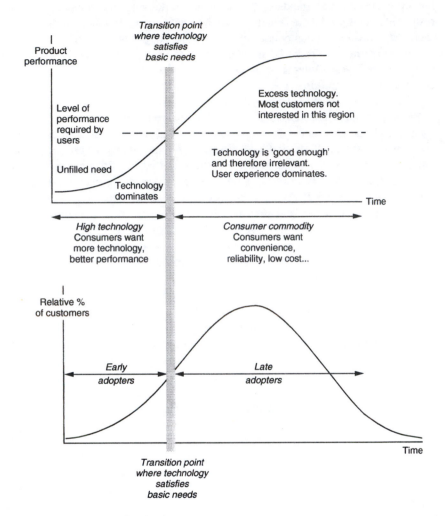

Figure 2.3 Life cycle of technology.

Source: Norman, D.A. (1998) *The Invisible Computer: Why Good Products Can Fail, the Personal Computer is So Complex, and Information Appliances are the Solution*, Cambridge, MA: MIT Press. Reprinted with Permission from MIT Press. © MIT Press.

because a demand curve is defined for a single time period. Each inverted 'U' represents a 'new model' and each peak of the TCC represents a new technology. For instance, the first peak may represent VCD players and the second peak may represent DVD players. Alternatively, the first peak may be a mobile phone (with a camera) and the second may be a palm top cum cell phone.

This shows that supernormal profits can be obtained even in the long run. Resources from all over the world are being attracted because of this phenomenon and output cannot be fixed at OA – the sustainable level of consumption. However, there is a phase difference between rich and poor countries. The technologies, products and 'models' that are waning in the rich countries are transferred by MNCs to poor countries.[5] Hence, globally there is an excess consumption of environmentally unfriendly goods, to a great extent, even if the EKC argument about rich countries having cleaner technologies is valid.

The above analysis points towards a convergence of production and consumption patterns between rich and poor countries. Consequently, the danger to the environment could worsen over time. The high population growth in poor countries is not so much a threat to the environment today, but it shall become a major threat if technologies percolate from rich countries and consumption and demand patterns follow suit. These arguments are verified in a full model of growth, global consumption and GED in Chapter 8.

Is growth a panacea for the environment's ills?

Our arguments thus far involve choice in regard to production and consumption across countries in an atemporal framework. One strong line of argument has been that such choices need not be forced, as there is scope for development for all countries. It is argued that countries are set apart only in time and that poor countries need only follow suit so that both growth and a better environment are attained. This argument has been called the sustainability debate.

Traditionally the literature has distinguished between two types of such relations. Daly (1977), Georgescu-Roegen (1971), and Hall *et al.* (1986) believe that the higher the income level, the greater the environmental degradation. However, Beckerman (1992, 1993), Bartelle (1994) and Panayotou (1997) believe that, after a point, income growth lowers environmental degradation, that is the relationship between environmental degradation and the income level is non-linear – positive up to a point and negative thereafter, implying that the income elasticity of demand for the environment is higher than one after a high level of income. This is the so-called EKC. We shall refer to the disagreement between the two schools as the 'growth-environment debate'.

Arrow *et al.* (1995) argue that the treatment of this debate in mainstream economic theory is inadequate. Economic growth theory almost ignores the environment. Where it does allude to the environmental effects of growth it suggests that these could be dealt with separately or that they would take care of themselves. Trade theory's approach is an anthropocentric one[6] as it is concerned with environmental issues[7] from the narrow perspective of 'trans-boundary pollution', 'permits', and so on.[8]

There is a substantial literature now on EKC – for a recent summary of the alleged links between economic growth and individual pollutants see Panayotou (2000). Here we attempt only a selective review. Grossman and Krueger (1995) carry out a cross-country study using a number of environmental variables. However, the data sets are non-uniform in that data on some variables refer to individual cities and, in other cases, to countries. The coverage of data over time is also not uniform. Shafik and Bandyopadhyay (1992) use a large number of variables to test for an EKC type relation in 149 countries but they study the effects of these variables separately and do not compute a composite index of these variables. Selden and Song (1994) studied pollution within a framework that distinguished between countries with high, low and medium incomes. They however restricted themselves to air pollution and did not articulate a composite index of environmental degradation. Janicke (1989) used an aggregate indicator for volume of throughput based on four indicators relating to energy, steel, cement, and rail and road freight. But their study was limited to 31 COMECON and OECD countries and covered the period 1970–85. They confirmed the presence of an EKC relationship. Later this was challenged by the 're-linking' hypothesis. Birdsall and Wheeler (1991) studied air pollution in the manufacturing sector of Latin America using developed and developing country data. They concluded that pollution intensity, measured as the ratio of air pollution to GDP, declined with income in open economies and rose in relatively closed economies. A pertinent question to ask at this juncture is that even if the EKC were to hold, have the rich countries reached the threshold level of income at which the EKC is purported to turn back Khanna and Plassmann (2004) address this question. Their results indicate that even high-income households in the US have not yet reached the income level at which their demand for better environmental quality is high enough to cause the income–pollution relationship to turn downwards for many pollutants.

Another relevant branch of the literature considers the relation between EKC and sustainable development. Pearce (1993) states that all versions of 'sustainable development' are based on the principle of equity. In the 1970s, the growth–environment debate was dominated by approaches based on the Law of Entropy (also see Daly 1977; Daly and Townsend 1993; Ekins 1997; Georgescu-Roegen 1971).[9] These physical entropy models rest on a global view of physical stocks of matter and flows of energy. This approach was opposed to the then prevailing 'growthmania' since it advocated the establishment of a 'steady state' that not only implied a constant capital stock but also a 'constant stock of people' (Daly 1977, p. 15). Daly questions not only the *feasibility* of growth but also its *desirability*. Such a view is *clearly anti-developmental*. Entropy models cannot be ignored, since they are based on physical phenomena. However, these models ignore the distributive aspects of growth and environment, which are the crux of the matter. These models recommend that developing countries, which are already at a low level of economic development, contain their rate of growth. Since developing countries possess natural resources, they must pay the price for the depleted global 'free energy' (low entropy), while the developed world has already amply benefited and has been largely responsible for the depletion. To the extent that the pattern of development of advanced countries continues to burden the global environment and insofar as global environmental management needs 'global solutions', this inequality is likely to be perpetuated and the prospect for the developing world shall remain dismal.

It is pertinent to inquire when, and in what form, world bodies responsible for development and global management took to the issue of growth and environment.

As opposed to the 1970s, in the 1980s concern turned towards 'sustainable development' (World Commission on Environment and Development 1987; see also Ruttan 1994). Only thereafter did chambers of business and world bodies (ICC 1990; UNCED 1992 – hereafter the World Bank 1992 and the WTO) start taking interest in the issue of sustainability (Ekins 1997). However, there remained an underlying belief that economic growth would lead to protection of the environment. Unfortunately, even this stand does not augur well for developing countries because, in the context of the EKC, as long as these countries are below the threshold at which the EKC bends back, growth would only increase their environmental degradation. Further, this approach requires developing countries to sacrifice growth if they want a healthy global environment. This would imply that to achieve global intertemporal efficiency we should sacrifice some global atemporal (spatial) equity. Our view on this, developed in Chapter 5, is that 'the applicability of the notion of sustainability has ultimately got to be *universal and refer to the indefinite future* and must be related[10] to consumption'.[11] One of the concerns of the present volume is to emphasise the spatial dimension of sustainability, in relation to economic development. Neither side of this debate highlights this dimension.[12]

Even later developments (broadly classified as 'weak' and 'strong' sustainability approaches), do not focus on the spatial dimensions of environment and the special problems of developing countries.[13] The 'weak sustainability approach' argues that while growth entails environmental degradation either the levels of degradation would fall after a threshold (in the EKC) or degradation could be decoupled or de-linked from growth.[14] Subsequent studies attempt to detail the manner in which this de-linking could be possible.[15] Bernstam (1991) attempts to link the fate of the South to that of the North. He argues that economic growth in the South depends on growth in the North. Hence accelerated growth in the North would result in the South surmounting the EKC hump. This argument is 'anti-developmental' because it indirectly justifies the existing gap between the North and South and provides a rationale for further accelerating the growth of the North.

In addition to these, Stern *et al.* (1996) and Ekins (1997) argue that:

1   There may be a negative feedback from environmental degradation to income growth, especially in the case of LDCs. This may be the cause of the inverted U- shape. However, Holtz-Eakin and Selden (1992) find no evidence of such simultaneity.
2   North exports its pollutants to the South. This may give rise to the inverted U-shaped EKC.
3   Ekins (1997) argues that OECD countries have passed the hump of EKC. Even a casual observation of data in this study does not support this position. Further, as indicated earlier Khanna and Plassmann (2004) show that most affluent US households could not be said to have reached the level of income where the EKC crosses its hump. In Chapter 6 we show that a consistently defined measure of environmental degradation shows no tendency to decline at high levels of PCI.[16] Further, Harbaugh *et al.* (2000), among others, find

no evidence of EKC relationship. Moomaw and Unruh (1997) and van den Bergh *et al.* (1998), suggest that what appears as de-linking may not persist in the long run. Further, there is the re-linking hypothesis (de Bruyn 1997; Pezzey 1989) that purports an *N* -shaped curve, wherein environmental degradation is ultimately positively linked to income levels.

The costs of unsustainability: some examples

Such non-sustainability is now leading to increasing human vulnerability to environmental problems. We now mention some instances of these high costs. McMichael (2001) documents the increasing dependence of human health on the environment. According to WHO (1997):

1   Deteriorating environmental conditions are a major contributory factor to poor health and poor quality of life. Mismanagement of natural resources, excessive waste production and associated environmental conditions that affect health pose major challenges to sustainable development.
2   Impoverished populations living in rural and peri-urban areas are at greatest risk from degraded environmental conditions. The cumulative effects of inadequate and hazardous shelter, overcrowding, lack of water supply and sanitation, unsafe food, air and water pollution and high accident rates, as well as greater susceptibility to disasters, have serious effects on the health of these vulnerable groups. Poor environmental quality is directly responsible for some 25 per cent of all preventable ill health, with diarrhoeal diseases and acute respiratory infections heading the list.
3   Two-thirds of all preventable ill health due to environmental conditions occurs among children.
4   Air pollution is a major contributor to a number of diseases, and to a lowering of the quality of life in general.

Overall it is estimated that 25–33 per cent of the global burden of disease is attributable to environmental factors (Smith *et al.* 1999). Murray and Lopez (1996) estimate that environment-related premature death and illness account for 18 per cent of the total burden of diseases in the developing world. This comprises contributions from water supply and sanitation (7 per cent), indoor air pollution (4 per cent), vector-borne diseases (3 per cent), urban air pollution (2 per cent) and agro-industrial waste (1 per cent). WHO (2002) estimates that every year environmental hazards kill 3 million children under the age of 5. Of these, 40–60 per cent are due to acute respiratory infection resulting from environmental factors. Microbiological contamination of the sea by sewage pollution has precipitated a health crisis of massive proportions globally. Bathing in polluted seas is estimated to cause some 250 million cases of gastroenteritis and upper respiratory disease every year, with an estimated annual cost worldwide of about USD 1.6 billion. Some of these people could be disabled over the longer term, suggesting that the global impacts of marine pollution are comparable to those of diphtheria and leprosy. Some authors have argued that food security is also affected by environmental factors. Agricultural growth as a consequence of the Green Revolution has also had an adverse impact on the environment in terms of nutrient mining, increases in soil salinity, water logging, depletion of underground water and the release of nitrogen into watercourses.

Human well-being is inextricably linked to ecosystems through the goods and services that the ecosystems provide. These include both marketed goods and services, such as food or forest products, and non-marketed ones such as water flow regulation. The cost of environmental damage to India in 1992 has been put at USD 11,867 billion a year or 4.5 per cent of GDP. A breakdown of the estimated costs shows that urban air pollution costs India USD 1.3 billion a year, and water degradation has associated health costs of USD 5.7 billion a year. Land degradation causes productivity losses of around USD 2.4 billion and deforestation leads to annual losses of USD 241 million. In Japan the damage to agricultural crops caused by tropospheric ozone amounts to an estimated USD 166.5 million yearly in the Kanto region alone. The potential economic losses of non-marketed ecosystems goods and services and the impact on human vulnerability are likely to be even higher than for marketed goods and services. Equally, little attention is paid to the high economic cost of more gradual environmental degradation and loss of natural resource potential. As daunting as current conditions are, they pale into insignificance when compared with ultimate results of further exploitation of the environment. Thus, for example, most of Asia is in the midst, not at the end, of an urban-industrial led development transition unparalleled in its scale and intensity. Urban population in Asia has been doubling in size every 15–20 years and will increase by another 69 per cent by 2025. Roughly 80 per cent of the industry that will be operating in 2020 (primarily in urban areas) has yet to be built. If trends continue, by 2010 Asia will produce more SO_2 than Europe and the US combined, and by 2020 the Asia region will become the world's largest source of GHGs. Hence existing trends are unmistakably pointing in the direction of a fundamentally unsustainable environmental future in the *Business-as-usual* case (UNEP 2003).

Obstacles to internalisation and global environmental management

A pertinent question to ask at this juncture is given that incomplete internalisation – at the local, trans-boundary and international levels – is perhaps the single most important contributor to environmental problems, why does not such internalisation take place – particularly in view of the high costs associated with such lack of internalisation.

A complex set of (familiar) reasons is behind the lack of progress towards internal industrialisation in the developing countries. These include weak and ill-defined property rights over resources, inefficient enforcement (Prasad 2004), large transactions costs, poor technology of surveillance and poor governance.

However, the experience of the developing countries in this regard is not very different from those of developed countries. Developing countries have often been thought of as following the development experience of the developed countries with a compressed lag. OECD countries have grown over some 200 years and transformed from primary agricultural to primarily high-technology service providers. Developing countries are following this experience at varying speeds and in different ways, but the transition time is clearly shorter. Korea, for instance, may have transformed itself from a country with lower income per capita than India in the mid-1950s to a lower income OECD country in 40 years. However, whereas the OECD countries during their years of rapid industrialisation could follow a policy of 'grow now and clean up later', the developing countries of today are under considerable pressure to clean up now. These pressures come from donor governments, international organisations and developed country NGOs, and sometimes carry the threat of punitive action. At the height of OECD country industrial revolutions, effectively no environmental controls were in place.

Thus, developing countries are subject to the twin pressures of having to raise PCIs rapidly and yet clean up during the process. What should be their response? Following developed country experience would seem to indicate adopting few environmental controls, and assuming that with income growth–environmental quality will improve. Indeed, a great fear is that attempts to heighten environmental regulation will only serve to slow growth, and hence slow eventual achievement of higher environmental quality through growth. On the other hand, with problems of compliance, one can argue that perhaps developing countries have no choice but to follow the older developed country industrial revolution experience of largely benign neglect.

There are key differences in the developing country experience in this area compared to the industrial revolution of old. First, the time periods involved are compacted, and hence the flow of environmental damage per year during industrialisation is larger. Second, the shocks which hit the economies are also much more severe than that underwent the industrial revolution in the nineteenth century. These economies simply did not experience population growth rates of 3 per cent per year plus massive growth in urban vehicle densities, or other elements contributing to today's environmental ills in the developing world. Not only is the process more compact, the severity of damage time adjusted probably exceeds that experienced in the OECD one hundred years ago. Third, even though weakly administered, there are abatement technologies, which can and are being employed, and even though there is political opposition, environmental management is taking root.

The process of internalisation of environmental external effects has gone much further in developed OECD economies. For instance, in the OECD countries we observe a strong decoupling of emissions of local air pollutants from economic growth. OECD countries have also achieved a strong decoupling between energy use and economic growth over the past 20 years, with the economy growing by 17 per cent between 1980 and 1998 and energy use falling by about the same percentage. Water and resource use continued to grow but at a rate slower than GDP growth, reflecting a weak decoupling of the two. Thus, decoupling of emissions in OECD countries and generally the developed countries has been accomplished through a combination of technological change and a strong environmental policy. The latter consists of 'greening' of fiscal policy, removing subsidies to environmentally harmful activities and the use of economic instruments to internalise environmental cost. For example, a number of European Union (EU) policy initiatives – the Broad Economic Policy Guidelines 2001, among others – have promoted a gradual but steady and credible change in the level and structure of the tax rates until external costs are fully reflected in prices. Such initiatives are attempting to cope with most of the fundamental structural problems in all developed countries: the unsustainable patterns of production and consumption. In the energy markets these guidelines aim to use taxes and other market-based instruments to rebalance prices in favour of reusable energy sources and technologies. Other EU initiatives in this direction are the European Climate Change Programme (ECCP), the directive establishing an EU framework for emissions trading, and the Integrated Product Policy (IPP) – all of which aim at realigning price relations and stimulating investments in new technologies that promote sustainable development. Member states are encouraged to improve market functioning by addressing market failures such as externalities through 'increased use of market-based systems in pursuit of environmental objectives as they provide flexibility to industry to reduce pollution in a cost-effective way, as well as encourage technological innovations' (UNEP 2003, p. 326). The tax instruments are promoted as the most efficient means of decoupling economic growth from pollution, as they alter price relations and thereby also drive changes in technology and consumer behaviour (preference) that lie behind the growth–environmental relationship. As exemplified by the energy and transport sectors, the EU decoupling policy consists of demand management through full cost pricing and development of more environmentally friendly alternatives by promoting technological innovations. The United Nations Economic Commission for Europe has repeatedly called upon its members to raise the prices of various energy sources to their full economic costs and adapt economic instruments to internalise the costs to human health and the environment associated with energy production and consumption. The aim is to decouple emissions from energy use and energy use from economic growth.

Commensurate progress in these areas in the case of developing or transition countries has been lacking, although some progress has been achieved. Thus, since 1990 all economies in transition have made efforts to restructure their energy and transport sectors along market principles and to raise energy prices closer to economic and international levels. However, because of the political sensitivity of energy pricing and the lagging reforms in many transition economies, a gap of 20–85 per cent continues to persist between energy prices in economies in transition. For example, electricity prices for households in Eastern Europe are only 50 per cent of those of the EU; for industrial consumers, electricity prices are closer to their economic and international levels, being 20 per cent lower than those of the EU. Subsidies on electricity for agriculture continue to be extremely high in India (Jha and Thapa 2003).

Although gains from internalisation (at the international level) are jointly shared and are substantial, why are custodians of assets not able to agree to manage and conserve assets in return for payment by those who benefit from such practices? From the viewpoint of the developing countries, given the large cost estimates for their environmental problems, it is likely that these countries will continue to pursue a much more activist environmental policy. However, given the greater cost of local degradation issues, such efforts will have a dominant focus on degradation over pollution. International external effects are more likely to be emphasised in any international environmental co-operation. To make such co-operation more attractive to the developing countries, concessions would have to be made to enable them to address their domestic environmental concerns – in particular, environmental degradation. In fact, an enlightened international environmental policy would link the issue of support for domestic internalisation policies in developing countries to co-operation in international environmental agreements such as those on GHGs.

There are several other reasons for this observed lack of internalisation at the international level. First, it is difficult to put together negotiations between groups who have an interest in the management practices used for environmental resources. For instance, governments may agree to conserve forests but may find it difficult to pursue this if encroachments into forests are done primarily by the poor. Similarly, in OECD countries there may be a willingness to pay for environmental protection in poorer countries, but any attempt to estimate this (by survey methods, for instance) will be subject to free riding. The benefits from environmental protection abroad are a public good which is hard to finance through voluntary action. A related problem is that individual countries can free ride on the environmental quality improvement by other countries. Hence some countries may hang back from multilateral negotiation in which they need to pay a price to achieve environmental quality improvements that others will benefit from. This has been emphasised by Barrett (1994). Environmental enforcement also has an important time-inconsistency dimension. OECD countries may strike deals with countries to meet environmental targets such as forest cover or species populations over a number of years. But if payment for these concessions takes place immediately, more money could potentially be repeatedly requested for environmental compliance. On the other hand, if payment is postponed until the end of the agreement, countries that conserve environmental assets have no assurance of getting paid.

This lack of internalisation denotes an institutional failure. In fact the international institutional architecture reflected in the present global environmental regime, and some 35 years in evolution, does not take as its starting point the design of mechanisms that seek to achieve internalisation of environmental externalities across countries. No agency attempting to achieve Coase's internalising deals across countries recognises the many problems in deal-making to improve environmental quality. The modern economics literature shows why private negotiation cannot easily complete the deals needed for international environmental internalisation, why intermediary agencies are needed, why scientific standard-driven arrangements produce only low-level environmental outcomes – in short, why a new global or at least regional agency for the environment is needed.

Progress in these areas has been scant and faltering. International environmental negotiations in the region are still in their infancy. In fact the present global economic institutions still reflect their 1940s origins and focus primarily on trade and finance as the dominant economic linkages between countries, rather than physical linkages.

The central global environmental problem is the relative lack of internalisation of cross-border and global externalities. We need an institutional form that seeks to achieve internalisation internationally, and one that does this by facilitating Coasian deals based on the perceived interests of the participants. At least since Coase (1960) it is known that bargaining between the parties to an externality would serve to achieve internalisation – no Pigou-type tax was needed. Coase argued that the issue of who should pay the additional costs of internalisation was a matter of property rights – who has the rights to what? Bargaining between the parties to an externality would serve to internalise it, with payments of compensation for damage to those having the legal rights to pursue redress and payment to induce reduction of damage by those parties having no such rights. Economic analysis is silent on the issue of who should have such rights. Also in the presence of an externality, bargaining (or Coasian deals) may already have been entered into and imposition of taxes or other measures could actually worsen the allocation of resources. Coase's discussion was largely centred upon narrowly defined externalities. In the case of global externalities the number of people affected is in the millions and the transaction costs of such bargaining (which Coase approximated to zero) are likely to be large. In fact we have seen some of the reasons why such bargaining may be hard to put in place. However, there is need for an international mechanism to facilitate such bargaining on this large scale. Other ancillary functions that need to be addressed are allowing for verification of completion of contracts and acting as a financial guarantor. While the WTO is cast within a bargaining framework, it is restricted since no cash is involved and the rules of the WTO Charter (via GATT 1994) constrain bargaining (such as the MFN rule).

The approach to consumption and sustainable development in this book

Our approach to sustainability (developed in some detail in Chapter 5) argues that current deliberations on sustainability are incomplete. This is because of two principal reasons. First, there is a somewhat narrow interpretation of sustainability in terms of reductions in consumption; the spatial dimension of stability is not considered or given only inadequate importance. Second, even in the context of reductions in consumption, the literature does not make clear the crucial role of behavioural changes and transfer of property rights over natural and environmental resources from the current generations to future generations.

The analysis in this book underscores these shortcomings. But it chooses to concentrate only on the problem of consumption reduction and advocates a strategy for attaining the reductions in consumption necessary for attaining sustainability. It advocates the use of group taxes on producers as well as consumers. Second, the tax revenues so collected should be earmarked for spending for the purpose of the environment. The resulting lowering of the discount rate and behavioural changes would lead to a drop in the rate of increase of prices of natural resources and, therefore, to a postponement of their consumption. All these involve the design of an intermediate run policy that treats environmental goods as *merit goods* as a prelude to their (ultimately) being treated as common resources.

In the long run, it is expected that behavioural changes and well-defined property rights would set-in a social dynamics that would endogenise the process of sustainability (The Endogenous Sustainability Hypothesis). Of course, it may be necessary to introduce and withdraw both taxes in an iterative manner because social behaviour may not change irreversibly, at one go. A distinct problem relates to the different treatment for renewable and non-renewable resources. This may be looked upon as a problem of the speed of adjustment. In the case of non-renewable resources the speed has to be faster, if such resources are essential to production. In such cases, greater reliance must be placed on exogenous changes in technology and tastes. In the case of renewable resources the expected change is essentially endogenous.

This analysis of the reduction in consumption is complemented with an analysis of the influence of the spatial distribution of consumption on sustainability developed in Chapter 5. The emphasis here is on developing an aggregate index of degradation rather than concentrating on individual degraders. We relate this aggregate index to a comprehensive index of economic development – the human development index – in order to better capture the links between environmental degradation and economic development.

Conclusions

Global environmental conditions have changed greatly during the recent past (UNEP 2003). Along with this have come immense changes in human conditions. The population of the planet has increased sharply, consumption levels in rich OECD countries remain high and high economic growth in some developing countries holds out promise for substantial increase in their consumption levels. As a consequence the environment has been heavily drawn upon to meet a multiplicity of human needs. In many areas, the state of the environment is much more fragile and degraded than it was in the 1970s.

Thus the world can now be categorised as consisting of four major divides (UNEP 2003):

1 The environmental divide. In many countries of the OECD environmental quality is high and may indeed have improved in recent times. In contrast the environmental quality in many parts of the developing world has deteriorated sharply. With no institutional mechanism to internalise transnational externalities an emerging threat is the sustained degradation of the global environmental commons.

2 *The policy divide.* There is sharp inequality between developed and developing countries in regard to both policy design and policy implementation. Whereas some developed countries are adept at both, many developing countries lack the institutional capacities to formulate, let alone implement, policies.

3 *The vulnerability divide.* As argued in this chapter some countries are increasingly vulnerable to environmental change. In view of existing trends, the environmental outlook for the near future appears grim for many parts of the developing world.

4 *The lifestyle divide.* There are large gaps in lifestyles between the developed and developing worlds. The former houses just one-fifth of the world's population but accounts for 90 per cent of total consumption whereas poverty is widely prevalent in the developing world where 1.2 billion live on less than USD 1 per day.

The four gaps are a serious threat to sustainable development. This book suggests that one component of a solution should be the redistribution of consumption from the rich to the poorer countries. It argues that it need not exacerbate environmental degradation, appropriately assessed. A complementary policy measure would be the internalisation of environmental externalities – at various levels. Incomplete internalisation – at the local, trans-boundary and international levels – is perhaps the single most important contributor to environmental problems globally. In view of the high costs associated with such lack of internalisation it is pertinent to inquire into the reasons why such internalisation is not forthcoming. This chapter has advanced some reasons for this phenomenon.

3 Methodological issues

A review

Introduction

A number of empirical studies on the relationship between pollution and economic growth have been conducted in recent years (e.g. Grossman and Krueger 1993, 1995; Hettige *et al.* 1992; Holtz-Eakin and Selden 1995; Selden and Song 1994). These studies report an inverse U-shaped relation between pollution and the level of economic development for some pollutants and, on account of its similarity to the pattern of income inequality documented by Kuznets (1955), this inverse U-shaped pollution–income pattern is often called an EKC (Figure 3.1). However, it should be emphasised that these empirical findings are debated (e.g. Ekins 1997; Harbaugh *et al.* 2000, Jha and Murthy 2003a; Jha and Whalley 2001; Perman and Stern 2003) and that there are warnings against exaggerated optimism based on them (Arrow *et al.* 1995).

In this chapter we will examine methodological issues raised in the extant literature on this topic. It could be argued that review articles exist and hence, there is no need to review the EKC literature any further. However, we feel that there is a need to do so because of three reasons. First, the extant discussion on EKC is so vast that any single review is not sufficient. Second, there is a need to review such review works themselves so as to get a synoptic view. Third, such a review would permit us to point out shortcomings in the extant literature and sharpen our point of view. The present chapter is in the nature of a review work and draws from[1] several other reviews.[2] In doing so the aim is to (i) evolve our conceptual framework; (ii) critically evaluate the extant empirical approaches; (iii) evolve our empirical constructs; and (iv) identify our causal framework. In a basic way we would look at all these aspects from the perspective of GED and GEM.

Previous literature on the EKC has identified some explanations for its particular shape. Among these are (i) changes in the composition of aggregate output as economies evolve from agricultural to industrial to service-based goods and services, (ii) technological progress, and (iii) increases in demand for environmental quality as income grows (Anderson and Cavendish 2001; Ansuategi and Escapa 2002; Grossman and Kruger 1995; Heerink *et al.* 2001; Panatoyou 1997). These three factors constitute a general approach to explaining the EKC.[3] In addition there are several other approaches, which we now discuss.

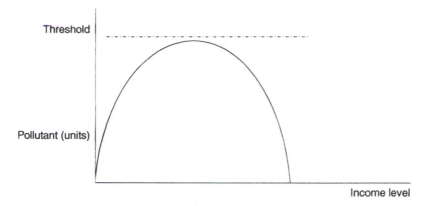

Figure 3.1 Environmental Kuznets Curve.

Role of institutions

Several authors have advanced theoretical models of the EKC and emphasise the preferences of consumers or institutional factors. Chichilinsky (1994), Lopez (1994) and Bohn and Deacon (2000) focus on property rights and institutions. Several analysts have included explanatory variables to explicitly account for the role of political institutions in the income–environment relationship. The specific institutions studied include The State, Democracy, Private Power and Demographics. For instance, Bhattarai and Hammig (2001) study the causes of deforestation in Latin America, Africa and Asia, by using a measure of institutional quality. They use an index that measures political rights and civil liberties, to account for the role of different policy regimes. Torras and Boyce (1998) use a similar technique based on panel data on a variety of air and water pollution indicators. These studies, however, do not explicitly attempt a decomposition of the demand for environmental policy based on heterogeneous population characteristics. They do not address the potential for distortions of the environmental quality preferences by different political regimes.

This approach believes that one of the major determinants of environmental policy is 'governance' (Rivera-Batiz 2002), identified as the socio-political regime of a particular country. Lopez and Mitra (2000) argue that corruption and rent-seeking behaviour can influence the relationship between income and the environment. They develop a theoretical model to show that corruption causes the turning points of an EKC to rise above the social optimum. On the other hand, Magnani (2000) suggests that well-defined property rights, democratic voting systems and respect for human rights can create synergies that lead to increased levels and efficacy of environmental policy. Eriksson and Persson (2002) have augmented the Stokey (1998) model by allowing agents to differ with respect to preference for environmental quality and income. They then analyse the impact of income and environmental inequality, and of democratisation on aggregate pollution. They find that the impact of a more equal income distribution depends on the degree of democracy.

Bond and Farzin (2004) have developed and estimated an econometric model of the relationship between air and water pollutants – CO_2, BOD, NO_x, VOC, SO_2 and $GEMSO_2$ and economic development while allowing for critical aspects of the socio-political economic regime of a State. Their hypothesis is that democracy and its associated freedoms provide the

> conduit through which agents can exercise their preferences for environmental quality more effectively than under an autocratic regime, thus leading to decreased concentrations or emissions of pollution. However, additional factors such as income inequality, age distribution, and urbanization may mitigate or exacerbate the net effect of the type of political regime on pollution, depending on the underlying societal preferences and the weights assigned to those preferences by the State.
>
> (Bond and Farzin 2004, p. 0)

Their explanation of this argument is based on the relationship between the demand and supply of environmental quality. Environmental quality, it is believed, in most cases, is a public good because the capital costs of the required infrastructures to abate pollution are huge, and individuals or groups within a society are unable to effectively provide them. Hence the state provides these goods and the realised environmental policy is a function of the preferences of society. The correlation between preferred and actual levels of environmental quality will depend on the weights placed on the various heterogeneous societal preferences by the policy-makers. This can be characterised as the policy regime. Specifically, it is suggested that environmental quality expenditures are, in part, a function of the preferences of society, but these preferences are subject to distortion (e.g. under political pressure from interest groups), interpretation and neglect by the State. The more open and democratic the society, however, the more likely it is that the preferences of society will be reflected in actual policy decisions.

With this as background it is straightforward to formulate an empirical model that assumes that policy can be instrumented solely by the democratic/autocratic structure of political institutions of the country. Thus we have:

$$X_{it} = \alpha_i + \sum_{j=1}^{3} \beta_j Y_{it}^j + \sum_{k=1}^{3} \beta_{k+3} P_{it}^k + \beta_7 D_{it} + \beta_8 D_{it} Y_{it} + \delta t + \varepsilon_{it} \qquad (3.1)$$

where X_{it} denotes the pollutant measure in country i at year t, Y_{it} is GDP per capita in year t for country i, P_{it} is population density in year t for country i, D_{it} is the democracy measure in year t for country i, t is a linear time trend to account for technological change over time, β_j and δ are regression coefficients, α's are country-level fixed effects and ε_{it} is an error term. Note that the policy variable enters both additively and multiplicatively, allowing for both intercept and slope shifts of the estimated relationship between national income and the pollution indicator. Equation (3.1) is utilised as a benchmark in the analysis, and used to test the EKC hypothesis and the effect of political institutions on environmental quality.

This equation is then extended to include variables which are expected to be correlated with (the heterogeneous) preferences of society at large, thus explicitly incorporating the demand for environmental quality into the specification. It is assumed that these preferences can be exercised only through the political system of the state, and as such the democracy variable is used to interact with each shifter. This specification implies that strongly autocratic regimes will be unresponsive to societal preferences relative to more democratic societies.

There are potentially many preference shifters. One such preference shifter discussed in the extant literature is inequality, both in political power and economic power. The former is incorporated through its interaction with the democracy variable. There is little agreement, however, on the causal relationship through which the latter, that is, income inequality, is manifested. One hypothesis suggests that there is evidence of a positive correlation between preferences for environmental degradation and individual's income and/or power due to ownership and consumption patterns (Torras and Boyce 1998). Bimonte (2002) advocates this hypothesis with respect to public lands. Magnani (2000) finds that reduced income equality decreases public expenditure on pollution abatement. This is, however, disputed by Scruggs (1998), who argues that higher levels of education and wealth are often associated with 'pro environment' preferences, so that movements in these directions (implying greater income inequality) within a country may result in better environmental quality.

Heerink *et al.* (2001) use individual household models with households both consuming and producing. They conclude that convexity and concavity properties of the individual household EKC determine the marginal effects of income redistribution when aggregated to the macro level, so that generalisations are inaccurate. While Bond and Farzin's (2004) model cannot distinguish between these competing theories, it helps in empirically testing whether and how income and political inequality significantly affect pollution indicators, implying a certain weighting structure by the State.

Other variables used in literature to explain policy preferences are demographics such as the proportion of youth in the population, the education level of the population and the degree of urbanisation. Age distribution is largely ignored by literature. John and Pecchenino (1994) and Jones and Manuelli (1994) focus on intergenerational conflicts, where the young strive for income while the elderly are interested in conservation. Ono and Maeda (2001) study the effects of an ageing population on environmental quality. Their analysis, based on the interaction of income and substitution effects from a change in longevity, concludes that the marginal impact of age distribution on environmental quality depends on the risk-aversion properties of individual agent's preferences. Particularly, if relative risk aversion with respect to consumption is less than one (implying that the population is not avert to intergenerational inequality in consumption), ageing may be beneficial to the environment. Furthermore, they indicate that technological change and growth in income can either mitigate or exacerbate the uncertain effects of age distribution on environmental quality, given different assumptions about the state of preferences and economic growth. Bond and Farzin hypothesise that a younger population tends to demonstrate a larger propensity to demand environmental quality. But this reasoning is based primarily on casual observation.

Bimonte (2002) argues that higher educational attainment is accompanied by a shift in preferences towards a higher level of environmental amenities. At the same time, education levels may affect the governance of a nation as well, since a more educated workforce contributes to a more educated (and possibly democratic-minded) public sector (Rivera-Batiz 2002). The net result of this preference shifter is thus expected to be reduced pollution with greater education levels, as the two effects complement each other in sign.

Finally, urbanisation is included to account for differences in preferences between rural and urban populations, as well as the potential economies of scale effects with regards to pollution abatement (Torras and Boyce 1998). Increased urbanisation may also improve the quality of governance, as costs of transportation and other communication means are lowered, thereby increasing the weights of citizen groups' preferences in the State's decision (Rivera-Batiz 2002). Of course, high degrees of urbanisation may result in increased pollution concentrations as well, as fossil fuel consumption per capita and per unit area increase (Panayotou 1997).

Formally, Bond and Farzin decompose equation (3.1) into these preference shifters and remodel this equation. The additional variables included are (i) U_{it} a measure of urbanisation, (ii) G_{it} the GINI coefficient measuring inequality, (iii) A_{it} the proportion of the population 14 years of age and under and (iv) I_{it}, the illiteracy rate of the adult population as a proxy for the education level. They maintain the assumption that the regime and preference shifters can affect both the intercept and slope of the income–environment quality curve, resulting in a significantly flexible functional form with marginal effects that may depend on the current state of development.

Inequalities, democracy and preferences

We now review the literature sketched above. Magnani (2000) emphasises well-defined property rights but does not provide a framework for including them. Similarly, Bond and Farzin (2004) emphasise environmental quality as a public good but do not provide a conceptual framework. On the other hand, in Chapter 5 of this book we clearly state the conceptual basis of what makes environmental quality a public good. In fact it is argued that it is a 'merit good'. Chapter 5 also provides a theoretical basis for the link between sustainability and property rights.

In the analysis in the section titled 'Role of institutions' four types of inequalities were discussed – those of age, education, income and rural–urban inequalities. Bond and Farzin, simplistically assume on the basis of 'casual observation', that youth have a greater concern and preference for a better environment. Such a misconception comes from equating democratic protests, about the environment, emanating from activists, to the behaviour of youth, in general. There is ample evidence on the basis of 'casual observation' that it is the youth who indulge the most, consume the most, waste the most and possess eco-unfriendly patterns of consumption as well. Similarly, the causal framework of income inequality and economic power is over-simplified. Scruggs (1998) assumes that higher inequality reduces environmental degradation. However, he does not provide empirical evidence and we need to ascertain through hard empiricism whether this actually happens. Second, even if it was granted that higher incomes would lead to such an effect, the question remains whether what holds true for individuals also holds for nations. Since our concern about and understanding of sustainability is global, the question remains unanswered. Across different studies there is no clarity on the question of inequality. Magnani (2000) finds that reduced income equality decreases public expenditure on pollution abatement. On the question of inequality in education Bimonte (2002) has argued that increases in education are often accompanied by 'increases in preferences that favour a higher level of environmental amenities'. Gangadharan and Valenzuela (2001) on the other hand, empirically show that education leads to a significant shift in the patterns of consumption towards those that are environmentally unfriendly. With regards to urbanisation the views of Torras and Boyce (1998), Rivera-Batiz (2002) and Panayotou (1997), conflict.

Such conflicting results may, at least, partly be due to the approach. Our approach is that education, urbanisation and inequality do not directly affect the environment but have to be understood within a causal framework. The HDI includes education and an age variable. We shall be incorporating HDI and other variables, such as urbanisation through a system of equations and a composite index of environmental degradors. In contrast, Bond and Farzin (2004) use six single equation models for six individual pollutants. Their main purpose is to establish that democratic polity leads to a better environment. Unfortunately, the results lead to ambiguous conclusions. First, the R^2's are low (not exceeding 0.44) and p-values are high indicating a poor fit. Even the sign of the main variable, polity, was not unambiguous: it was negative in the case of certain pollutants while for others it was positive. This reveals that the estimates are not robust. Most importantly it implies that conclusion regarding the main variable – polity – is questionable. This is because the argument about preferences exerting themselves more positively, in a democratic polity could either be true or false. It is not adequate that it holds good for certain pollutants and does not hold good for others. Once the structures exist in a democratic polity the impact should be felt across all pollutants. Preferences cannot be exerted only in the case of certain pollutants. In a democratic set-up what prevents similar influence in the case of other pollutants?

Eriksson and Persson (2002), argue that in a well-functioning democracy a more equal income distribution generates, *ceteris paribus*, less pollution, which is consistent with indirect empirical evidence, whereas the opposite is the case if democratic rights are highly restricted. Furthermore, democratisation typically lowers both the income and the environmental quality preferences of the median voter. In this case, if, in utility terms, the fall in environmental quality is worse than the fall in consumption the median voter decides to tighten environmental legislation so that aggregate pollution decreases.

Apart from the methodological question on inequality this raises a moot conceptual question. This question is about the relationship between preferences and policy. As emphasised in the statement by Dasgupta and Mäler (1995):

> The connection between environmental protection and civil and political rights is a close one. As a general rule, political and civil liberties are instrumentally powerful in protecting the environmental resource-base, at least when compared with the absence of such liberties in countries run by authoritarian regimes.
>
> (p. 2412)

Thus, they emphasise conscious choices of environmental policy emanating from civil rights to express preferences are the key to understanding the relationship between economic development and environmental quality.

While this may be true in principle, many questions arise. How are preferences shaped? In the democratic (market-oriented) economy what is the influence of advertisement and ethos on the preference formation process? How does consumerism influence demand for environmental quality? Even if all these questions are wished away the paramount question that remains is whether State policy (on environment) is unambiguously aligned to the choices of environmental policy emanating from civil rights? If this were the case it would imply that other forces (like private lobbies) do not influence State policy. It also assumes that the State acts in the best interest of the people. Here the problem is that while, under ideal conditions, it can be assumed that the State may actually act impartially, it cannot be assumed that the State 'knows' what is right for the environment.

Recent trends in the ecological economics literature emphasise the role of Participatory Processes, wherein it is 'people' who are at the grassroots that are assumed to have the knowledge (Stagl 2003; van den Hove 2000) of what is right for the environment.

Growth models

The tradition of growth models in the area of EKC bases itself on the notion that EKC is a correlation in search of an underlying theoretical explanation. Since it was discovered in panel data, there is no a priori reason to expect an EKC-type path to describe the evolution of an individual economy over time. Furthermore, little is known about why different time paths are observed for different pollutants and why the data for many degraders other than pollutants fail to fit the inverted U-shaped pattern.

Previous attempts to provide a theoretical explanation for the EKC owe much to the work of Forster (1973a,b) who introduced models of growth and environmental quality. Later, Selden and Song (1995) showed the possibility of a 'J' curve for abatement expenditures and an inverted 'U' curve for pollution when the marginal utility of consumption is initially higher than the marginal benefit from abatement. However, Selden and Song indicate that this need not always occur. Whether it occurs depends on the rate of growth of capital and consumption, and the response of pollution to abatement effort.

Stokey (1998) derives the conditions for the existence of the EKC when more productive techniques of production are also more pollution intensive. In her analysis, the marginal utility of consumption is high at lower income levels and pollution increases. If the marginal utility of consumption is not inelastic, then substitution of cleaner and less productive technologies for the dirtier and more productive ones causes pollution to eventually decrease. She analyses variants of neoclassical growth models and derives conditions for realising an optimal growth-environment path in a decentralised economy. She derives the result that the price of a pollution permit should equal the optimal tax on pollution for either a flow or a stock pollutant. She further shows that pollution standards cannot produce the optimal outcome. Although the focus of Stokey's analysis is not on technological improvements in emissions, but on substitution among techniques of production, her model implies a long-run movement towards the use of cleaner but otherwise less-efficient techniques. Furthermore, along with Forster (1973b), Stokey (1998) treats pollution as an increasing and convex function of capital. There is growing evidence, however, that capital efficiency increases and the pollution intensity of capital decreases in the long run as technology advances and market distortions are removed (Khanna and Zilberman 1999; Reppelin-Hill 1999). Thus, a fundamental driving force in the standard neoclassical approach to the EKC is open to doubt.

In their seminal paper, Andreoni and Levinson (2001) (henceforth AL) set-up a simple static model to analytically derive sufficient conditions for an EKC. We sketch the AL model below. Utility of the representative agent depends on consumption (C) and pollution (P) and can be expressed as:

$$U = U(C, P) \tag{3.2}$$

where $U(C, P)$ is quasi-concave in C and $-P$ (disutility) and both arguments and are normal goods. Pollution is a function of consumption and environmental effort E given by:

$$P = C - B(C, E) \tag{3.3}$$

Pollution increases one to one with consumption (gross pollution) as represented by the first term on the RHS of equation (3.3). On the other hand, pollution decreases due to abatement as represented by the second term of the RHS, $B(C, E)$. This is the abatement technology, which is increasing in both arguments, consumption C and environmental effort E. Both inputs are essential for abatement, that is, $B(0; E) = B(C; 0) = 0$. One the one hand, it is clear that abatement requires a positive amount of environmental effort, that is, $E > 0$. On the other hand, effective abatement necessarily requires pollution, that is, $C > 0$. Otherwise, cleaning up would simply be ineffective.

The next basic equation is a standard budget constraint given by:

$$M = C + E \tag{3.4}$$

where M denotes the resources available (income) and is spent either on consumption or environmental effort.

Also abatement is given by

$$B(C, E) = C^\alpha E^\beta \tag{3.5}$$

Such that $\alpha + \beta > 1$ (Increasing returns to scale – IRS- exist).

AL show that there are two conditions which guarantee the existence of an EKC. The first condition (related to the preference side of the model) requires that the marginal willingness to pay to clean up the last speck of pollution does not go to zero as income approaches infinity. As AL notice, this is a rather weak condition and is easily satisfied since pollution abatement can be regarded as a normal good. The second condition (related to the abatement technology) requires that there must be increasing returns to scale (IRS) in abatement. Together both conditions are sufficient to guarantee the existence of an EKC.

Subsequently, Chimeli and Braden (2002) presented a two-sector endogenous growth model with an initial imbalance in capital. This chapter and Song's analysis share a similar driving force for the EKC. But Chimeli and Braden extend Song's work by formally characterising the transitional dynamics of the economy when environmental quality is initially abundant relative to capital, solving for the implementation of the social optimum in a decentralised economy, explicitly deriving the time when environmental quality starts to improve, and analysing the difference in timing for the improvement of different environmental problems as a function of the efficiency of environmental protection.

Chimeli and Braden's model severs the link between capital and environmental quality by distinguishing pollution from environmental quality, with the latter also being affected by public investments. They do not assume that capital productivity is positively associated with pollution intensity, and instead of assuming that pollution increases at an increasing rate with the accumulation of productive capital, they focus on the possibility of a linear relationship that may nevertheless overstate the long-term prospects for pollution. This model differs from the previous work not only in its characterisation of the environment and the technical relationship between productive capital and pollution, but also in admitting the possibility of public investment in environmental improvement apart from pollution reduction. As a result, they provide a more general result for the optimal set of public policies for growth and environment in a decentralised economy. Furthermore, their derivation of the EKC is not affected by the elasticity of marginal utility.

Their analysis is an advance beyond previous works in three respects. First, they provide a simpler and more powerful explanation for the EKC than had previously been offered – an explanation based on the relative scarcity of different types of capital during a country's development. Second, they showed that typical environmental policy instruments that implement the social optimum in a static framework, such as taxes and permits, by themselves are insufficient to produce the desired result in a dynamic model. In a dynamic model inducing the optimal level of pollution through pollution taxes and permits goes only part way towards the optimal provision of environmental quality. Third, their model was able to solve for the time when environmental protection starts to improve and to investigate its determinants. In particular, they showed how different efficiencies of expenditure[4] can coexist.

In their model, individuals care about both the consumption of a private good and the stock of environmental quality, which is a public good. The advantage of modelling environmental quality in the utility function, as opposed to pollution, is in revealing that achieving the optimal level of emissions is only part of the problem of optimally providing environmental quality. The creation of nature reserves, ecosystems rehabilitation, pollution sequestration and species reintroduction are among the other means of environmental improvement. They introduce these options in a stylised form and solve for the transitional dynamics and balanced growth paths (BGPs) of environmental quality, consumption, environmental protection expenditures and productive capital. They show that their model can account for important empirical regularities in the relationship between growth and environmental quality.

Their model is also distinctive in representing environmental quality as a stock rather than as a flow. Pollution degrades environmental quality, which can be restored only after the passage of some period of time – shorter for some aspects of environmental quality than others. For example, SO_2 emissions are less important for their effects on ambient SO_2 concentrations than for their enduring effects on soil chemistry, forest stocks, lake chemistry and aquatic biodiversity (Alewell *et al.* 2000; Likens *et al.* 1996). Persistent effects on environmental quality also result from chlorofluorocarbons (CFCs) (Schrope 2000) and many other industrial pollutants. Therefore, the focus is on the state of the environment, characterised as a stock that can change as a result of emissions on one hand and corrective actions on the other. Further, in contrast to much of the EKC literature, their model concentrates primarily on the relationship between growth and environmental quality – a public good – rather than between growth and pollution. Since pollution diminishes environmental quality, in their framework, the EKC translates into a U-shaped relationship between income and environmental quality. They are interested in the growth path that is optimal for an economy over time and model this from the perspective of a social planner in an economy characterised by low initial income, abundant initial environmental quality and the potential for endogenous growth.

The transitional dynamics of the economy to an optimal BGP are consistent with three empirical regularities. First, environmental quality diminishes initially during a phase of intensive income growth, but eventually environmental quality improves as income growth continues, albeit at a slower rate. Thus, the optimal growth path for an individual economy is consistent with the EKC. Second, the planner will begin to invest in environmental improvement only after income and environmental quality reach threshold levels of capacity to invest in public goods and perceived need for environmental protection. At that point, investment in environmental improvement ratchets up quickly and thereafter continues to grow. This picture of benign neglect until reaching a threshold income level and stock of productive capital is consistent with the history of most of the developed countries. In the US, for example, most of the public commitment to environmental protection dates from the late 1960s and early 1970s, long after the introduction of regulations addressing other types of market failure (Portney 1990). Third, when environmental protection begins to be a focus of significant investment, income growth rates decrease leading some commentators to suggest that environmental protection is a drag on income growth (see, for example, Denison 1985; Jorgenson and Wilcoxen 1990; Stokey 1998). Their analysis also sheds light on the timing of reversal of environmental trends. For example, while acid precipitation has declined in North America and Europe (Krajick 2001) and there is hope that stratospheric ozone may rebound with the international elimination of ozone-destroying compounds (Schrope 2000), global temperatures appear to be headed upwards as a result of ever-increasing GHG emissions (Holtz-Eakin and Selden 1995; Schmalensee *et al.* 1998). These models show how variation in the efficiency of expenditures on prevention and remediation across different environmental problems can help to explain differences in rates of progress towards reversal.

Egli and Steger (2004) extend the AL model. They employ a simple dynamic macroeconomic model to investigate issues related to the EKC. Their attempt is to show that an EKC arises naturally in the course of economic development. The resulting EKC represents a smooth development path and does not rely on abrupt changes (giving rise to discontinuities) as in most previous dynamic approaches. Their analysis demonstrates that an EKC can be represented both as a transitional dynamics phenomenon as well as a balanced growth phenomenon.

By focusing on the social solution, they are able to derive analytical solutions for the critical thresholds of income and the point in time at which pollution starts to decline. The consequences of external effects and public policies on these critical thresholds are investigated numerically by simulating the transition process. It turns out that the impact of even small market failures is tremendous and hence there is a strong role for public policy. Moreover, they show that an observed N-shaped pollution–income relation (PIR) can be plausibly explained from the interaction of public policy measures and the intrinsic properties of the model. The model implies that this N-shaped PIR is actually an M-shaped PIR. They first consider the socially controlled economy. Subsequently, the decentralised equilibrium is derived taking external effects associated with polluting consumption and environmental effort into account. Finally, optimal taxes are determined.

Egli and Steger simulate their model to answer some important questions. (i) If an EKC can be shown to exist theoretically, how long does it take until pollution starts to decline? Similarly, provided that pollution vanishes, at which point in time does this occur? (ii) At what levels of income does pollution reach its peak and finally vanishes? (iii) Provided that the optimal long-run stock of overall pollution is finite, how large is this optimal long-run stock of overall pollution?

The results of Egli and Steger can be summarised as follows:

1   They confirm the basic finding of AL according to which increasing returns to scale in abatement can explain an inverted U-shaped PIR. This is important to the extent that the analysis of AL completely ignores the intertemporal dimension of the problem.
2   By focusing on the social solution, they derive closed-form solutions for the resulting dynamic system. It is possible then to analytically determine the critical level of income and point in time at which pollution starts to decline.
3   They investigate the consequences of market failures and public policy. By simulating the transition process of the market economy, they show that the critical thresholds are highly sensitive with respect to external effects.
4   They show that an empirical pattern which is observed for some specific pollutants (i.e. an N-shaped PIR) can plausibly be explained as a consequence of the interaction of public policy measures and the intrinsic properties of the model.
5   They observe that an N-shaped PIR may indeed turn out to be an M-shaped PIR implying that pollution eventually starts to diminish.

Growth and demography

We now shift our focus on another model in the context of EKC, that of Marquez and Tamarit (2004). They construct an endogenous growth model. They rightly point out that:

> only a naive interpretation of the EKC hypothesis may lead people to believe that the best role for policy-makers is to keep away from active environmental protection policies.
>
> (p. 19)

But their subsequent statement that:

> There is no reason to believe that the eventual positive relationship linking growth and environmental quality is inevitable, because even though economic growth directly fosters higher abatement expenditures it also increases pollution. In this context, policy has a very important role to play by promoting both sustained growth and the environment.[5]
>
> (p. 20)

is not well substantiated.

Marquez and Tamarit go beyond short-run dynamic interpretations and provide a long-run alternative view based on the variability of population growth rates and the willingness to pay for a cleaner environment, while they leave technical and preference parameters unchanged. Theirs is a simple model of endogenous growth that builds upon the traditional Rebelo's (1991) one-sector AK model into which pollution has been incorporated. In their model welfare depends not only on consumption but also on the quality of the environment and pollution arises from production, as a by-product, and enters the consumer's utility function as an externality. Pollution may be mitigated by means of emissions abatement activities, which allow control of the degree of dirtiness associated with production technologies as well as for the net flow of pollutants to the environment. Since these activities are costly they reduce investment and consumption possibilities.[6]

Aznar-Marquez and Tamarit model a one-sector closed economy. Gross output, Y, is obtained according to an aggregate production function of the AK type where capital is the only factor needed to produce,

$$Y(t) = AK(t) \tag{3.6}$$

Input K is an aggregate composite of broad capital, which includes physical as well as human capital. In this economy there is an aggregate pollution flow $P(Y(t), B(t))$, which arises as a by-product of economic activity Y and B (abatement). The emissions flow is increasing with respect to gross output and decreasing with respect to abatement B, that is, $P_1 > 0$ and $P_2 < 0$. Function $P(.)$ is assumed homogeneous of degree zero, that is, an equally proportional increase in both output and abatement leaves the emissions flow unchanged independently of the population size.

Consequently, we may write

$$P(Y(t), B(t)) = E(B(t)/Y(t)) \tag{3.7}$$

There is an effective upper bound for the emissions function. The structure of the model yields a long-run BGP, defined as an allocation in which consumption per capita grows at a constant rate and the dirtiness index, Z, is constant.

$$Z = 1 - [B(t)/Y(t)]\varepsilon[0,1] \tag{3.8}$$

The dirtiness index, Z, in turn, depends positively on the productivity parameter when the intertemporal elasticity of substitution is greater than one, but the sign of this relationship cannot be analytically determined for values of such elasticity lower than one. Moreover, to ensure a positive BGP, the higher the patience of agents the higher should be the value of Z. When consumers show a high level of patience, the central planner optimally decides to reallocate resources towards capital accumulation, which enhances growth. This is done so intensively that it may even divert some resources previously devoted to pollution abatement. This leads to production with a more dirty technique. Because of the crowding out effect, the higher the weight of environmental care in the utility function the smaller would be the dirtiness index. Finally, they also state that the greater the population growth rate the higher the dirtiness associated with the effective production technique because with higher population growth the central planner decides to divert more resources from abatement effort.

The Aznar-Marquez and Tamarit growth model has some distinguishing characteristics. They go beyond the three most conventionally assumed channels – scale, composition and technique effects – through which income growth is assumed to affect environmental quality. Grossman and Krueger (1995), McConnell (1997) and Panayotou (1997) consider that the state of the environment may deteriorate (improve) over time if consumer tastes shift towards less (more) environmental concern, causing an autonomous shift in the demand for environmental safeguards. In general, different levels of institutional and organisational development are accompanied by corresponding varying levels in education and awareness of the effects of pollution. Hence, three fundamental states can be identified. The first is the agricultural state, where people live in a stationary equilibrium with nature. Given that survival depends on environmental sustainability people show high environmental concern, which is incorporated in traditional habits of consumption and inherited techniques of production. This equilibrium is low in pollution intensity. The second state is industrial where people are more concerned with earning their own living and other material needs and show low concern for environmental quality. Individuals cannot afford much expenditure on abatement and, consequently, this state is high in pollution intensity. Finally, there is the post-industrial state where people demand higher levels of environmental quality. This state is low in pollution intensity not only because individuals show a high environmental concern, but also because they have the needed resources to abate pollution. According to this, an eventual improvement of the environment may arise from the increased demand for environmental protection, based on the increased willingness to pay for environmental care at higher levels of income per capita.

Some authors feel that there exists an empirically well-documented demographic relationship between PCI levels and population growth rates, the demographic transition phenomenon, which is a consequence of the development process. This transition has very clear implications for the rates of population growth in agricultural, or subsistence, industrialising and services-oriented economies, respectively (Dahan and Tsiddom 1998; Kremer 1993; Mincer 1995; Tabata 2003). In general, the demographic transition occurs in three stages of development. In stage I both birth and death rates are high, and the population grows slowly. At stage II, because of the improved sanitation and health care, the death rate falls. However, the birth rate remains high, and the population grows rapidly. In stage III, because of the changes in marginal costs and benefits of having children, the birth rate falls approaching the death rate, which has remained low. The population now grows more slowly.

Combining the two previous ingredients Aznar-Marquez and Tamarit conclude that:

> development and income growth provoke fundamental changes in the economy, in such a way that we can first postulate for low rates of population growth and high environmental concern at the initial stages of the development

process, when economies are essentially agricultural and they suffer a limited impact from economic activities on the environment. Then, at the intermediate stages, when economies become fundamentally industrial, the rates of population growth are higher and the environmental concern lower. Thus, increased emission of pollutants and more dirty technologies lead to increase the environmental damage. Finally, for high developed and basically services oriented economies the rates of population growth is again low and the environmental concerns care high.

(p. 3)

Their assumption is that there now exist cleaner technologies and a growing ability and willingness to pay for a better environment, which tend to reduce environmental degradation. They conclude, 'Therefore, we can modelise a long-term EKC on the basis of the evolution and changes experienced by two structural parameters of the model alone', that is, the population growth parameter and the environmental concern parameter (p. 3).

Critical evaluation of growth models

While there may be individual differences, a general (across models) evaluation of growth models in the area of EKC literature can be advanced under the following six headings:[7]

1   Types of models
2   Features of models
3   Assumptions
4   Advantages of models
5   Problems with models
6   General issues.

Types of models

The literature has considered four broad categories of models.

* Static
* Transitional dynamics
* BGP
* Endogenous growth.

While some have been empirically estimated, in most cases the empiricism is limited to some numerical simulation. The dominant formulations are theoretical.

Features of models

The models are largely based on patterns of consumption and abatement, their parameters and interaction. The utility function is primarily based on consumption and pollution. In certain cases the emphasis is on environmental quality rather than pollution. The policy alternatives and scenarios considered in the models include decentralised vs. centralised economies, state intervention as optimal taxes, public policy and the role of a Social Planner.

The models mostly predict an inverted U-shaped EKC. However, Chimeli and Braden's model severs the link between capital and environmental quality by distinguishing pollution from environmental quality, where the latter can also be affected by public investments. They arrive at a U-shaped EKC, rather than an inverted U-shape. Their model is also distinctive in representing environmental quality as a stock rather than a flow. It is admitted that, 'the impact of even small market failures is tremendous and hence there is a strong role for public policy'. Egli and Steger argue that the model implies that the N-shaped PIR is indeed an M-shaped PIR.

Assumptions

Assumptions may differ from model to model, however there are some common strands.

1 Pollution results from consumption.
2 Individuals care both about the consumption of a private good and the stock of environmental quality, which is a public good.
3 $B(C, E)$ is the abatement technology, which is increasing in both arguments consumption C and environmental effort E. Both inputs are essential for abatement, that is, $B(0; E) = B(C; 0) = 0$.
4 There are two formulations of abatement technology (and expenditure). One depicts abatement without external effects, with abatement being in the form;

$$B(C, E) = C^\alpha E^\beta$$

Such that $\alpha + \beta > 1$ – implying IRS. The second formulation allows for external effects as well, with abatement being of the form;

$$B(C, E) = C^\alpha E^\beta Ex^\eta.$$

5 In her analysis Stokey states that at lower income levels, the marginal utility of consumption is high and pollution rises with income. If the marginal utility of consumption is not inelastic, then substitution of cleaner and less productive technologies for the dirtier and more productive ones eventually causes pollution to decrease. This is one example of a production-based approach.
6 The transitional dynamics of the economy to an optimal BGP are consistent with the three empirical regularities corresponding to agricultural, industrial and service-oriented societies noted above.
7 For a positive BGP, the higher the patience of agents the higher the value of Z (dirtiness index).
8 Aznar-Marquez and Tamarit assume that the post-industrial society is one where people demand higher levels of environmental quality. This state is low

in pollution intensity because individuals show a high environmental concern, but also because they have the needed resources to abate pollution. According to this view, an eventual improvement of the environment may arise from the increased demand for environmental protection, based on the increased willingness to pay for environmental care at higher levels of income per capita.

9   Finally, for highly developed and, basically, services-oriented economies the rate of population growth is low and environmental concerns are high.

10   Aznar-Marquez and Tamarit conclude that the EKC can be explained with just two parameters, that is, the population growth parameter and the environmental concern parameter.

Advantages of models

These models succeed in providing a theoretical basis of the EKC, although the main basis of the EKC is empirical. They are able to identify the sufficient conditions for the existence of an EKC. The two conditions are – there must exist willingness to pay for cleaning up and IRS in abatement technology, although this raises vital questions in the global context. These two factors help explain the time paths shown in Figures 3.2(a) and (b) in addition to some issues considered below. Following Egli and Steger (2004) Figure 3.2(a) relates pollution to income, while Figure 3.2(b) relates pollution to time and the two figures address the questions when the downturn would occur and how much time it would take for pollution to come down to zero. The time horizon, under conditions of moderate externalities is predicted to be 250 years! Egli and Steger's model in the process also highlights the ineffectiveness of market solutions (Figure 3.3). The market solution takes a much larger income range for the downturn to be effective, while the social solution enables it at a much lower level of income.

Problems with the models

1   Consider the utility function $U = U(C, P)$. As per our understanding pollution depends upon consumption, that is, $P = f(C)$. This raises a vital question: if

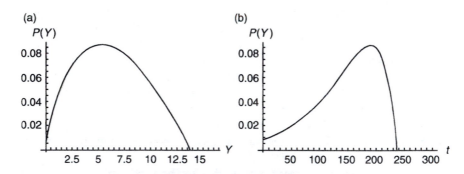

Figure 3.2 Time paths: (a) pollution to income and (b) pollution to time.

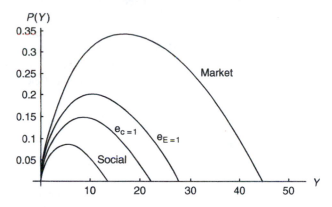

Figure 3.3 Market solutions.

we consider utility to be a function of C and P are they both separable? While it might pass for the theoretical model, how would this affect estimation?

2   Consider the relation $P = C - B(C, E)$ with $B(0; E) = B(C; 0) = 0$. In many poor economies it is possible that abatement expenditures is (nearly) zero. If E is zero $P = C$ and the utility function in a poor economy would be a 45° line. This would yield only corner solutions, if any.

3   Consider the claim that IRS is a necessary condition for EKC to exist. What about IRS in the global context (a GEKC)? How can abatement technologies be instituted across the globe? Who will pay for these technologies? How can abatement technologies have IRS across the globe?

4   Consider the assertion that the EKC depends only on two parameters; the first relating to population growth and the other to environmental preferences. We have shown that even the impact of population growth on the environment is not straightforward (in Chapter 2) even if we ignore various influences on preferences, like advertisement, consumerism and so on. Again, empirically speaking it shall be seen that even if per capita measures are taken for pollution (which accounts for the population growth), the relatively populous and poor countries do not display high levels of pollution (see Jha and Murthy 2003a, or Chapter 6 in this book).

5   Consider $Z = 1 - [B(t)/Y(t)] \varepsilon [0,1]$. If abatement is zero $Z = 1$. In poor economies there may not be any B but it has been empirically shown in various chapters in this book that their P is near to zero.

6   Consider IRS with externalities, that is, $B(C, E) = C^{\alpha} E^{\beta} Ex^{\eta}$ and $\alpha + \beta + \eta > 1$. In the global context the problem of GED depends upon internalisation of local externalities (see Chapter 9). Moreover, there could be many externalities like carbon sinks found in developing countries while pollution is generated in developed countries. The developed countries have the capacity and willingness to pay for abatement measures in their own countries. Would they be prepared to pay for these in developing countries?

The benefits are global. How would these models deal with such complex situations?

7   In general, these models assume that developed economies, post-industrial and service economies, have high demand for environmental quality. This assumption begs the question. The more pragmatic approach is to test whether this assumption is true. Stern (2003) suggests that 'the income elasticity of emissions is likely to be less than one – but not negative in wealthy countries as proposed by the EKC hypothesis' (p. 30). Also, de Groot (1999) asserts that 'although changes in the sectoral composition may give some relief and may explain temporary declines in emissions, they are insufficient to persistently delink (real) income and emissions' (p. 35).

8   Recent empirical studies have shown that, for some countries and pollutants, the best functional form is cubic, implying that for very high levels of income per capita environmental degradation starts to increase again (Torras and Boyce 1998; Jha and Murthy 2003a). Moreover, it can be shown that high-income elasticity for environmental quality is indeed helpful for an EKC conformable pattern, but it is neither sufficient nor necessary (McConnell 1997). Since recent empirical analyses suggest that relationship between income and pollution is influenced by consumer preferences for environmental quality, Plassmann and Khanna (2003) separate the impacts of consumer preferences and technological factors in the commonly used static model by shifting the focus from the disutility generated by pollution to the utility generated by activities that reduce pollution. They first show that it is always possible to obtain an EKC relationship with suitable preferences, regardless of the properties of the pollution function, while there is no pollution function that leads to an EKC relationship under all types of preferences. They then prove that a sufficient condition for an inverted U-shaped relationship between income and pollution is that the returns to scale in pollution abatement exceed the returns to scale in the generation of gross pollution, and that increasing returns to scale in abatement by themselves are not sufficient for an EKC relationship.

9   Consider the assertion that the higher the patience of agents the higher the value of Z (the dirtiness index). Contrary to this (in Chapter 5) we show that the problem arises because of the undue preference for present consumption, which has an adverse influence on the discount rate. Empirically, it is clear that the consumption patterns of developed countries display a higher dirtiness index (see Chapter 8 on GEKC and Chapter 7 on ESI).

10 Consider the assertion that the EKC is not N-shaped but M-shaped. This is based on a switching of transition from a market path to a social path while internalising externalities. 'At some point in time, policy instruments are implemented to internalise external effects and pollution diminishes accordingly' (Egli and Steger 2004, p. 19). We have already pointed out how difficult it is to effect such internalisation, especially in the global context.

11 It is common to assume that pollution results from production (e.g. Xepapadeas 2004) rather than from consumption and both assumptions

are plausible in principle. However, there are other theoretical studies, which assume that consumption generates pollution (Andreoni and Levinson 2001; John and Pecchenino 1994). Most importantly, however, polluting consumption represents a simplifying assumption, which does not affect the qualitative results. Within the current framework, production-induced pollution has two unfavourable consequences: (i) the model then shows transitional dynamics and (ii) a BGP does not exist.

Concluding remarks – general issues

Many of the conceptual planks that have been used by these models were proposed by our paper (Jha and Murthy 2000, reprinted as Chapter 5 of this volume). This work was the first to emphasise the Sustainability Hypothesis and the role of a Social Planner (State) in attaining it. This work precedes most of the growth models discussed in this chapter.

Egli and Steger propose some interesting questions for future research. For instance, it is well known that in the real world there are PIRs with very different shapes depending on the specific pollutant under consideration. Some of these individual pollution paths follow the EKC pattern, while others do not. To shed light on the importance of pollution heterogeneity for the overall level of pollution and welfare, it would clearly be interesting, they state, to extend their model to allow for different consumption activities (giving rise to the emission of different pollutants) as well as pollutant-specific abatement activities. 'Then the question arises whether the pollution structure that affects the overall level of pollution can be investigated' (2004, p. 21). This relates to our main criticism of extant literature. Most empirical and theoretical models only estimate EKCs based on single pollutants. Our methodology overcomes this problem.

Our second concern relates to the global environment. Strand (2002) points out 'that the evidence indicates that estimated EKC relationships appear to hold largely for local pollution indices, but less so for environmental and resource variables where effects occur on a global scale, such as biodiversity and carbon emissions' (p. 4). Further, Dijkgraff and Vollebergh (2001) cast doubt on empirical results based on panel estimations of an 'inverted-U' relationship between per capita GDP and pollution. Using a new data set for OECD countries on CO_2 emissions for the period 1960–97, they find that 'the crucial assumption of homogeneity across countries is problematic. Decisively rejected are model specifications that feature even weaker homogeneity assumptions than are commonly used. Furthermore, their results challenge the existence of an overall Environmental Kuznets Curve for carbon dioxide emissions' (p. 39). This brings us to one of our principal points: Does a GEKC exist?

The attempt of the growth models discussed in this chapter is to look for an economic rationale and an appropriate methodology to explain the inverted U-shaped EKC. This is where the analysis of growth models started. Our criticism brings the discussion full circle. Insofar as the EKC is an empirical model the prime concern should not be to build up a justification for the purported 'inverted

U-shaped EKC' through a well-developed theoretical model but to verify whether the EKC really exists and, if yes, what is its shape, level and downturn, in the global context with environmental degradation defined more broadly than one or a few pollutants. Since environmental degradation is a global problem and environmental sustainability needs a global approach there is a need to conceptually define GED, empirically estimate a GEKC, verify its shape and finally develop the causal framework for estimating such a construct globally.

Much of the rest of this volume is devoted to addressing these issues.

4 Global environmental degradation

Concept and methodology of measurement

Introduction[1]

The advent of EKC raises many questions: What have we learnt about the statistical relationships between various measures of environmental quality and income? Do all aspects of environmental quality deteriorate or improve systematically with economic development? At what point on the Y-axis does the turn of the EKC arise? What is the threshold income level at which it falls? In doing so does it go all the way to the X-axis (Figure 3.1)? What is the proportion of the area under the curve before the threshold? Most of all our concern is about a prime question. Does a global EKC exist?

In this chapter we explore the theoretical and empirical foundations of the EKC literature and emphasise the need for verifying the existence of a global EKC. We then outline our methodological approach to such estimation.

Income–environment relationship

It is possible to distinguish three main channels through which income growth affects the quality of the environment. In the first place, growth has a scale effect on the environment: a larger scale of economic activity leads to increased environmental degradation, per se. More output implies increased waste and emissions as by-products of economic activity. Second, income growth can have a positive impact on the environment through a composition effect: as income grows, the structure of the economy tends to change, with the share of cleaner components of the GDP gradually rising. Finally, technological progress often occurs with economic growth since a wealthier country can afford to spend more on research and development. This generally leads to the substitution of obsolete and dirty technologies with cleaner ones, further improving the quality of the environment. This is known as the technique effect of growth on the environment.

An inverted-U relationship between environmental degradation and PCI suggests that the negative impact on the environment of the scale effect tends to prevail in the initial stages of growth, but that it is eventually outweighed by the positive impact of the composition and technique effects that tend to lower the emission level. The income elasticity of environmental demand is often invoked in the literature as the main reason to explain this process. As their incomes grow, people achieve higher living standards and care more for the quality of the environment they live in. All extant studies on the EKC address the following common questions: (i) is there an inverted-U relationship between income and environmental degradation? (ii) If so, at what income level does environmental degradation start declining? As we shall see, both questions have ambiguous answers.

There are major differences across indicators as to the turning point of the EKC: carbon monoxide and especially nitrous oxides show much higher turning points than SO_2 and suspended particulate matters. Similar large differences occur in the case of SO_2. In the absence of a single environmental indicator, the estimated shape of the environment–income relationship and its possible turning point generally depend on the factors considered. This raises the basic question as to how we can explain the behaviour of developed countries. How can we explain their being sensitive and 'caring' about some pollutants while they are not so about other pollutants? This points towards the need to study environmental degradation as a composite rather than as individual pollutants. Jha and Murthy (2003a) (reprinted as Chapter 6), is one of the rare works that does so. We achieve this with the help of our original methodology.

Studies suggest that the EKC may only be a valid description of the environment–income relationship for a subset of all possible indicators. This points towards the need to use data reduction methods. In particular, both early and recent studies find that emissions of global pollutants (such as carbon dioxide (CO_2)) either monotonically increase with income and start declining, if at all, at income levels well beyond the observed range. This finding also points towards the need to study global environmental degradation rather than that of individual countries or that of a group of particular countries. This is further strengthened by the fact that some local pollutants (e.g. SO_2), may travel for hundreds of miles, so that they can be considered as both local and global air quality indicators. Selden and Song (1994) measure the flow of emissions of local air quality indicators in 22 countries, whereas Shafik (1994) focusses attention on the stock of the same indicators using a much larger database (up to 149 countries). Nevertheless, neither do so from the point of view of studying a global EKC. The only study that does so is Jha and Murthy (2003a) (Chapter 6 of this book). This study is based on 174 countries and is conceptualised as a Global Environmental Kuznets Curve (GEKC).

Possible patterns of the EKC

Dasgupta *et al.* (2002) point towards various possible patterns of the environment–income relationship as derived from extant literature. This is portrayed in Figure 4.1.

The EKC model has elicited conflicting reactions from researchers and policy-makers. Applied econometricians have generally accepted the basic tenets of the model and focused on measuring its parameters. Their regressions, typically fitted to cross-sectional observations across countries or regions, suggest that air

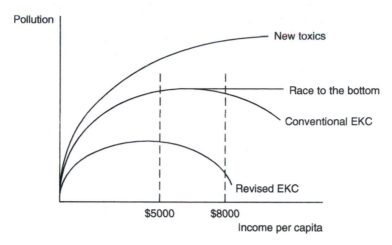

Figure 4.1 Environmental Kuznets Curve: different scenarios.

and water pollution increase with development until PCI reaches a range of $5000–8000. When income rises beyond that level, pollution starts to decline, as shown in the 'conventional EKC' line in Figure 4.1. In developing countries, some policy-makers have interpreted such results as conveying a message about priorities: Grow first, and then clean up. Numerous critics have challenged the conventional EKC, both as a representation of what actually happens in the development process and as a policy prescription. Some pessimistic critics argue that cross-sectional evidence for the EKC is nothing more than a snapshot of a dynamic process. Over time, they claim, the curve will rise to a horizontal line at maximum existing pollution levels, as globalisation promotes a 'race to the bottom' in environmental standards, as shown in Figure 4.1. Other pessimists hold that, even if certain pollutants are reduced as income increases, industrial society continuously creates new, unregulated and potentially toxic pollutants. In their view, the overall environmental risks from these new pollutants may continue to grow even if some sources of pollution are reduced, as shown by the 'new toxics' line in Figure 4.1. Although both pessimistic schools make plausible claims, neither has bolstered them with much empirical research. In contrast, recent empirical work has fostered an optimistic critique of the conventional EKC. The new results suggest that the level of the curve is actually dropping and shifting to the left, as growth generates less pollution in the early stages of industrialisation and pollution begins falling at lower income levels, as shown by the 'revised EKC' in Figure 4.1.

Cross-country studies

Given the lack of long time-series of environmental data, most empirical studies have adopted a cross-country approach. At the outset we should make a distinction between panel regression and cross-country analysis. While the former is a technique of estimation the latter is concerned with the level at which the EKC is being captured. In this section we lay the foundations for the estimation of a GEKC. Therefore, our emphasis is on the level aspect and not the technique aspect.[2]

Grossman and Krueger (1991) were the first to model the relationship between environmental quality and economic growth. Their methodology involved a cross-country panel of comparable measures of air pollution in various urban areas. In all, 42 countries are represented in Grossman and Krueger's sample for SO_2, 19 countries for smoke or dark matter, and 29 for suspended particulates. They found that ambient levels of both SO_2 and dark matter (smoke) suspended in the air increase with per capita GDP at low levels of national income but decrease with per capita GDP at higher levels of income. These findings provided statistical evidence for the existence of an EKC relationship for these two indicators of environmental quality. Following closely on the heels of the Grossman and Krueger study, Shafik and Bandopadhyay (1992) estimated the relationship between economic growth and several key indicators of environmental quality reported in the World Bank's cross-country time-series data sets. They found a consistently significant relationship between income and all indicators of environmental quality they examined.[3]

Discovering turning points requires a data set that contains PCI or GDP ranging from very low to high levels. Without this range of incomes, one might observe a monotonically rising or falling relationship between pollution concentrations and income rather than a curve. The appropriate range of incomes is not always available for higher-income countries, such as the US. If an EKC relationship is observed, it will likely be for the rightmost part of the curve, that portion where rising income levels are associated with environmental improvement. This result is found in the work by Carson *et al.* (1997). They found that emissions per capita decrease with increasing PCI for all seven major classes of air pollutants. In this respect, their results are consistent with those from country studies that find an EKC. In their work on auto lead oxide emissions across the developed world Hilton *et al.* (1998) found a more complete EKC. They opine that there is a related EKC identification problem when data are examined for all countries worldwide. The heterogeneity of the sample makes it extraordinarily difficult to account for institutional differences (Stern and Common 2001).

Our understanding is that if an EKC is to be estimated across the world then such factors would level off across countries in a cross section. Furthermore, our approach is to highlight the fact that essentially the EKC is an economic phenomenon. In a regression framework any 'unexplained variation' can be attributed to non-economic factors, like 'institutional differences'. If a model is under-specified there could be any number of social or institutional variables that can fill the gap. However, as long as the dominant underlying causal framework in the 'global population' is economic, a well-designed causal framework would adequately capture the 'economic causation', which needs to be distinguished from the social, institutional and above all 'ecological' influence. While these factors need to be taken into account they must be incorporated in the right manner and at the right time, and not obfuscate the main design of the model.

Bertinelli and Strobl (2004) employ a semi-parametric technique to investigate the existence of the EKC in a cross-country (135 countries) context. So far, results on cross-country studies measuring the relationship between economic growth and pollution have led to rather mixed results concerning the existence of an EKC (see, for instance, Shafik 1994; Selden and Song 1994; Grossman and Kruger 1995; Holtz-Eakin and Selden 1995; Stern and Common 2001; Hettige *et al.* 2000; Hamilton and Turton 2002 among others for recent evidence). However, all of these studies have imposed relatively restrictive functional forms. Their findings using the semi-parametric estimator suggest that in a cross-country sense, at least in terms of measuring pollution by SO_2 and CO_2, the link between environmental pollution and economic growth is actually monotonically increasing for low levels of GDP per capita, and flat thereafter.[4]

Single-country studies

As argued above, cross-country studies suggest that the EKC may only be a valid description of the environment–income relationship for a subset of all possible indicators. However, Roberts and Grimes (1997) have recently questioned the existence of an EKC even for indicators that seem to follow this pattern. They observe that the relationship between per capita GDP and carbon intensity changed from linear in 1965 to an inverted-U in 1990. How can we explain the modification in the curve shape over the last 30 years? Roberts and Grimes (1997, p. 196) argue that the Kuznets-type curve that we observe for carbon intensity today is the result of environmental improvement in developed countries in these last decades and 'not of individual countries passing through stages of development'. In fact, the data set shows that carbon intensity fell steadily among high-income countries in the period 1965–90, but increased among middle- and low-income nations, with a marked increment in the latter group. Therefore, the EKC that emerges in the cross-section analysis

> may simply reflect the juxtaposition of a positive relationship between pollution and income in developing countries with a fundamentally different, negative one in developed countries, not a single relationship that applies to both categories of countries.
>
> (Vincent 1997, p. 417)

For this reason, Vincent (1997) claims that the cross-country version of the EKC is just a statistical artefact and should be abandoned. In fact, as Stern *et al.* (1994) have argued, that more could be learnt from examining the experiences of individual countries at varying levels of development as they develop over time.

These considerations have given rise to a new line of research based on single-country analysis. This econometric approach achieves some surprising results that cast serious doubts on the reliability of the indications emerging from cross-country studies. Vincent (1997) examines the link between PCI and a number of air and water pollutants in Malaysia from the late 1970s to the early 1990s. Two main conclusions emerge from this study. First, cross-country analysis may fail to predict the income–environment relationship in single countries, as it occurs in the case of Malaysia. Second, none of the pollutants examined by Vincent shows an inverted-U relationship with income. Contrary to cross-section analysis, several measures indicate that increments in the income level may actually worsen environmental quality. It can be argued that the results achieved by Vincent hinge heavily on specific features of the country in question and cannot be extended to other countries. However, de Bruyn *et al.* (1998) reach similar conclusions following other individual countries over time. They investigate emissions of several air pollutants (SO_2, CO_2 and nitrous oxides) in four OECD countries (Netherlands, West Germany, UK and USA) between 1960 and 1993 and find them to be positively correlated with growth in almost every case. However, these conclusions are questioned by Carson *et al.* (1997) who find the opposite result in a single-country study on the US. Using data collected by the Environmental Protection Agency from the 50 US states, Carson *et al.* (1997) find that per capita emissions of air toxics decrease as PCI increases. In conclusion, all current single-country studies seem to suggest that the EKC need not hold for individual countries over time. However, different studies reach conflicting results as to the effects of growth on the environment. Therefore, further research is needed to understand the evolution of environmental degradation relative to income in a single country over time. In particular, both Vincent (1997) and Carson *et al.* (1997) are cross-regional studies, therefore they are also subject to the critiques to the cross-country approach mentioned above. In fact, cross-country studies implicitly assume that all countries will follow the same pattern in order to infer the environment–income relationship of a single country over time. As mentioned above, this assumption does not seem to be supported by empirical evidence. Similarly, in order to infer the environmental degradation of the whole country over time, cross-regional studies implicitly assume that all regions in a given nation will follow the same pattern. For some countries, however, regional differences can be very significant. Thus, the environment–income relationship may not only differ across nations, but also across regions of the same country.

Hence, although current single-country studies tend to go in the right direction, a time-series approach seems more appropriate than a cross-regional one to examine individual countries over time and this is the line of research that single-country analyses should develop in the future. However, our interest is in studying global environmental degradation. Therefore, these conclusions regarding single-country studies are of little relevance.

Empirical problems

We have argued above that cross-sectional studies (both cross-country and cross-region) limit the validity of the evidence at our disposal. In this section, we look at some other drawbacks of the current literature that should induce to view the available results with particular caution – particularly for policy purposes.

Data problems

The first and most obvious limitation of the studies on the EKC is the lack of good data on environmental indicators. Even when such data is available; it appears to be unreliable in some low-income countries because of data collection problems. In parts of the extant literature this has been taken to be an absolute limitation and the very need to estimate the EKC has questioned, by some. We do not subscribe to this view and have a more positive approach. Our methodology of data reduction (Jha and Murthy 2003a) would enable low-income countries to collect much fewer data series, such that data collection cost to them goes down and the reliability goes up. Beyond data quality and comparability, current studies may also suffer from sample selection bias. Our methodology does not suffer from these problems because we are not using sample countries but a large set of 174 countries, in the world.

Reduced-form models

Both cross-and single-country studies are based on reduced-form models. Reduced-form relationships 'reflect correlation rather than a causal mechanism' (Cole *et al.* 1997, p. 401). Hence, a simultaneous equation model may be more appropriate for understanding the environment–income relationship. There has only been one attempt (Dean 1996) to use this approach so far. However, Dean applies this method to investigate the impact of trade liberalisation on environmental quality in developing countries. Our methodology, in its final step, uses a simultaneous equation model (see Chapter 8 in this book).

Non-parametric estimation

Millimet *et al.* (2003) have shown with data for US states that parametric modelling can be rejected in favour of a semi-parametric estimator, since this does not impose any a priori restriction on the functional form of the relationship. However, given its semi-parametric nature, the estimate cannot be subjected to the kind of standard statistical tests (such as an F-test or a t-test) of parametric regressions. However, it is possible to calculate upper and lower point-wise confidence intervals, as suggested by Haerdle (1990). It should also be noted that the use of the semi-parametric estimator leads to the problem of non-identification of an unrestricted intercept term, which leads to a scaling issue when comparing the semi-parametric results with any parametric alternative.

Thus, Bertinelli and Strobl (2004) conclude:

> This paper re-examines the existence of an Environmental Kuznets Curve (EKC) across countries using a semi-parametric regression estimator, which places no restrictions on the functional form. Our results using cross-country panel data on Sulfur and Carbon Dioxide strongly suggest that the relationship

between wealth and environmental degradation is not bell-shaped, as suggested by an EKC. Rather that there is a positive link for the very poorest countries and no clear relationship for richer countries.

(p. 1)

Other variables

Most of the EKC studies use GDP per capita. When other living standard variables have been used the results have not been encouraging. Bertinelli and Strobl (2004), conclude:

> We also experimented with other controls, such as openness and population growth rate. However, these made little qualitatively or quantitative difference and only reduced sample size, ... The main problem is that any attempt to incorporate other variables without an adequate theoretical or conceptual framework is bound to yield ambiguous results.

(p. 3)

Evolving our approach

In his review Stern (2003) comments, 'The EKC is an essentially empirical phenomenon, but most of the EKC literature is econometrically weak.'[5] He also points out that

> When we do take diagnostic statistics and specification tests into account and use appropriate techniques *we find that the EKC does not exist* (Perman and Stern 2003). It seems that most indicators of environmental degradation are monotonically rising in income though the 'income elasticity' is less than one and is not a simple function of income alone.

(p. 3)

Therefore, from the above quote, it is fairly clear that the shape of the EKC can no longer be taken for granted. In fact the criticism is much more fundamental because not only direction of change, after the 'threshold' but also the cause of environmental degradation are being questioned.

However, one of Stern's assertions needs to be examined critically. He states that 'most studies assume that if the regression coefficients are individually or jointly nominally significant and have the expected signs then an EKC relation exists. However, one of the main purposes of doing econometrics is to test which apparent relationships, or 'stylised facts', are valid and which are spurious correlations'. To further this argument we take an analogy from Real Business Cycle Theory (RBCT). In RBCT it is known that with some exceptions, price level, interest rate, wages, employment, income, production and so on, all move in the same direction, during each phase of the cycle. These are the 'stylised facts' about a business cycle. There is a universal appeal about these happenings and there is virtually no controversy over this. The debate in macroeconomic theory is about why business cycles occur and how they are propagated.

In a similar vein the EKC is considered to be an empirical construct in search of a theory or a conceptual framework. The growth models, considered in Chapter 3, are an attempt at providing such a conceptual framework. The problem with them is that they are unable to explain GED and a possible GEKC phenomenon. We are in agreement with Stern that the method of study of the EKC rests on evolving a method that explains the 'stylised facts', at the global level. But the disagreement is over the notion that the hub of the problem rests upon the econometric methods used, although improvement of econometric methods helps in better estimation. According to our understanding, the debate in EKC should no longer be about which of the 'stylised facts' are 'valid' (*a la* Stern) but about *what are* the 'stylised facts'. This needs to be examined from the point of view of developing a more fundamental approach to environmental sustainability. It is this methodological consideration that has guided our approach to environmental sustainability, which we have coined as 'The Consumption Approach'. While there may be certain areas of overlap with ours, by contrast, the other approaches can be termed as 'The Production Approach', 'The Structural Approach', 'The Technology Approach' and so on. The differences arise because the concerns are different. It is not as though one approach could or should overthrow the other approaches but we must recognise that different approaches may and should coexist because the issue of environmental sustainability is too complex. Then how do we decide which approach is better. Once again we can draw a parallel with RBCT. As is the case with RBCT, the efficacy of different approaches is sought to be evaluated with the help of the following criteria:

1   ability to explain the 'stylised facts'
2   simplicity
3   consistency with economic theory
4   plausibility.

These criteria are straightforward. However, the interpretation of the evaluation through these criteria is rather complex and may not be straightforward in the sense of enabling the establishment of the superiority of one approach over the other. On the one hand, the evaluation of different approaches may lead to a judgement that considers one approach as being more plausible while the other being more simple and yet another being more consistent. Therefore, the end result could point to the coexistence of approaches. Yet, it might just be that one approach scores over others in an overwhelming way. Thus, this overall critical methodology helps in clarifying to ourselves the state of ignorance or knowledge, in which we find ourselves, at the present juncture. It helps in answering the question, as to whether our 'state of knowledge' can afford a *unique* answer to fundamental questions like – Does a GEKC exist? What is its shape? And so on. Or whether we would have to reconcile to the coexistence of various approaches, each having its importance in literature, till such time that the 'state of knowledge' enables us to throw-up a unique answer?

It is to make such an assessment that we would like to elaborate upon our methodology and attempt a preliminary comparison with other approaches. For this it is necessary to first specify our understanding of the 'stylised facts'. The 'stylised facts' quoted in extant literature are quite different.

> (i) only some indicators (mainly air quality measures) follow an EKC; (ii) an EKC is more likely for pollutants with direct impact on the population rather than when their effects can be externalised; (iii) in all cases in which an EKC is empirically observed, there is still no agreement in the literature on the income level at which environmental degradation starts decreasing.

As per our understanding the stylised facts are as follows:

1   The consumption levels are phenomenally higher in developed countries, in absolute and relative terms, as compared to developing countries, as a class.
2   The level of environmental degradation, as measured by a set of environmental degraders, is also much higher, in the case of developed countries, as a class, in absolute and relative terms.
3   There is a high degree of correlation amongst these environmental degraders, in general.
4   There is a convergence of consumptions patterns across the globe, as between developed and developing countries.
5   There is a convergence of the 'type of economic development', with the advent of globalisation, as between developed and developing countries.
6   Finally, all the above 'stylised facts' have a bearing on global environmental sustainability.

Therefore, it is necessary to conceptualise, evolve and estimate a construct that explains global environmental sustainability and to develop a causal framework for the same. This entire gamut spells out our approach. The elements of our approach are as follows:

1   our notion of sustainability (Chapter 5);
2   our critical evaluation of extant studies (this Chapter and Chapter 3);
3   our concept of GED (Chapter 4 and 6);
4   the envisaged mesoeconomic structures (Chapter 2);
5   our construct – the GEKC (Chapter 6);
6   our econometric methodology (in this chapter and elsewhere);
7   the causal framework (Chapter 8).

Having said all this about the framework of our methodology, in response to Stern, we wish to raise another more fundamental question. What is the level at which the phenomenon of EKC needs to be captured and studied? We take-up this question later.

Extant approaches

'The Production Approach', 'The Structural Approach' and 'The Technology Approach', all complement each other. It is therefore, difficult to separate them. We shall attempt to give a combined critique.

There is an intuitive appeal about the shape of the EKC and its evolution through different stages of economic development. At low levels of PCI in agrarian economies based on subsistence farming, one might expect environmental conditions to be relatively unaffected by economic activity. Pollutants associated with industrial activity would be virtually absent or low. With development and industrialisation environmental damage increases due to greater use of natural resources, more emission of pollutants and the operation of less-efficient and relatively dirty technologies. As economic growth continues and life expectancies increase it is expected (or assumed) that cleaner water, improved air quality and a cleaner habitat become more valuable as people make choices at the margin about how to spend their incomes. It is also expected (or assumed) that much later, in the post-industrial stage, cleaner technologies and a shift to information and service-based activities combine with a growing ability and willingness to enhance environmental quality (Munasinghe 1999). Thus, Aznar-Marquez and Ruiz-Tamarit (2004) state that, 'an eventual improvement of the environment may arise from the increased demand for environmental protection, based on the increased willingness to pay for environmental care at higher levels of income per capita' (p. 18).

This has been the conventional argument justifying an inverted U-shaped EKC. While there is agreement about the very early stages of economic development and environmental change the later developments need to be questioned. The essence of research in the area of EKC relates to the later developments and leads to an intense debate as to whether the latter changes take place so certainly, systematically and predictably. In fact there is enough literature to completely put to doubt the hypothesis of a downturn taking place at all.[6] There are four assumptions on which the downturn of the EKC, in the case of rich countries, is based.

1   Rich countries have access to better production technologies and that they export bad technologies to developing countries (pollution haven hypothesis).
2   Rich countries have better abatement technologies and the capital to invest in them.
3   Poor countries have a high marginal utility of consumption.
4   Rich countries and societies value a better environment because their basic needs have been met.

Stokey (1998) derives the conditions for the existence of the EKC. She states that 'at lower income levels, the marginal utility of consumption is high and pollution increases. If the marginal utility of consumption is not inelastic, then (at higher-income levels) substitution of cleaner (and less productive technologies) for the dirtier (and more productive ones) causes pollution eventually to decrease'. A casual examination of Figure 4.2 reveals that 40 per cent of the richest countries

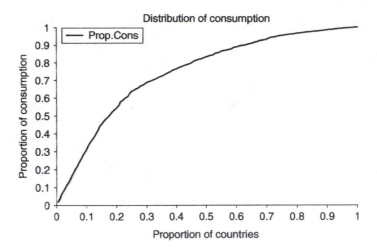

Figure 4.2 Distribution of consumption.

Source: Based on data from Human Development Report 2000, UNDP.

have, almost 80 per cent of real consumption, in per capita terms. Therefore, even though the marginal utility of poor countries is high it is wrong to conclude that they would be polluting more (Figure 4.3).

Utility, consumption patterns and environmental degradation

The pollution generated from production, ultimately, depends on consumption because consumption creates derived demand for production. Consumption is primary and production is secondary. In general, hence, environmental degradation (Ed) or pollution (P) is a function of consumption (C).

Utility function in extant studies

In extant studies, utility is conventionally measured by the following utility function:

$$U = U(C, -P)$$

where total utility depends on utility due to consumption and disutility ($-P$) due to pollution.

There are many implications of such a function (apart from those suggested in Chapter 4). Some are laid out below:

1   P is endogenous to a consumption decision;
2   the relationship between C and P is hyperbolic;

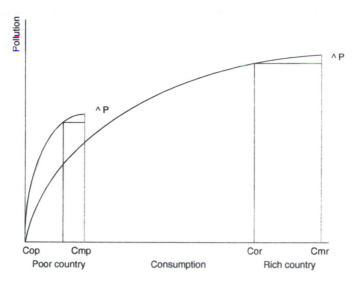

Figure 4.3 Pollution and consumption.

3   the utility function underlying this relationship does not lead to a downturn in the EKC;
4   the sacrifice required by rich countries is much greater than that of poor countries, if, we have to 'care for the environment' at the global level.

It is an unrealistic behavioural assumption to posit that individuals would actually decide to choose a set of combinations of pollution and consumption as being equally acceptable to them. Therefore, such a utility function cannot be interpreted within an indifference map framework. We believe that pollution need not be endogenous to any consumption decision, in the sense that they could be consciously, jointly decided and determined. Consumption is primary and essential. Pollution is incidental to consumption. If we were to endogenise both it would imply that individuals are conscious of the impact of their pattern of consumption and are capable of adjusting their consumption accordingly. Such an assumption would obviate any need for policy correctives and would amount to wishing away the problem. In fact, consumption decisions are undertaken independently of their consequences for pollution. This is the crux of the problem of environmental sustainability. In other words, net welfare is determined by the difference between the utility of consumption, which is endogenous, and disutility of pollution, which is exogenous to consumption, especially because pollution has externalities (more so in the global context). We shall take-up the implications of such issues for economic calculations later.

   If it cannot be treated as an indifference relationship how can the utility function be interpreted? In the following analysis we shall consider the utility function to be the time path of utility. The purported shape of the utility function as desired by the logic of the inverted U-shaped EKC must be quadratic. We shall now consider this possibility.

Given that:

$$dU = \partial U/\partial C * dC - \partial U/\partial P * dP$$

the time path of utility will be given by:

$$dU/dt = \partial U/\partial C * dC/dt - \partial U/\partial P * dP/dt$$

Figure 4.3 depicts the Pollution–Consumption ($P–C$) function that is based on the extant utility function. The first curve is the $P–C$ function of a poor country, and shows that at low levels of income their pollution is higher, as purported by the EKC literature. The second curve shows the $P–C$ function of a rich country that is less polluting, initially. But the maximum level of consumption is vastly different.

In the extant literature the marginal utility of consumption is higher in poor countries. But this does not imply that the overall pollution by poor countries is higher as is evident from the second path that belongs to rich countries. The level of consumption of poor countries is much less than that of rich countries. This corresponds to the 'stylised facts'. Accordingly, the maximum consumption of a poor country is 'Cmp' while that of a rich country is 'Cmr'. This, by itself, however, does not ensure that the utility or welfare is the maximum, in either case.

In general, as is apparent, both pollution and consumption rise along the $P–C$ path. Pollution creates disutility, simultaneously with the utility of consumption. The net utility is generated while marginal utility of consumption declines and marginal disutility of pollution increases. The net utility from such a function will decline very rapidly because the second term grows more rapidly since P also rises along with the marginal disutility. To ensure that utility grows constantly, C must grow very fast. Therefore, we have a fast growing C associated with a slow growing P yielding a hyperbolic relationship between the two. An implication, however, is that ΔP tends to zero as ΔC tends to become very large, especially in the case of rich countries. For an EKC (inverted U) to occur the relationship between pollution and consumption (or income) must take a quadratic form, that is, the relationship between P and C must turn negative after a point. It is difficult to envisage consumption behaviour that is based on a sudden shift from a positive relationship between environmental degradation and consumption to a negative one. The only sudden change that can be envisaged with such a utility function is that the marginal utility of consumption becomes zero. At this point the maximum total utility from consumption is reached. That is:

$$\int dU/dt \Rightarrow \text{Maximum gross utility}$$

when

$$\partial U/\partial C = 0$$

But the net utility is not necessarily maximised unless we assume that the ΔP becomes zero at this very point. If it does then it signals dU/dt being zero.

$$\int dU/dt \Rightarrow \text{Maximum net utility}$$

when $dP/dt = 0$ (along with the gross utility condition), that is, the total net utility (or global net welfare) is maximised. Incidentally, this is also the point at which global pollution is maximised! At this point, therefore, there is no more incentive to consume (Satiety Condition). There can be no further consumption and hence this pre-empts any downturn. *Hence, an inverted U-shaped EKC cannot exist.* The relationship between consumption and pollution cannot be negative because either of these conditions must obtain.

1    $dP/dt < 0$
2    $\partial U/\partial C < 0$.

Both these conditions can obtain only if there is abnormal consumption behaviour. On the other hand, it can be shown that if either of these conditions were met before the maximum point of the P–C function it would not result in maximum net utility or maximum net global welfare. Hence, a downturn of the EKC is theoretically impossible, under normal circumstances, because either it is pre-empted or it implies abnormal behaviour. This implies that the EKC cannot be a quadratic relationship. Hence, the downturn, if any, may be explained only in terms of abatement measures and not on account of rich countries' (consumers) being inherently caring for the environment.

Let us consider the possibility of abnormal behaviour. This would require that countries voluntarily restrain consumption below the maximum. This would imply that they are altruistic and show restraint out of concern for future generations, in deference to intergenerational equity. This involves a sacrifice of present consumption. Under such circumstances, the optimal consumption of rich countries is 'Cor'. Under similar circumstances the optimal consumption of poor countries would be 'Cop'. Even under such assumptions two points become clear, of which one relates to 'stylised facts' and the other to policy:

1   that the absolute level of pollution by poor countries is still much less than rich countries;
2   that the sacrifice (Cmr – Cor) desired of rich countries is much more than (Cmp – Cop) that desired of poor countries, for the same reduction in global pollution, that is, ΔP.

Even without an inverted U-shaped EKC the first result is confirmed by 'stylised facts'. The second conclusion, above, questions the basis of sacrifices being sought of poor countries so as to protect the global environment. It is amply clear from the above analysis that rich countries need to make the maximum sacrifice.

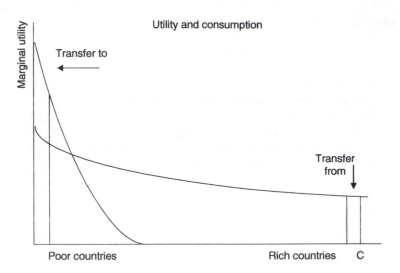

Figure 4.4 Utility and consumption.

Normal and abnormal consumption behaviour

Let us next consider the question of a natural limit on environmental degradation. For gauging the natural limit it is necessary that total utility (or total welfare) be maximised at the point where consumption is maximised.[7] This is achieved when the marginal utility from consumption is zero. Further since the utility function is intertemporal there is an implicit assumption that there are no budget constraints that can be made redundant through an appropriate reallocation of resources over time. Once maximum consumption is reached there is no additional consumption and there would not be any additional pollution. The shape of the above utility function does not imply any specified limit on pollution unless the restrictive conditions laid out are met. However, as shown below, for an ordinary utility function proposed in our framework there is a natural limit on pollution imposed by normal consumption behaviour.

Normal utility function

We now consider an ordinary utility function and ordinary behaviour and its implications for global pollution and welfare (Figure 4.4). On one hand, since the marginal utility of poor countries is high their marginal utility would fall faster, assuming consumption is a normal good. Total utility would start to rise slowly, much earlier. Therefore, to achieve the maximum level of total utility (total welfare – $W1$) poor countries would consume much less. This means that very soon they cease to consume at the margin. This result holds good even if we ignore the low income and the consequent budget constraint. If the constraint is introduced they end up consuming even less. But for the sake of welfare comparisons we ignore such constraints. The relevant point is that such a constraint is only going to reduce the consumption of poor countries further, although they already have very low levels of consumption. On the other hand, since rich countries have a low marginal utility of consumption that falls slowly, they tend to consume much more to achieve the maximum level of total utility (total welfare – $W2$). This is corroborated by the 'stylised facts'. Presumably, their satiety level is reached much later. Also, rich countries do not face such a severe budget constraint. This allows them to consume more. The vast difference in consumption, *in per capita physical units*, can only be explained by such behaviour being buttressed by consumerism, advertisement, excessive waste, all of which encourage over-consumption. These influences discourage abstinence and deferment of consumption. They encourage present consumption and hence impose an extra levy on the discount rate of future consumption. This implies that the present generation in rich countries is not concerned about the environment because such a concern must translate into postponement of present consumption so that resources are saved for future generations. The argument of the downturn rests heavily on the assumption that the present generation of rich countries is more concerned about the environment. It is believed that they are prepared to spend on abatement because of such a concern. Even if it were assumed to be true that they are concerned about the environment because their basic needs are met, unlike poor countries, there is an apparent contradiction between the following 'stylised facts' and this proposition.

1   Rich countries have phenomenally high consumptions levels.
2   Rich countries have very high environmental degradation levels.
3   Rich countries care for the environment.

This contradiction cannot be resolved.

The real issue is whether actually rich countries and societies value a better environment. In fact, poor countries and their peoples do not need large amounts of energy and natural resources, in absolute terms. Their needs are simple and living is frugal. They are forced to re-cycle waste out of necessity and economic compulsion. Their environmental practices in production, technology use and consumption are more sustainable, in the first place. Their resources constrain them from over-use of environmentally significant goods. They cannot afford environment-unfriendly products such as cars, refrigerators and air-conditioners. Their scale of consumption of plastics, paper, chemicals and fertilisers, are miniscule as compared to rich countries. Furthermore many of them export resources to the developed world.

The above pattern of consumption and utility can be summed up as:

$$U = U1(C1)$$

$$U = U2(C2)$$

$C1$ = consumption of poor country; $C2$ = consumption of rich country

$U1'$ = marginal utility of poor country; $U2'$ = marginal utility of rich country

It must be noted that the level of consumption is determined at the point where there is maximum satisfaction, unconstrained by a budget. This is the level of satiety of consumption. Once this is attained there can be no more generation of pollution because pollution or environmental degradation (Ed) depends only on consumption.

Satiety Condition

$$\text{Max} \int U1' dC1 = W1 \text{ when } C1 = \hat{C}1;$$

$$\text{Max} \int U2' dC2 = W2 \text{ when } C2 = \hat{C}2$$

$W1$ = welfare of poor country (maximum total utility)

$W2$ = welfare of rich country (maximum total utility)

If

$$[dU1/dC1] > 0 \quad \text{and} \quad [dU2/dC2] > 0$$

and

$$[d^2U1/dC1^2] < 0 \quad \text{and} \quad [d^2U2/dC2^2] < 0$$

while

$$|d^2U1/dC1^2| > |d^2U2/dC2^2|$$

it can be seen that

$$W1 < W2$$

such that

$$\hat{C}1 < \hat{C}2$$

The satiety condition shows that the unconstrained maximum consumption by poor countries would necessarily be less than that of rich countries. In the event of introducing income (a budget constraint) the consumption of poor countries would necessarily be further lowered. This implies that if there were a monotonic functional relationship between P and C then poor countries would always be less polluting in absolute terms than rich countries.

Net global welfare condition

It appears as though a maximisation of consumption by both groups of countries should be a sufficient condition for global welfare maximisation. Under such conditions a fundamental question is that if the above patterns are stabilised (by virtue of patterns of global economic development) is there any scope for improving global welfare? We now consider a transfer or consumption as a means of enhancing global welfare.

When

$$C2 \Rightarrow \text{Max}; \quad U2' \Rightarrow 0$$

$$C1 \Rightarrow \text{Min}; \quad U1' \Rightarrow \text{Max}$$

Even if we assume that the pollution is higher in poor countries, initially, at the margin, such a transfer maximises net global welfare, which is the net utility due to consumption minus the disutility due to pollution. Therefore, a transfer of consumption from the richest to the poorest countries maximises global welfare and minimises consumption and hence minimises GED.

Factoring environmental degradation

We have seen that if we consider only the relationship between pollution and consumption and if it is monotonically increasing, clearly poor countries are much less polluting. We now consider a more complex relationship that involves other factors also. We first address the question whether there is a monotonically positive relationship between Ed and Y, or whether it is possible to have a negative relationship as well. For answering this question we shall take into account all the related aspects of domestic production per capita (Dp), per capita income (Y), consumption (C), abatement effort (A) and pollution (environmental degradation – Ed). We shall attempt to reconcile these aspects with the patterns that conform to the 'stylised facts', through a decomposition of pollution intensity of income (PII). It is this measure that is the hub of the argument of an inverted U-shaped EKC. Now

$$\text{Ed}/Y = (\text{Ed}/C)*(C/\text{Dp})*(\text{Dp}/A)*(A/Y) \tag{4.1}$$

where

Ed/Y = Pollution Intensity of Income (PII)

Ed/C = Pollution Intensity of Consumption (PIC)

C/Dp = Propensity of Real Consumption (PRC) – out of domestic production

Dp/A = Production Abatement Factor (PAF)

A/Y = Pollution Abatement Ratio (of Real Income) (PAR)

Taking logs:

$$\text{Log}(Ed/Y) = \text{Log}(Ed/C) + \text{Log}(C/Dp) + \text{Log}(Dp/A) + \text{Log}(A/Y) \quad (4.2)$$

Taking the first difference:

$$\Delta\text{Log}(Ed/Y) = \Delta\text{Log}(Ed/C) + \Delta\text{Log}(C/Dp)$$
$$+ \Delta\text{Log}(Dp/A) + \Delta\text{Log}(A/Y) \quad (4.3)$$

Summarising equation (4.3), we arrive at an elasticity condition jointly determining η_{PII}.

$$\eta_{\text{PII}} = \eta_{\text{PIC}} + \eta_{\text{PRC}} + \eta_{\text{PAF}} + \eta_{\text{PAR}} \quad (4.4)$$

Homogeneity condition

This holds when C, Dp and A change in the same proportion and

$$dEd/dY = 0 \quad (4.5)$$

Function (4.1), above, is homogenous of degree zero. Seen in a dynamic context, this implies that there would be a monotonic increase in Ed if there were steady-state growth amongst C and Dp, along with optimal policy intervention in the form of commensurate abatement measures (A), along with economic growth. This has been the import of most of the BGP models discussed in Chapter 3.

This brings us to the interpretation of these elasticities and ratios. The PII signifies the overall measure of the degree of environmental degradation of a country. If this measure is stable and remains at such a level that is sustainable then the differences in environmental degradation as between countries boils down to differences in scale. Essentially, pollution is caused by consumption, therefore PIC is the single most important measure of environmental sustainability. PRC – out of domestic production, has been chosen to represent the openness of the economy. In the case of open economies that are net importers it is possible that they are causing environmental degradation in other countries by consuming goods produced by other countries. This ratio would be greater than one for such countries. The PAF describes how large the production effort is in comparison to the abatement effort and PAR (of Real Income) explains how much a society is prepared to spend out of its income on abatement. For instance, in the case of a growing middle-income country the former ratio would be high and the latter would be low leading to a high PII. The impact of these ratios can be assessed by means of individual elasticities of each of these

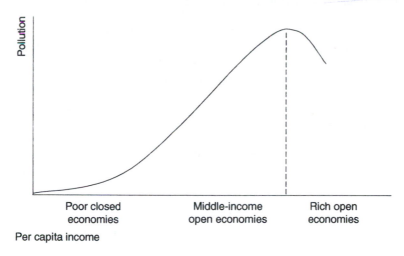

Figure 4.5 Hypothetical Global Environmental Kuznets Curve.

factors whose value would depend on the change in these variables. The total effect can be measured by the relative effect of each of these factors, taken jointly, in terms of magnitude and direction.

Is a downturn in the EKC possible?

Taken at face value equation (4.2), above, appears to be very straightforward. But the basic problem is that for the existence of an EKC the necessary condition is not a constancy of elasticity of Ed with respect to income but a rise and fall pattern that can explain the inverted U-shape of the EKC. The partial elasticities of the four factors must combine in both magnitude and direction so that elasticity of Ed to income is quadratic in form.

Let us consider the following cases:

1   a poor closed economy;
2   a middle-income open economy;
3   a rich open economy.

If these economies were lined-up in ascending order of development, it would emulate the sequential order of a global economy (Figure 4.5). Correspondingly, if their levels of environmental degradation were associated with their development levels the pattern would emulate a hypothetical GEKC, as proposed by the EKC literature. Accordingly, in the first case, the η_{PII} should be positive and very low. In the second case, η_{PII} should be positive and large and in the third case it should be large and negative, if the EKC should follow an inverted U-shaped curve. We now take up each of the above cases.

In a poor closed economy the following trends would obtain:

η_{PIC} $\Rightarrow$ Insignificantly small positive elasticity – less than one (in an agrarian economy).

η_{PRC} $=$ 0 (Since saving equals investment).

η_{PAF} $\Rightarrow$ Extremely large positive elasticity – greater than one (since abatement is much smaller than Dp).

η_{PAR} $\Rightarrow$ Insignificantly small positive elasticity – less than one (since abatement is much smaller than income).

The net η_{PII} is bound to be large and positive.

Let us now consider a middle-income open economy that is a net exporter.

η_{PIC} $\Rightarrow$ Small positive elasticity – less than one (growing economy).

η_{PRC} $\Rightarrow$ Small positive elasticity – greater than one (Dp $>$ C).

η_{PAF} $\Rightarrow$ Extremely large positive elasticity – greater than one.

η_{PAR} $\Rightarrow$ Small positive elasticity – less than one (since abatement is much smaller than income).

The net η_{PII} is bound to be large and positive.

Finally, we consider a rich open economy which is a net importer. We now assume, as is purported by some of the extant literature, that pollution falls with consumption, in the case of such a rich country, although we have rejected such a possibility earlier. However, this assumption is necessary to examine the central argument that the EKC has a downturn after a threshold level of income, that is, in the case of rich countries.

η_{PIC} $\Rightarrow$ Small and negative elasticity.

η_{PRC} $\Rightarrow$ Positive and somewhat greater than unity ($C >$ Dp).

η_{PAF} $\Rightarrow$ Extremely large positive elasticity.

η_{PAR} $\Rightarrow$ Small and positive elasticity.

The net η_{PII} is bound to be large and positive. Here, we should also emphasise that in this case there is an additional factor that ensures that it would be positive – η_{PRC}. *Therefore, a downturn is not possible, in general, and especially in the case of rich countries that the η_{PII} be negative.* Thus, there are three arguments against an inverted U-shaped EKC: the 'stylised facts', the utility function and the factoring of Ed. These clearly reject any possibility of a downturn of the EKC.

Our methodology

Our approach consists of the following components:

1 Conceptualisation of GED.
2 Emphasising the need for composite indices.

3 Critical appraisal of regression framework of analysis.
4 Principal Component Analysis methodology.
5 GEKC – functional form.
6 Analysis of variance (ANOVA) of environmental degraders and country (development) classes.
7 Causal framework.
8 Canonical Discriminant Analysis.
9 Analysis of outliers and influential observations.
10 Consumption-based HDI.

Of these components of our methodology the first five form the core methodology and are basis of the next few chapters (6–8). The ANOVA analysis is relevant to Chapter 6 and is discussed only in that chapter. The rest of the components ((7)–(10)) are discussed in the specific context in which they appear in Chapter 8.

Global environmental degradation

A number of questions about country-level EKC are pertinent. First, is it a local phenomenon restricted to individual countries or is it a global phenomenon? Second, is the EKC uniformly declining or an inverted U-shaped curve as is suggested in literature? Hence there is a need for a fresh examination of the empirical form and analytical content of the GEKC. If one admits the possibility of a GEKC then one has to probe its underpinnings. If EKC is a purely local phenomenon, then is this construct independent in each country? Is one country's EKC related to other countries' EKC? When analysing GED, a number of issues have to be addressed: does it arise from local phenomenon restricted to individual countries? Is income per capita an appropriate basis for tracing the EKC? What are the specific causative factors responsible for GED? What is the structure of causal factors? What are the implications of these questions for methodology?[8] A considered response to these questions would involve a fresh examination of the empirical form and analytical content of the GEKC as a manifestation of GED. In this respect, if the intention is to study the composite phenomenon, all factors responsible for GED must be included in the analysis.

Is GED a consequence of geophysical phenomena or is it anthropogenic in nature? Often GED has been treated as a geographic and natural phenomenon and not explicitly as an economic phenomenon, more particularly one that arises out of a certain 'type of economic development', arising out of the consumption patterns. There is another important question in this context. Is GED a composite? GED is a composite because such phenomena mutually influence each other. For instance, excessive paper consumption would result in deforestation, which would cause a fall in water resources and a growth in CO_2 levels, which would then cause global warming, soil degradation and denudation, which would adversely affect biodiversity and so on. It must be noted that all these factors are not 'causes' of environmental degradation but effects of degradation. However, since they are mutually linked, with one influencing the other, we would prefer to call them indicators of GED. In net, the composite of GED is caused by a consumption pattern, which is related to a certain type of development, perpetuated by developed countries.

An extension of the EKC rationale to the GEKC would imply that at low levels of PCI environmental degradation would rise with economic development and at high levels of PCI there would be a decline in environmental degradation (as depicted in Figure 4.5). The level of PCI at which the hump in the GEKC occurs is, of course, critical. If the GEKC was indeed quadratic it could be concluded that the LDCs are responsible for environmental degradation and developed countries reduce environmental degradation. Even assuming that the GEKC exists and that developed countries are on the right side of the hump, the large gap between the HDI of developed and developing countries could imply that the absolute level of environmental degradation index (EDI) is much higher for developed countries as compared to developing countries. The extant literature on EKC has emphasised the direction of change of one or more indicators of environmental degradation with respect to PCI, not its absolute level. However, two studies confirm such a rise in the absolute level.

There seems to be a consensus that the following four factors are primarily responsible for environmental degradation: (i) Pollution – of various types; (ii) lack of biodiversity; (iii) waste-toxic and non-toxic; and (iv) erosion of the natural resource base due to phenomenon like deforestation, depletion of fresh water resources, paper consumption, etc. Levels of these indicators or the like, define the 'state of the world' in context of entropy. In the pristine natural state there is no entropy. Hence, there is no degradation or disorganisation of the 'state of the world'. Entropy occurs as unwarranted human activity takes place. As long as anthropogenic activity is in consonance with and commensurate to the 'state of the world' there is no environmental degradation. Our basic hypothesis is that excessive and lop-sided human consumption patterns are the most fundamental 'cause' of entropy. Especially, extreme events cause severe degradation. Therefore, it is important to identify outliers and influential observations and to measure their contribution to GED.

A maintained hypothesis of our approach is that global environmental problems are rooted in local phenomena. If this were true then the GEKC would arise within a collective cross-sectional (cross-country) framework. A major problem with regard to the EKC, in extant studies, relates to their conceptualisation. They view environmental degradation as a phenomenon, whereby the level individual pollutants, (most often) in individual countries, are related to the level of an individual indicator of development, namely, PCI. In its empirical basis, GED is an economic phenomenon being 'caused' by certain 'latent' factors, related to economic development. We conceptualise GED as a 'composite' since it would be simplistic to assume otherwise and conceive of this as a conglomerate of many factors that may be acting as vectors in different directions, with the resultant vector having a certain central tendency (the grand mean). A secular increase (both temporally and spatially) in this conglomerate of factors would 'cause' entropy and would be indicative of the phenomenon of GED. The composite of GED is in this sense, 'caused' by another composite of economic development, with each of the composites appropriately weighted. It is important to both conceive of and measure this composite and relate it to the 'type of development' that leads to degradation.

The fact that extant EKC studies concentrate on individual pollutants has led to two practices while modelling this phenomenon. The first is the use of regression analysis (without adequate justification) and the second is relating individual degraders to individual (and perhaps partial) indicators of economic development. A part of the problem arises from not delving into the data generating processes, that is, the factors responsible for the phenomenon, their characteristics, the interrelationships and, most of all, the appropriate level for the empirical study.

Composite index

Why is GED a composite? GED occurs as a result of an accumulation of local phenomenon such as: pollution – of various types; destruction of biodiversity, accumulation of toxic and non-toxic waste and the erosion of natural resource base due to deforestation, depletion of fresh water resources, paper consumption, etc. Given values for this set of indicators could be said to define a 'state of the world'. If the intention is to study the composite phenomenon, all factors responsible for GED must be included in the analysis.

We now clarify the concept of 'composite' in the context of the GED. A composite is a conglomerate of many factors that may be acting as vectors in different directions, with the resultant vector having a certain central tendency (*the grand mean*). A secular increase in this tendency would be indicative of the phenomenon of GED. The composite of GED is in this sense, 'caused' by another composite of economic development with each component appropriately weighted. It is inappropriate to isolate one indicator of each (pollution and level of development) and attempt to explain the phenomenon of GED by relating the two. This would be beset with several problems. First, it would be biased because while GED and economic development are composites, each country HDI group (high, low or medium) would have specific dominating characteristics with regard to GED incorporated in a specific indicator. Second, the choice of different factors would give varying results and isolating one factor and embedding it in a regression framework could lead to inconsistency. In addition the problems of multicollinearity, simultaneity and loss of information may exist in the regression framework. Neither the use of regression analysis nor isolating individual pollutants in order to relate them to PCI may always be appropriate.

In contrast, to extant studies, our approach is to study the phenomenon at the level of country groups, as well as, globally, for all countries and all degraders. The preferred method is to relate an EDI with HDI, a composite index of economic development. This enables us to understand GED as an economic, rather than a geographic and natural, phenomenon being 'caused' by certain 'latent' factors, related to economic development. Factor analysis allows such phenomena to be gauged on the basis of latent factors and permits alternative, plausible sets of latent factors for explaining the same phenomenon (of say, GED). While the same could be said of many economic phenomena, it is truer of GED that alternative latent factors may be responsible for it.

Limitations of regression

The composite of GED is in this sense, 'caused' by another composite of economic development where each of the composites is measured with the help of appropriate weights. It is, in this sense, inappropriate to isolate one indicator of each (pollution and PCI) and attempt to explain the phenomenon of GED by relating the two. This method would not only be biased but would also be inconsistent: biased because while GED and economic development are composites, each country HDI group (high, low or medium) would have specific predominating characteristics with regard to GED incorporated in a specific indicator. It would be inconsistent because first, the choice of different factors would successively give varying results and second, because isolating one factor and embedding it in a regression framework would result in inconsistency. Three problems may be expected of the regression framework:

1   multicollinearity
2   simultaneity
3   loss of information.

An examination of the above problems reveals the weakness of regression analysis and the limitations of isolating individual pollutants for relating them to PCI, which is the usual methodology employed.

Two points need reiteration. First, there is merit to the approach that conceptualises GED as a composite, overall measure. Second, in so far as *real world economic phenomena* need to be gauged by inductive rather than deductive methods (which may, nevertheless, be appropriate for physical phenomena) some amount of exploratory empiricism is called for. Factor analysis allows for such exploratory and confirmatory analysis. Further, such exploratory empiricism would not only help in identifying the contours of the phenomenon of GED but would also reveal the weakness of the regression analysis in general, and in particular, the weakness of the usual procedure of isolating some pollutants and attempting to relate these to PCI.

At the empirical level, the indicators of environmental degradation suffer from both simultaneity and multicollinearity. The regression approach to the EKC is subject to multicollinearity, as well as the need to assume normality. In contrast, Principal Components Analysis (PCA) performs well in relation to removing these weaknesses of regression analysis. PCA is based on a linear transformation of the 'regressors' such that they are orthogonal to each other by design. Hence, the information contained in all the points in the event space is retrievable. None of it is treated as a random error (i.e. orthogonal to the best fit line). Second, the normality assumption is not essential. In the real world, where there are wide differentials amongst countries, and between individual effects of indicators, such an assumption is dispensable. Third, with such a dispersed set of outcomes, PCA is ideally suited because it maximises the variance rather than minimising the least square distance. For these reasons we chose PCA.

Problem of multicollinearity

Most studies take-up individual indicators (say CO_2 emissions) and attempt to explain their behaviour independently of the other indicators. Hence, CO_2 levels are taken to be an effect of economic development, rather than 'a contributor' to GED. Furthermore, it is highly likely that movements in other indicators (auxiliary regressors) could be causing multicollinearity. A reliable method of testing for multicollinearity is to carry out k auxiliary regressions if there are k such indicators, with each of the regressors being treated as regressands.

Formally, consider a regressand y and a matrix of regressors $X = [x_1, x_2, \ldots, x_k]$. The regressand y is an n vector and the matrix of regressors X is an $n \times k$ matrix with each column x_i being an n vector. The regressand y and each of the k regressors can be thought of as points in the n-dimensional Euclidean space, E^n. The k regressors span a k-dimensional subspace of E^n, denoted by $\delta(X)$. If γ is a k vector then all points Z in E^n constitute the subspace $\delta(X)$ such that $Z = \gamma X$. The dimension of $\delta(X)$ is $r(X)$, which is the rank of X. The problem arises when the k regressors are not linearly independent. They would then span a subspace of a dimension less than k, say k', where k' is the largest number of columns of X that are linearly independent. In such a situation, $\delta(X)$ will be identical to $\delta(X')$, where X' is an $n \times k'$ matrix. In an extreme situation, all k regressors may be mutually dependent. Here X reduces to an n vector. In a more realistic situation, it may be possible that pairs of x_i's are linearly independent, so we would have subspaces denoted by $\delta(x_1, x_2)$, $\delta(x_1, x_3)$ etc. But the two vectors define each of these subspaces jointly. Hence, the regressand y is to be explained either by a single variable, which makes the model highly restricted and deterministic, or by sets of variables that are linearly independent, which would introduce an ambiguity because $\delta(X) = \delta(x_1, x_2) = \delta(x_1, x_3)$. Moreover, explaining y in terms of a linear transformation of regressors incorporated in one of the auxiliary regressions assumes exact multicollinearity. If this were not be to the case, that is, if sampling variations are allowed for, there would be a loss of information because of the error of prediction.[9] Hence there would be a loss of information at the level of predicting the regressand y also. Apart from multicollinearity a limitation of the regression framework is that it assumes normality.

Basic analytics of principal components

We now discuss some basic issues in PCA. For a fuller treatment see Lewis-Beck (1994).

If we need to choose the essential variables and arrive at relative weights for the purpose of consolidating these variables into a single index we choose PCA.

This is popular in the literature since it has a number of desirable properties. Consider p random variables – x_1, x_2, x_p such that

$$y_1 = a_{11}x_1 + a_{12}x_2 + \cdots + a_{1p}x_p = \sum_{i=1}^{p} a_{1i}x_i \qquad (4.6)$$

PCA is a statistical technique that linearly transforms an original set of variables into a smaller set of uncorrelated variables that represents most of the information in y_1, the first principal component, is defined such that the variance of y_1 is maximised subject to the constraint that the sum of squared weights is equal to 1, that is,

$$\sum_{i=1}^{p} a_{1i}^2 = 1.$$

If the variance of y_1 is maximised then the sum of the squared correlations with the original variables is also maximised. This is written as:

$$\sum_{i=1}^{p} r_{y,xi}^2$$

PCA finds the optimal weight vector $(a_{11}, a_{12}, \ldots, a_{1p})$ and the associated variance of y_1, which is denoted as λ_1.

The second principal component y_2, is

$$y_2 = a_{21}*x_1 + a_{22}*x_2 + \cdots + a_{2p}x_p \qquad (4.7)$$

such that the variance of y_2 is maximised subject to the constraint that the squared weights of the second weight vector $(a_{21}, a_{22}, \ldots, a_{2p})$ is equal to 1:

$$\sum_{i=1}^{p} a_{2i}^2 = 1$$

Here, y_2 is orthogonal to y_1 so that

$$\sum_{i=1}^{p} a_{1i}a_{2i} = 0$$

Hence, y_2 has the second largest sum of squared correlation with the original variables. As successive components are extracted the variance of the principal components gets smaller. The first two principal components have the highest possible sum of squared correlation with the original variables. Therefore, the variance is maximised by extracting the first two principal components.

$$\sum_{i=1}^{p} R_{x_i, y_1, y_2}^2$$

This is a measure of the explanatory power of the components.

Component scores

The principal components are an exact mathematical transformation of the raw variables. If the objective is a simple summary of the information contained in the raw data the use of component scores is desirable. It is possible to represent the components exactly from the combination of raw variables. The scores are obtained by combining the raw variables with weights that are proportional to their component loadings. Thus, if b_{ij} is the component loading of the jth variable on the ith component and λ_i is the associated eigenvalue then the component score is given by b_{ij}/λ_i ($= w_i$).

Division by the eigenvalue assures that the resulting index has a variance equal to 1. In our case the component scores have been used for determining the weight of each

$$EDI_i = \sum_{j=1}^{5} w_j . x_{ji}$$

of the raw variables in constructing a composite EDI for the ith country and, similarly, for other countries, where $j =$ index of selected variables.

Similarly, GED is specified as:

$$GED = \sum_{i=1}^{174} EDI_i$$

There are two types of component scores – rotated and unrotated. They explain the same amount of total variation but sometimes it helps to obtain the orthogonally rotated scores. They help in better interpretation. There are various procedures for rotation. The most popular orthogonal rotation procedure is Kaiser's Varimax rotation.

Modelling the GEKC

As pointed out earlier our main contribution lies in developing a model of the EKC on a global scale. The estimation has been done on the basis of data for environmental variables on 174 countries, drawn from *Human Development Report* (1999). The model relates a composite index of environmental degraders – The EDI (whose details are given in Chapter 6 along with some other estimation details) that is regressed on another composite index of development (overall – not just economic), that is, on the ranks of the HDI for three classes of economies – low, middle and high human development countries.

The contentious issue was that of the functional form. We have chosen a cubic form since it fits the best. Hence, the basic model of GEKC can be written as:

EDI $= F$ (HDI Ranks)

where F is a cubic function. Moreover, as we have argued, we believe that for all reasons quoted above, the *EKC is not a quadratic*.

Hence our model for estimating GEKC is as follows:

$$EDI = a + b_0\,HDIR + b_1\,(HDIR)^2 + b_2\,(HDIR)^3 + e$$

Regression of EDI on HDI rank (Selected model).

In the process of modelling a number of issues cropped up. We now consider these.

1 HDI VS. PCI. It is true that in light of the high correlation between HDI index and per capita GDP some people have questioned the superiority and informational validity of HDI. It is sometimes felt that PCI would give similar results. However, in our specific case this does not appear to be the case. We can make a number of arguments that favour HDI as against PCI. For instance,

a   The very construction of the HDI involves other indicators (apart from PCI). Therefore, a priori HDI has additional information. HDI is a more complete indicator of development than PCI since it is based on social variables as well (e.g. life expectancy, educational attainment – which is itself a composite of literacy, primary, secondary and tertiary levels of enrolment – and PCI). Mahbub ul Haq has described the HDI as an index 'as a measure that is not blind to social aspects of human lives as GNP is' (*Human Development Report* 1999, p. 23). Social indicators do not necessarily present the expected result, namely, a fall in environmental degradation along with increase in incomes. Hence, they cannot to be subsumed under PCI. At least one study shows that education level is negatively related to environmental degradation (Gangadharan and Valenzuela 2001). In Table 4.1 we provide numerical indicators of the relative significance of HDI and PCI.

b   We have empirically tested for the correlation between PCI and HDI index and estimated alternative models for the final equation for the determination of GEKC. (The summary results are given in Table 4.1.) First, it is clear that PCI and HDI are not highly correlated since the relevant measure is R^2 (0.4252) (and not R), happens to be low. The fact that HDI has additional information is also obvious from the results. The selected equation has a higher adjusted 'R^2'. The Summary results of relative significance of HDI and PCI are given in Table 4.1.

Table 4.1 Correlation between HDI index and PCI

	R	R^2/Adjusted R^2
	0.6521	0.4252
1 Regression of EDI on HDI rank (Selected model)		0.7641
$\quad$ EDI = a + b_0\,HDIR + b_1(HDIR)^2 + b_2(HDIR)^3 + e		
2 Regression of EDI on PCI rank (Alternative model)		0.7190
$\quad$ EDI = a + b_0\,PCIR + b_1\,(PCIR)^2 + b_2\,(PCIR)^3 + e		

Notes
HDIR = HDI ranks and PCIR = PCI ranks.

In view of this, the results with respect to PCI, although fully worked out, have not been reported, in Chapter 6.

c   It is also possible to argue that the method of calculating HDI has inherent advantages for the following reasons. First, it uses real GDP per capita in PPP $ terms which would be important since there is better treatment of the fact that many countries may have large non-traded good sectors. Second, each variable (say, X_i) is measured as an index that is normalised. This normalisation is based on the following formula:

$$\text{Index} = (\text{Actual } X_i - \text{Minimum } X_i)/(\text{Maximum } X_i - \text{Minimum } X_i)$$

The average of the individual indices is then used for calculating the overall index of HDI and the corresponding ranks. Third, per capita GDP in the calculation of the HDI index has been appropriately discounted. Prior to 1999, an explicit non-linear discounting procedure was adopted but since 1999 an implicit logarithmic discounting method is used (based on Anand and Sen 1999). Such discounting is 'driven by the fact that achieving a respectable level of human development does not require unlimited income' (*Human Development Report* 1999, p. 159). Fourth, HDI is neither the same thing as index of per capita GDP nor does it yield same results. For instance, in the case of China (in 1999) the HDI index is 0.701 while the PCI index is 0.575. Hence, not only does HDI have greater information content but also the information is different. This is significant because our study is concerned about distribution of EDI as well.

In view of these reasons the full results of a comparison using both models involving HDI and PCI are not reported. Only the results of the selected model based on HDI are reported.

     2 Data reliability While we admit that there are data problems, there is always a choice between studying and not studying a problem on account of data problems. We decided to measure EDI and study the phenomenon GED in spite of the problems for the following reasons:

1   If we question international data sources beyond a point then it becomes impossible for individual researchers to study such phenomenon (that need to be studied globally). We have to rely on the data provided to the international source, by the individual countries.
2   It is impossible for individual researchers to gather primary data on such a scale.
3   Most studies of this nature follow this same practice (i.e. use secondary sources).

The source that we have used gives reasonably good data for the purpose, for almost all countries, for both variables involved in EDI and HDI.

3 HDI ranks vs. Index. There was a choice between using HDI ranks as against the HDI index, as the regressor. For several reasons the ranks were chosen. First, the fit in terms of ranks is better than the index. Second, the distinction between different countries in terms of the index is often very narrow (only in the second decimal place). Hence, the rank provides a greater variation in the data and thus a better basis for generating the predicted 'trend' of EDI. Third, the graphical results clearly favour the model based on ranks. This is important because the concept of EKC strongly rests upon the graphical construct. The analysis with respect to HDI index has also been done but we prefer to report results with respect to ranks. Heggestad *et al.* (1976) provide another application using ranks and rationale for using these.

4 Time series vs. cross-sectional analysis. While we could have considered time-series analysis there were many reasons for choosing a cross-sectional method.

1   The first and foremost significance of developing the concept of GED in the cross section is to verify, *a priori*, that a GEKC exists. There are many studies in which individual pollutants (not necessarily other 'degraders') are studied for individual countries over time. There are works that study the same in the cross section. There are a few that study individual pollutants in panel (for a limited set of countries). The attempt to study a composite GED at a point of time for almost all countries in the world has not been made.

2   Further, while it is true that, a measurement of GED in a panel framework could have provided useful information, it could not be done, at the present time, due to incomparability of data over time. The change in the method of discounting PCI is an important reason because of which data becomes incomparable (prior to 1999). Subsequently, *Human Development Reports* do not report data, on a comparable basis on environmental degradation.

3   Moreover, the distribution of EDI (area under the curve), the outliers and the influential observations (that have been identified), all have an impact on the cumulative phenomenon of GED. Hence, the study of GED is relevant even at a given point of time. There is no such readily available measure in the literature.

GED as a level variable

As for the relevance of GED as a *level* measure we wish to emphasise the level rather than the shape of the GEKC. Most extant studies tend to emphasise the latter. This makes it appear that the essential relationship between development and GED is that developing countries tend to raise GED, while developed countries reduce GED. But this is not borne out by our study.

While it might be argued that the GED is based on marginal contributions and hence may not represent a *level* variable, the measure is of interest in itself especially, since we are interested in the changes in the global measure, which is the sum of the marginals. Further, although the GED constitutes marginal contributions, EDI (which is our RHS variable) is a level variable for at least three reasons. First, the variables are measured in per capita or per cent terms. Even the HDI is based on two indicators that are in per capita terms and two that are in per cent terms. Yet, HDI is universally recognised as a level variable. In the construction of the HDI, all countries in the world have been classified on the basis of computed HDI as low, middle and high countries by level of human development. This is in spite of the fact that the HDI is in the form of a normalised index. Hence, the variables used are more in the nature of averages. Second, our measure of EDI is not a normalised (index), as is the case with HDI. Third, the methodology of PCA requires that factors bear common scale and code. Thus, it is not possible to include absolute values of degraders (they have to be in per cent or per capita terms).

Conclusions

This chapter has critiqued the extant approach to modelling the environmental degradation economic development relation. It has indicated fundamental draw-backs in the theoretical approach as well as the methodology adopted in the extant studies and argued that a fresh consumption-based approach to environmental degradation needs to be developed. It has advanced a detailed rationale for such an approach and provided the methodological structure for such an analysis. The results of the analytical work itself are reported in Chapters 6 to 8.

5 Sustainability

Behaviour, property rights and economic growth

> The advantage of economic growth is not that wealth increases happiness, but that it increases the range of human choice... We certainly cannot say that an increase in wealth makes people happier... We do not know what the purpose of life is, but if it were happiness, then evolution could have stopped a long time ago, since there is no reason to believe that men are happier than pigs, or than fishes. What distinguishes men from pigs is that men have greater control over their environment; not that they are more happy. And on this test, economic growth is greatly to be desired. The case for economic growth is that it gives man greater control over his environment, and thereby increases his freedom.
>
> (Sir Arthur Lewis 1955, pp. 420–21)

Introduction

Sir Arthur Lewis' quote amply summarises the rationale for economic growth in human society. Economic growth is desired because it increases opportunities and thereby provides greater scope for action. Clearly, there is an intertemporal dimension to this. Enhanced scope for action today may be available only by reducing such scope in the future. The environment is the principal example of this. But it is, by no means, the only one. For example, the no-Ponzi game condition restricting the growth of public debt (see Blanchard and Fischer 1989, for example) such that the state (or private individuals) do not borrow indefinitely from future generations in order to finance current consumption, is surely part of the same concern as, for example, that of preserving biodiversity. The stock of natural, human and physical capital must all be maintained at some, as yet vaguely defined, 'optimal' levels over time. The message that we live off resources borrowed from future generations rather than those inherited from our ancestors has to be enshrined as a basic principle of economic constitutions the world over.

The notion that economic growth has to be sustainable is part of this constitution. But sustainability can have several alternative definitions. Before we discuss some of the notions that have been used in the literature and propose our own, it should be realised that just as important as the definition of sustainability is the notion of sustainable for whom. Surely, for a sufficiently high price, rich OECD countries can continue to dump nuclear and toxic waste onto poor LDCs. Thus, sustainability of growth can be attained for the OECD countries but not for the LDCs. Surely, this option although feasible at a point in time, cannot be continued indefinitely. Thus, the applicability of the notion of sustainability has ultimately got to be universal and refer to the indefinite future. Germane to this whole argument is the notion that sustainability involves a switch in consumption possibilities both across space at a point in time and from the present to the future. When we say that a contemporaneous profile of consumption is not sustainable, then it probably means that a switch in consumption either spatially and/or over time would improve global welfare, again perceived as a magnitude referring to the indefinite future.[1]

It is one of the principal concerns of this chapter to point out that the notion of sustainability has not been sufficiently well developed in the extant literature. In particular, the full import of sustainability defined as a universal phenomenon and one that applies to the very long run, is insufficiently articulated in the literature. Developing this notion in its full generality is an important task as yet incomplete. Here we take the first step in this direction by trying to focus on the consumption reducing aspect of the sustainability agenda. The consumption switching component is discussed in Chapter 8.[2] In doing so, we at once critically examine the notion of sustainability as espoused by noted commentators and extend it in areas that seem to have been ignored. In particular, we are interested in the implications of sustainability for consumer behaviour and the outlining of property rights.

The rest of the chapter is organised as follows. The section titled 'Existing approaches to sustainability' details and evaluates some of the more popular existing approaches to the concept of sustainable economic development. The section titled 'A new approach towards sustainability' pays out the contours of an alternative approach which seeks to redress some shortcomings of the extant literature. The section on 'Sustainability: the present approach' emphasises the role of behavioural reform and property rights in the attainment of sustainability. The last section concludes the chapter.

Existing approaches to sustainability

Defining sustainable development even broadly is a non-trivial task. A further difficulty arises when we have to decide what has to be done to achieve it. The term 'sustainable' is relatively easy to define: it means 'enduring' or 'lasting'. So sustainable development is development that lasts.[3]

The term 'development' is a value-loaded concept inviting any number of interpretations. Economic development may be a relatively narrow term defined as growth in GNP per capita, or real consumption per capita and perhaps expanded to include educational and some social development indicators. The UN develops a HDI which emphasises literacy, life expectancy and GDP per capita. The World Commission on Environment and Development (WCED) focuses on needs and underscores its emphasis on poverty alleviation as the prime objective of sustainable development. The WCED position might be regarded as the minimum level of access to commodities and resources alone beyond which well-being or utility has meaning. In doing this, it achieves a starting point to an inquiry into the determinants of sustainable development.

If defining sustainable development is hard, enunciating the conditions under which it could hold is harder still. Clearly, long-term need not be equivalent to infinity – it could be a century or thereabouts with the clear indication that this would be a rolling arrangement with future generations having their own hundred-year horizons. But one point that essentially remains is that the present generation is the arbiter of value.

The literature on sustainable development is large and growing rapidly. Several surveys exist, for example, Pearce *et al.* (1990), Chichilinsky *et al.* (1998), and Carraro and Siniscalco (1997). A thematic representation of some of the notions of sustainability discussed in the literature is attempted in Table 5.1.

All these models have some important weaknesses which reduce their appeal as providers of a framework to analyse sustainability. For example, in the models of Dasgupta and Heal (1979) and others, no absolute degradation of the

Table 5.1 The notions of sustainability in the literature

Criteria used	Type of model	
	Non-renewable resources	*Renewable resources*
Maximising per capita consumption or maintaining a certain minimum consumption over time. Also includes models that require the attainment of a vector of desirable social objectives	Dasgupta and Heal (1979) Supply-side models of Pearce *et al.* (1990) and others	Golden Green Rule Models of Johansson (1993) and others
Impure Altruism	Models of Andreoni (1989, 1990), Kopp (1991), Qiuggin (1989) and Rosenthal and Nelson (1991)	
Net welfare measure		Resource–environment interaction models of Seibert (1998), Baumol and Oates (1988), Maler (1991), Tahvonen (1991) van der Ploeg and Withagen (1991) and Xepapadeas (1996)

exhaustible resource is permitted. However, this may be too pessimistic since it presumes that future technological growth will not reduce substantially the rate of growth of such resource use or that substitutes for this resource may not be found. In this connection Solow (1974) had shown that an economy with two factors of production (produced capital and a non-renewable resource) could achieve a constant level of real per capita consumption over time if the Hotelling efficiency rule was satisfied and any one of the following three conditions held:

1   the elasticity of substitution between natural and produced capital is greater than unity (i.e. the natural resource is technically inessential for production, so that there is no need to substitute for its depletion during production);
2   the elasticity of substitution is equal to unity (so that the natural resource is essential for production) but the share of produced capital in output is greater than that of the natural resource;
3   technological progress increases the productivity of the natural resource faster than the discount rate depletes it.

Hamilton (1995) shows that the elasticity condition is crucial. Only if this elasticity is less than one will the Dasgupta–Heal result hold.

In similar vein, models of the green golden rule genre (which says that the marginal rate of substitution between consumption and the natural resource should equal the rate of regeneration of the natural resource), ignores the possibility that there may be a divergence between private and social costs. Hence, the problem of attaining sustainability is viewed as one of reordering consumption over time only with no role for external effects. Models of impure altruism (which require members of the current generation to be 'somewhat' altruistic) are silent on how the present generation would reconcile its own tendency to maximise utility with the demand placed on it by the requirement of altruism as well as differences among people with respect to the degree of altruism they may have. Supply-side models have the shortcoming that they are tractable only under the restrictive Hotelling assumptions. Almost all these approaches are of the view that the Coase theorem using changes in property rights to attain sustainable consumption does not attain its goal.[4] This is essentially because of three well-known reasons: (i) the Coasian assumption of zero transaction costs is invalid; (ii) the bargaining process is not sufficiently analysed; and (iii) by assuming only one pollutee the theorem assumes away the existence of public goods or bads.[5] Resource–environment interaction models of the sort that use some measure of Net Welfare[6] are appealing, but they ignore the possibility that there maybe indivisibilities between capital and the natural resource. Models that require the attainment of a vector of social objectives take these objectives for granted and do not rationalise them in terms of individual behaviour.

One such aspect of individual behaviour that is critical to an analysis of sustainability is the discount rate. We now comment on its use in some models of sustainable behaviour.

The discount rate in models of sustainable development

As Pezzey (1989) argues a solution to the optimal growth problem:

$$\text{Maximise} \int_{t=0}^{\infty} U(C_t)e^{-\delta t}dt$$

subject to various resource allocation constraints, where U is utility of a representative individual, C is real consumption and δ is the rate of discount, may or may not be sustainable. To make the solution to the optimal growth problem to be coincident with that of the sustainability problem we have to have an appropriate discount rate. The higher the rate of discount, *ceteris paribus*, the greater is the risk that the path of consumption may not be sustainable. The smaller is the rate of discount the less the chance that the existing stock of natural resource will be extinct in finite time.

If welfare is based on consumption, then the appropriate rate of discount is the social rate of return on investment given by

$$\text{SRRI} = r + \eta[(dC/dt)/C]$$

where SRRI is the social rate of return, r represents the preference of a representative individual for consumption today rather than tomorrow. The term inside the square brackets [.], represents the rate of growth of consumption and η represents the elasticity. r is the pure rate of time preference and would induce people to prepone consumption whereas the second term captures the fact that since we are likely to be richer in the future, present consumption is more highly valued. There are two important points to be noted here: (i) if the pure rate of time preference is deemed to be 'too high', then it might be necessary to effect behavioural changes;[7] (ii) it may be misleading to make an assumption about the rate of discount without some plausible future scenario in mind. The most ordinary argument that seeks to explain the preference for present consumption is that people do so due to the fear of dying. While this might be justified for an individual, it has no relevance for the society as a whole. Society would or should survive generation after generation and, hence, sustainability concerns many generations. A concern of the sustainability literature and this chapter is that such myopic individual behaviour should not determine the fate of future generations.[8]

It is well known that there are immediate links between the rate of discount and the rate at which the price of an exhaustible resource rises. In a world with zero extraction costs, this price would rise at the rate of discount. An important question that arises here is that if current users do not expect any benefit from the future extractive activity and are maximising short-term utility, they would ignore the rent and consume everything now. Thus, along with determining an appropriate rate of increase of the price of the resource, we face the task of defining property rights over future consumption. If such property rights were not defined there would be an over-exploitation of resources.

The upshot of this argument is that if we wish to lower the discount rate to better target sustainability, we would have to work on the twin targets of behavioural changes and better defining of property rights.[9] The need to address these targets forms the basis for some of the key arguments of this chapter.

A new approach towards sustainability

In thinking about and developing a framework for analysing sustainability it is best to begin from first principles. Some of these principles are listed below.

1   Individual behaviour of members of the current generation should not completely determine the fate of future generations.
2   Future generations must be ensured the required minimum level of consumption.
3   The purview of sustainability must be expanded to include the possibility of divergence between social and private costs and the existence of public goods. Sustainability should not be narrowly interpreted in terms only of tradeoffs in intertemporal consumption.
4   The price path of natural resources and property rights to future consumption must be so defined as to avoid over-exploitation by the present generation.
5   In some situations the market may not have a solution.
6   Hence, there may be a rationale for non-market intervention.
7   The design of this intervention is an important aspect of a strategy to attain sustainability.

It is the contention of this chapter that an appropriate strategy for the attainment of sustainability would involve a change in behavioural patterns and a clearer definition of certain property rights. We elaborate somewhat on these themes.

Behaviour of agents

Utility maximising behaviour of the consumer (that forms the basis of most of the models of intergenerational optimisation) is based on the implicit assumption that the consumer does not face the possibility of extinction. This is explicitly stipulated in models of infinite horizon and implicitly so in models where finitely lived individuals leave bequests. This is justified only so long as adverse situations, with the potential of the consumer becoming extinct, are not encountered. An analogy with producer behaviour might be helpful here. When faced with adverse market conditions that may imply the possibility of his or her being driven out of business, a producer could switch from profit maximisation to loss minimisation (as opposed to cost minimisation) by avoiding variable costs, in the hope that, in the long run, fixed costs would vanish and profits would be revived. Thus, there is a change in the production plans in the face of adversity. This change is warranted by theory as well as by prudence. However, there is no such immediate parallel in regard to consumer behaviour. One could stipulate that the consumer should voluntarily reduce consumption to a level that would ensure sustainable consumption. But voluntary restraint in the absence of any obvious fixed cost would be difficult to expect from the consumer. Thus, unsustainable behaviour by the consumer ultimately leading to extinction cannot be ruled out. If the present generation persists with its existing behaviour, it may spell the extinction of future generations (Seibert 1998, p. 262). *Hence, with laissez faire, there is no conceivable welfare neutral, or welfare superior behaviour that is democratic and that can steer clear from the threat of extinction.*

An additional dimension of the problem is that even if alternative behaviour by the consumer could be conceived, the consumer does not *suo moto* perceive the threat of extinction. Hence, there is no scope for postulating switching behaviour. The expected behaviour of the present generation shall continue to be one of maximising utility, and therefore, consumption. This state of affairs cannot be allowed to prevail in the interest of posterity. It calls for some intervention not only because some degree of intergenerational equity must be established but also *because the portent of extinction must be perceived and stopped.*

Another way of visualising this problem is to say that, by virtue of not being born at the present point in time, future generations are not able to exercise their property rights over resources. Hence, they may be denied the rights to the flow of consumption from this resource stream.

Property rights

Property rights in the context of this chapter refer to the rights of future (yet unborn) generations. In principle, property rights need to be established over various categories of goods with the broad characteristics of: rivalry in use and exclusion provisos. Rivalry implies that individuals compete with each other in using the good. In addition to rivalry, if other potential users can be excluded from consuming the good would acquire the character of being a private good. When there is no such rivalry and no exclusivity can be established, the good becomes a pure public good. In the case of such goods, individuals cannot exercise private property rights. Within the category of public goods there are various levels of congestion. Thus, we may define the following terms:

Pure public good

This is a good which is consumed in its entirety by the whole population. The quality of this good is the same for all consumers.

$$Q = Q^1 = Q^2 = Q^3 \cdots = Q^n$$
$$U = U^1 = U^2 = U^3 \cdots = U^n$$

where Q = quantity and U = quality and $1, 2, 3, \ldots, n$ = individuals.

Rivalry-interpersonal

One consumer can increase consumption only at the expense of other consumers.

$$Q = Q^1 + Q^2 + Q^3 + \cdots + Q^n$$

Private goods would fall in this category.

Rivalry-Intertemporal

$$Q = Q_1 + Q_2 + Q_3 + \cdots + Q_t$$

where the subscript denotes time. A natural candidate is exhaustible resources.

Exclusion

For $(n - x)$ individuals (out of n) consumption is positive while for x individuals it is zero because some exclusion technology/proviso exists.

Congestion

As the number of individuals rises, the per capita quality of the goods declines.

Club goods

If there is no rivalry, amongst those who can use this good, but, in some form, the beneficiaries can impose exclusion on other individuals, it becomes a club good.

Merit goods

If it is thought on the basis of existing technology and consumer preferences that the commodity in question should no longer be produced yet it is deemed socially useful and production is encouraged, the commodity in question is a merit good. It is useful to summarise this classification of these goods as in Table 5.2.

Table 5.2 Property rights and classification of goods

Characteristics of goods	Institutional arrangement		
	Exclusive property rights	*Partially exclusive property rights*	*Non-exclusive property rights*
Rivalry in use	Private goods		Common resources
Partial rivalry		Environmental goods	Merit goods
Non-rivalry	Club goods		Pure public goods

This table helps us classify environmental goods. The two extremes represent private goods (north-west corner) and pure public goods (south-east corner). The definitional space consists of other intermediate goods that are placed in between.

Environmental goods

We define environmental goods as such intermediate goods in the case of which there is partial rivalry in use. This is because congestion exists amongst the users of one generation. In addition, there is intertemporal rivalry and exclusion is possible by virtue of the present generation's implicit ability to appropriate the resources, to the relative exclusion of the future generations.

Sustainability: the present approach

We may think of the environment as serving four functions: (i) providing public goods for consumption, for example, clean air; (ii) supplier of raw materials, for example, natural resources; (iii) receptacle for pollutants, for example, rain forests; and (iv) space locations. An environmental good is to be viewed as being composite in character and may possess one or more of the above functional qualities.

We see sustainability as *strategy for inducing a paradigm shift*, whereby environmental goods can be moved to the north-east corner of the definitional space in Table 5.2. We have remarked on the fact that, left to themselves, members of the current generation would not sufficiently honour the claims of the future generations to the environment. Hence, this transition is to be effected by first considering environmental goods as merit goods. Hence, we first move east to go north-east in Table 5.2. This movement makes clear the changes in property rights in respect of environmental goods that would have to be effected in order to make their use sustainable. In the absence of such a paradigm shift, environmental goods would slide into the north-west corner. Or, at the best, in certain cases, they may emerge as club goods. Such moves would militate against intergenerational equity as well as against sustainability. This paradigm shift can only be achieved through a multi-pronged strategy involving institutional change, behavioural changes, technological change and benign market interventions.[9] In the case of non-renewable resources the urgency lies in evolving a strategy such that the desired change takes place before the resource gets exhausted. Market for environmental goods in partial equilibrium is shown in Figure 5.1.

To make matters a bit more concrete we pursue (in Figure 5.1) the role of tax policy in bringing about changes in tastes, giving property rights to current resources to future generations, and thereby attaining sustainability. Figure 5.1 conceives of the market for environmental goods in partial equilibrium. DD' is the market demand curve and OS the supply schedule. Competitive equilibrium occurs at F with consumption equal to OX and price OK. It has been the contention of this chapter that this consumption is excessive. With a tax on producers to reflect the external diseconomy caused, the supply curve shifts to TS'. Equilibrium consumption is now OQ and the price OP. This would have been the

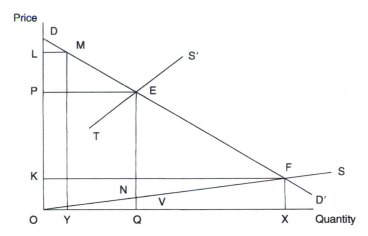

Figure 5.1 Market for environmental goods in partial equilibrium.

standard remedy for an externality problem. However, if we consider the consumption level OQ as non-sustainable, we can proceed as follows. We realise that the pre-tax producer price is OK. We can then impose a tax on consumers to the extent of TM, thereby inducing them to consume still less. The market price is now OL. The drop in consumption from X to Q was to correct for external effects whereas that from Q to Y is to address the sustainability issue. Thus, concerted action by the social planner results in a level of consumption that is sustainable and corrects for external effects.

The role of the Social Planner is crucial here. If the tax is imposed with certain conditions there is a possibility that it will induce certain long-term behavioural changes. If the producers/consumers are told that the taxes are medium-term measures and that they would be removed as soon as they take effective measures to arrest environmental degradation, they would hope to enjoy the benefits in the near future. In the process of tax imposition, property rights are indirectly being defined. This analysis, however, implicitly assumes that the funds collected from the taxes would be used for pursuing policies that would further the aim of attaining sustainable development. This would include expenditure on appropriate research and technology, consumer information campaigns, earmarking of funds for resource conservation and preservation, and so on. Through these tax-expenditure policies by a benign social planner in the present generation, society is able to implicitly transfer property rights over current resources to future generations.

The government must impose the tax as a group measure (say, upon an industry), so that peer pressure will work towards compliance by the errant producers. The producer would have to comply or quit. There would be a pecuniary interest on the part of the peers. The consumers would also be made to perceive the loss to society due to environmental degradation. They might become more aware of the future threat. Weisbrod (1964) and Bishop (1982) have pointed out that in such circumstances the consumer is prepared to pay a sum in excess of the expected consumer's surplus (access value) for enjoying the environmental good under conditions of uncertainty (say, the threat of extinction). Hence, as in Figure 5.1, the government imposes a tax on consumers. Once again, since it is a collective tax and the expectation is that the Isolation Paradox (Sen 1967) behaviour will be induced, the consumers would be prepared for the sacrifice. The future generation now receives a real bequest in the form of the balance of the environmental good and a monetary bequest in the form of the taxes. This is different from the case of Impure Altruism since it does not suffer from the problem of differences amongst individuals (egoists and altruists) because of being a social bequest. The taxes, it is assured will be used for reducing the congestion and ensuring the existence of the environmental good in the future. This also influences the implicit property rights and would, in the long run, lower the discount rate.

Conclusions

This chapter has argued that current deliberations on sustainability are incomplete. This is because of two principal reasons. First, there is a somewhat narrow interpretation of sustainability in terms of reductions in consumption; the spatial dimension of stability is not considered. Second, even in the context of reductions in consumption, the literature does not make clear the crucial role of behavioural changes and transfer of property rights over natural and environmental resources from the current generations to future generations.

This chapter has underscored these shortcomings. But it has chosen to concentrate only on the problem of consumption reduction, leaving the spatial dimension and an integration of the two for Chapter 8. It advocates a complex strategy for attaining the reductions in consumption necessary for attaining sustainability. It advocates the use of group taxes on producers as well as consumers. Second, the tax revenues so collected are earmarked for spending for the purpose of the environment. The resulting lowering of the discount rate and behavioural changes would lead to a drop in the rate of increase of prices of natural resources and, therefore, to a postponement of their consumption. All these involve the design of an intermediate run policy that treats environmental goods as *merit goods* as a prelude to their (ultimately) being treated as common resources.

In the long run, it is expected that behavioural changes and well-defined property rights would set-in a social dynamics that would endogenise the process of sustainability (The Endogenous Sustainability Hypothesis). Of course, it may be necessary to introduce and withdraw both the taxes in an iterative manner because social behaviour may not irreversibly change at one go. A distinct problem relates to the different treatment for renewable and on-renewable resources. This may be looked upon as a problem of the speed of adjustment. In the case of non-renewable resources the speed has to be faster, if such resources are essential to production. In such cases, greater reliance must be placed on exogenous changes in technology and tastes. In the case of renewable resources the expected change is essentially endogenous.

6 An inverse Global Environmental Kuznets Curve[1]

Introduction

The EKC[2] is purported to be an inverted U-shaped curve designed to explain the dependence of environmental degradation on the level of economic development. It is typically described for a given country, or cross section of countries, as a relation between PCI and select environmental indicators,[3] each taken separately. The EKC implies that global pollution is driven largely by the development efforts of LDCs as they traverse the upward rising part of the EKC.[4] On the other hand, the purported downturn of the EKC at high levels of PCI implies that developed countries are contributing to the amelioration of environmental degradation. However, such studies do not emphasise the level of GED,[5] which we conceive of as a worldwide phenomenon,[6] to be captured by a more composite index emphasising a wider notion of environmental degradation and not just pollution. Hence, these studies cannot address the distribution of GED and its relationship to economic development. This chapter develops an EDI, based on several indicators of environmental degradation or pollution, for each of the 174 countries represented in the HDI. An analysis of the spatial behaviour of the EDIs helps us to identify the contribution of various countries to GED, defined as an aggregation[7] of these EDIs, and to assess whether particular countries are contributing excessively to GED.

Linking individual pollutants to the level of PCI gives an incomplete picture because many pollutants are related to each other and to other indicators of environmental degradation. Furthermore, a country's PCI may be only an imperfect indicator of its development. The first problem can be addressed by computing a more comprehensive aggregate measure of environmental degradation, of which pollutants would only be a subset. The second problem can be addressed by relating this measure to a more complete measure of economic development, namely, the HDI. The existing literature has ignored these issues; the present chapter attempts to fill this lacuna. We present cross-sectional evidence on the relation between the EDI and the HDI for 174 countries. We call this relationship a GEKC and test to see whether it has an inverted U-shape. Several important conclusions relating to the spatial distribution of environmental degradation over these countries, the precise shape of the GEKC and the pattern of distribution of

GED are derived. The chapter organized as follows. The second section discusses issues of sustainability from the perspective of developing countries. The third section presents the conceptual basis for EDI and a methodology for its computation. The fourth section develops this methodology, the fifth section analyses the results and the last section is the conclusion.

The growth–environment debate

Although the growth–environment debate builds on Cole (2000), Jha and Murthy (2000), Jha and Whalley (2001) and Stagl (1999), we focus on the developing country perspective in a global context. The literature distinguishes two relationships between economic growth and environmental degradation. Associated with Daly (1977), Georgescu-Roegen (1971) and Hall *et al.* (1986), the entropy literature asserts that the higher the income level, the greater the environmental degradation. Entropy models[8] are based on a system-wide view of physical stocks of matter and flows of energy. This literature argues against the then prevailing growthmania and advocates the establishment of a steady state based not only on a constant capital stock but also on a constant stock of people. Daly (1977) questions both the feasibility and the desirability of growth. Such a view is anti-developmental because it prescribes growth containment for developing countries. Developing countries possess natural resources so that they must pay the price for depleted global free energy, that is, low entropy, while the developed world has already benefited amply from, and indeed is largely responsible for, this depletion. To the extent that the pattern of development of advanced countries continues to burden the global environment and insofar as GEM needs global solutions, this inequality is likely to be perpetuated so that prospects for the developing world remain dismal.

The literature on the EKC is voluminous. Grossman and Krueger (1995) carry out a cross-country study using several environmental variables. Their data sets are non-uniform in that some variables refer to individual cities and others to countries, and the coverage over time is uneven. Shafik and Bandyopadhya (1992) use a large number of variables to test for an EKC relationship in 149 countries; however they analyse the effects of these variables separately and do not compute a composite index. Selden and Song (1994) study air pollution across countries with high, low and medium incomes but do not compute a composite index of environmental degradation. Jänicke and Weidner (1997) use an aggregate indicator for volume of throughput based on four indicators, namely, energy, steel, cement, and rail and road freight for 31 COMECON and OECD countries from 1970 to 1985 and find an EKC relationship. However, this result is challenged by the re-linking hypothesis of Birdsall and Wheeler (1991). These authors study air pollution in the manufacturing sector of Latin America and conclude that pollution intensity, measured as the ratio of air pollution to GDP, declines with income in open economies and rises with income in relatively closed economies.

The weak sustainability approach argues that, although growth entails environmental degradation, either the levels of degradation would fall after a threshold, as in the EKC, or degradation could be de-linked from growth. Subsequent studies show how this de-linking could be possible.[9] Bernstam (1991) argues that economic growth in the South depends on growth in the North so that accelerated Northern growth leads the South to overcome the EKC hump. However, this argument is anti-developmental because it justifies indirectly the existing gap between the North and South and provides a rationale for further accelerating Northern growth. Ekins (1997) argues that OECD countries have passed the hump of EKC but casual observation of the data does not support this claim. Stern *et al.* (1996), Stern and Chapman (1998) and Ekins (1997) argue that a negative feedback from environmental degradation to income growth may occur, especially in LDCs, and cause the inverted U-shape. However, Holtz-Eakin and Selden (1992) find no evidence of such simultaneity. Furthermore, if the North exports its pollutants to the South, an inverted U-shaped EKC might occur.

Harbaugh *et al.* (2000) find no evidence of an EKC-type relationship. Moomaw and Unruh (1997) and van den Bergh *et al.* (1998), suggest that what appears as de-linking may not persist in the long run. Further, there is the re-linking hypothesis (Pezzey 1989; de Bruyn *et al.* 1998) that asserts an N-shaped curve, in which environmental degradation is positively linked to income levels eventually. Finally, Stern *et al.* (1996) argue that, in any estimation of the EKC, corrections for heteroskedasticity need to be undertaken, so that the estimates of the parameters of the EKC are not inefficient.

Apart from developing an index of degradation, this chapter addresses the problems of multicollinearity and heteroskedasticity and attempts to highlight the spatial dimension of sustainability with respect to economic development, which is an aspect that has been largely ignored in the literature.[10] We develop a composite index that is based on a broad range of degraders, not only pollutants. The analysis in this chapter is global in the sense that we consider data on 174 countries that are dispersed spatially around the world. Further, we show that the phenomenon of environmental degradation is worldwide and transcends country-specific effects.

The phenomenon of GED

EKC studies use regression analysis and relate individual degraders to individual, and perhaps partial, indicators of economic development. GED is treated often as a geographic and natural phenomenon and not explicitly as an economic one, especially one that arises from a type of economic development. A maintained hypothesis of this chapter is that global environmental problems are rooted in local phenomena in the individual countries, so that a GEKC arises in a cross-country framework.

Relating individual pollutants to partial indices of economic development, as in the regression framework, leads to biased results because each country group has specific dominating characteristics with regard to individual indicators incorporated in GED. Furthermore, the choice of different factors leads to varying results so that isolating one factor and embedding it in a regression framework could lead to inconsistency. In addition, the problems of multicollinearity and loss of information may arise in the regression framework. Movements in the dependent variable may be caused by movements in other indicators in the presence of multicollinearity. If a single variable explains the variation in the dependent variable, the model becomes highly restrictive and introducing another independent variable may lead to multicollinearity.[11] Information is lost in the regression framework because the data points that are not on the regression line are treated as errors of prediction[12] and ignored.

Our composite GED is a conglomerate of many factors that may act as forces in different directions having a certain central tendency. At the country level, the EDI is a weighted mean of the values of indicators for that country. Within each class of countries the composite is the average of the measures for the individual countries. At the global level, GED is the grand mean of the country-class means. A secular increase in the grand mean indicates temporal growth of GED. The variations in the EDI across countries characterise the distribution of GED. Hence, the composite GED is related to another composite of economic development with each component weighted appropriately. GED depends on an accumulation of local phenomenon, leading to pollution of various types, destruction of biodiversity, accumulation of toxic and non-toxic waste, the erosion of the natural resource base due to deforestation, depletion of fresh water resources and paper consumption. In this composite, constituent phenomena are interrelated, for example, excessive paper consumption results in deforestation, which causes a fall in water resources and a growth in CO_2 levels, which further causes global warming, soil degradation and denudation, which, in turn, affects biodiversity adversely. Given these linkages, it is impossible to separate cause from effect, so that we refer to these factors as indicators of GED, rather than treating them as individual pollutants.

To create a composite EDI and relate it to HDI to develop a GEKC, we choose the essential variables and determine the relative weights to consolidate them into a single index. Given a dispersed set of outcomes, PCA is the appropriate methodology because it maximises the variance rather than minimises the least-square distance. PCA transforms linearly the original set of variables into a smaller set of uncorrelated variables containing most of the information. Since the components are orthogonal to each other, multicollinearity is not present. This transformation is represented as:

$$y_1 = a_{11}x_1 + a_{12}x_2 + \cdots + a_{1p}x_p = \sum_{i=1}^{p} a_{1i}x_i \tag{6.1}$$

The first principal component is defined so that the variance of y_1 is maximised. Consider the p random variables $x_1, x_2, \ldots, x_p$ subject to the constraint that the sum of squared weights is equal to 1, that is, $\sum_{i=1}^{p} a_{1i}^2 = 1$. If the variance of y_1 is maximised, the sum of squared correlations, that is, $\sum_{i=1}^{p} r_{y,x_i}^2$ is also maximised. PCA determines the optimal vector of weights $(a_{11}, a_{12}, \ldots, a_{1p})$ and the associated variance of y_1, which is denoted λ_1.

The second principal component, y_2, is given by:

$$y_2 = a_{21} * x_1 + a_{22} * x_2 + \cdots + a_{2p} * x_p \qquad (6.2)$$

so that the variance of y_2 is maximised subject to the constraint that the sum of the squared weights of the second vector of weights $(a_{21}, a_{22}, \ldots, a_{2p})$ is equal to 1:, that is, $\sum_{i=1}^{p} a_{2i}^2 = 1$.

In this specification, y_2 is orthogonal to y_1 so that $\sum_{i=1}^{p} a_{1i}a_{2i} = 0$. Hence, y_2 has the second largest sum of squared correlations with the original variables. As successive components are extracted, the variance of the principal components gets smaller. The first two principal components have the highest possible sum of squared correlations with the original variables. Hence, $\sum_{i=1}^{p} R_{xi,y1,y2}^2$ is maximised by extracting the first two principal components, which is a measure of the explanatory power of the components.[13]

Data and methodology

We estimate a GEKC for the 174 countries included in the HDI in UNDP (1999). The data used are cross-section observations; most of the variables refer to the period from 1990 to 1996. The HDI reports data on nine environmental variables. Three of these variables are not included; data on SO_2 emissions per capita were too scanty to use. In addition, internal renewable resources per capita are very large in comparison to the other variables and are, therefore, dropped. For a similar reason, total CO_2 emissions were also dropped. Thus, we are left with the following six variables: annual per capita fresh water withdrawals (PCFWWs), annual fresh water withdrawals as a percentage of water resources (CENTFWWs), printing and writing paper consumed per capita (PAPCM), per capita CO_2 emissions (PCCO$_2$), the share of world CO_2 (CO$_2$SH) and the average annual rate of deforestation (DEFOR).

Additional indicators of GED, such as biodiversity, waste and soil degradation, may be important but paucity of comparable data prohibits their use. The variables selected are expressed as ratios or as per capita measures to minimise scale problems.[14] In certain cases, deforestation is negative implying reforestation. The few data gaps are filled by substituting means based on values for neighbouring countries.[15] The 174 countries are grouped into three classes: high human development (HHD), having a HDI greater than or equal to 0.8, which includes countries with a HDI rank from 1 to 45, medium human development (MHD) having a HDI between 0.5 and 0.799 and a rank from 46 to 139 and low human development (LHD) having a HDI less than 0.5 and a rank from 140 to 174.

While the formation of a composite index is necessary, it is important to ascertain whether there are any country-specific effects at different levels. A global index across all countries would be justified only if the phenomenon of GED is generalised. To verify this, we carry out a two-factor ANOVA with and without replication[16] at two levels, namely, the overall level and the three development classes. The two factors are the 174 countries and the six environmental degraders.

For the first model, we specify:

$$X_{jk} = \mu + \alpha_j + \beta_k + \varepsilon_{jk} \tag{6.3}$$

In equation (6.3), X_{jk} is a measure of environmental degradation due to the kth degrader (column) and the jth country (row). The random variable X_{jk} is distributed normally across the grand mean μ with three additive effects, namely, α_j, the country effect, β_k, the degrader effect and ε_{jk}, the random effect. The random effect is distributed normally with the total variance (V) given by:

$$V = V_R + V_C + V_E \tag{6.4}$$

Thus, the total effect is the sum of the country effect, that is, the between country-group variance (V_R), the degrader effect, that is, the between degrader variance (V_C) and the overall variance (V_E). The respective mean square errors are used to test the statistical significance of these effects.

For the second model, we include an interaction term and specify:

$$X_{jk} = \mu + \alpha_j + \beta_k + \gamma_{jk} + \varepsilon_{jk} \tag{6.5}$$

In equation (6.5), X_{jk} is a measure of environmental degradation due to the kth degrader (column) and the jth country-group (row-block). The random variable X_{jk} is distributed normally across the grand mean μ with four additive effects, namely, α_j, the country-group effect, β_k, the degrader effect, γ_{jk}, the group–degrader interaction effect and ε_{jk}, the random effect. The random effect is distributed normally with the total variance (V) given by:

$$V = V_R + V_C + V_I + V_E \tag{6.6}$$

The total effect is the sum of the effects defined in equation (6.4) and an added interaction effect variance (V_I). The respective mean square errors are used to test the statistical significance of these effects.

At the aggregate level and at the level of country classes, the country effect is not significant but the degrader effect is in most cases, as Table 6.1 indicates. For LHD countries, both effects are insignificant so that it is meaningful to estimate a GEKC across the entire set of 174 countries. An ANOVA for all countries together reveals that only the degrader effect is significant. The variable designed to capture interaction effects between country groups and degraders is not significant as the analysis for the three-country group indicates. However, the country-group effect and the degrader effect are significant in this model. The significance of the degrader effect does not prevent the development of a composite index because the methodology used to construct the index accounts for these differentials by using appropriate weights.

Table 6.1 Analysis of country and degrader effects

ANOVA-two factor	Effect					
	SS[a]	Df[b]	MS[c]	F	P-value	F-criterion
High HDI						
Country	1438919.34	44	32702.71	0.972	0.527	1.43
Degrader	430248.56	5	86049.71	2.56	0.028	2.25
Random	7398976.01	220	33631.71			
Total	9268143.92	269				
Medium HDI						
Country	1593473.98	93	17134.13	1.04	0.39	1.28
Degrader	469511.18	5	93902.23	5.69	4.11E-05	2.23
Random	7665457.05	465	16484.8			
Total	9728442.2	563				
Low HDI						
Country	28053.4	34	825.1	1.05	0.4	1.49
Degrader	6102.03	5	1220.4	1.552	0.17	2.26
Random	133631.75	170	786.07			
Total	167787.2	209				
All countries						
Country	3155981.54	173	18242.67	1.02	0.4	1.2
Degrader	713591.03	5	142718.2	8.02	2.09E-07	2.22
Random	159390335.6	865	17792.29			
Total	19259908.1	1043				
Three-country groups						
Country	91248.37	2	45624.19	3.63	0.027	3.01
Degrader	209141.11	5	41828.22	3.33	0.005	2.23
Interaction	145879.98	10	14587.99	1.16	0.31	1.85
Random	7688819.03	612	12563.43			
Total	8135088.51	629				

Note: The letters a, b and c denote the sum of squares, the degrees of freedom and the mean sum of squares, respectively.

To examine whether there are differences between the mean levels of degraders across country classes, the means and coefficients of variation of the degraders are estimated for each of the three country classes. The descriptive statistics in Table 6.2 indicate that, even though the country effect was found to be insignificant, the mean levels of degraders are highly correlated with the level of HDI. The HHD group has the highest mean values for all but one variable, namely deforestation, which is negative for that group because deforestation in these countries occurred at a much earlier time. The MHD countries display middle-range values for most degraders, while the LHD countries have extremely low values. The coefficients of variation follow almost the reverse pattern; hence, the HHD countries display high levels of degradation because their coefficients of variation are low in most cases. Therefore, a negative relationship between environmental well-being and the level of economic development may exist.

Table 6.2 Basic statistic of degraders

	PCFWW	CENTFW	PAPCM	PCCO$_2$	CO$_2$SHA	DEFOR
High HDI						
Mean	7.2	107.9	59.66	11.09	1.09	−0.1
S. dev.	4.0	445.1	51.1	9.16	3.36	0.74
CV	0.55	4.12	0.85	0.82	3.08	−6.97
Medium HDI						
Mean	7.08	80.29	4.21	3.03	0.46	0.73
S. dev.	8.93	315.3	5.57	3.24	1.65	1.51
CV	1.26	3.92	1.32	1.07	3.58	2.05
Low HDI						
Mean	1.56	15.02	0.22	0.56	0.017	0.73
S. dev.	3.09	68.8	0.38	1.87	0.05	0.64
CV	1.97	4.58	1.69	3.35	3.31	0.87

We have tested for multicollinearity among the indicators, with the help of auxiliary regressions, in which each degrader is taken as the dependent variable with the other degraders as independent variables. The values of the F-statistic were found to be 5.04, 4.94, 10.69, 12.33, 16.43 and 13.19, respectively, for CO$_2$SH, DEFOR, PCFWW, PCCO$_2$ and PAPCM, as dependent variable. Our results indicate significant multicollinearity among all indicators of environmental degradation at the 5 per cent level of significance. Hence, these tests justify using environmental variables as constituents of a composite index rather than as individual variables in a regression framework.

If the objective is to summarise the information from the raw data, the use of component scores is appropriate. These scores are obtained by combining the raw variables with weights that are proportional to their component loadings. We use the component scores to determine the weight of each of the raw variables in constructing a composite EDI for each country. As more and more components are extracted, the measure of explanatory power increases but it is necessary to strike a balance between parsimony and explanatory power (Lewis-Beck 1994). The most frequently used decision rule is Kaiser's criterion but it discards too much information. We use Cattell's scree plot, which indicates that we should retain three components because after the third component the plot becomes flat.[17]

Sometimes the principal components are rotated to allow a more conceptually appealing and simpler interpretation. Both the unrotated and rotated solutions explain exactly the same amount of variation in the variables so that the choice between them hinges upon their respective interpretative power.[18] The unrotated component scores with respect to the first component are 0.301, 0.243, 0.299, 0.383, 0.237 and −0.27 for PCFWW, CENTFWW, PAPCM, PCCO$_2$, CO$_2$SH and DEFOR, respectively. For the same variables, the corresponding rotated scores are −0.083, −0.06, 0.52, 0.39, 0.495 and 0.102. One problem with using the unrotated scores is that, except for DEFOR, the component scores are almost equal so that the index would behave like an unweighted one. Hence, we choose the rotated components to construct our index.

The principal components may be used in their entirety or a subset may be chosen. The criterion for selecting one variable to represent each of the retained principal components is to choose the variable that has the highest loading on a component, provided that it has not already been chosen. The criterion is invoked in *seriatim* (Lewis-Beck 1994). Following this procedure, we reduce the number of variables from six to four by discarding two variables, namely, CENTFWW and DEFOR. Hence, we define the EDI for the *i*th country as:

$$\text{EDI}_i = \sum_j w_j x_{ji} \tag{6.7}$$

where w_j is the *j*th component score and x_{ji} is the value of the *j*th variable for the *i*th country given *j* equal to 1, 3, 4 and 5.

One criterion to evaluate the efficiency with which a subset of variables represents the total set is the total amount of variation explained by the subset. This can be obtained by adding the sum of the variances for the retained variables to the sum of the variation that they explain in each of the discarded variables. Hence, we can write total variation explained as $n_r + \Sigma_{i \in d} R^2_{i,r}$, where the set *d* consists of the discarded variables, n_r is the number of retained variables, and $R^2_{i,r}$ stands for the squared multiple correlation of the *i*th discarded variable with the *r* retained variables, which is obtained by regressing each of the two discarded variables on the four retained variables. The number of retained variables is included because each of the retained variables explains its own variation. The measure $R^2_{i,r}$ is summed over the discarded variables because it represents the variation in the discarded variables explained by the retained variables.[19]

In the next section we present the core empirical results relating to the EDI ranks, the construction and decomposition of the GEKC, and the distribution of environmental degradation.

The empirical results

Table 6.3 contains countries listed in descending order by their HDIRs, with information about their EDI and their EDIRs. The EDIR presents environmental degradation in ascending order, with rank 174 representing the country with the most environmental degradation, that is, Finland. EDI in the US is 2.5 times average EDI in the HHD country-class, 11 times average EDI for MHD countries and 210 times that of LHD countries. As the table indicates, HDIR and EDIR are inversely related. There is a strong negative correlation between HDIR and EDIR (-0.727) in the HHD class. The correlation is lower for the MHD class at -0.55, but it is still negative. For the LHD countries, the correlation is low and positive; EDI is extremely low on average.[20]

Table 6.3 The human development and environmental degradation profile of 174 countries

HHD countries[a]		MHD countries[b]		LHD countries[c]	
Country	HDIR (EDI) [EDIR]	Country	HDIR (EDI) [EDIR]	Country	HDIR (EDI) [EDIR]
Canada	1, (57.57), [165]	Trinidad and	46, (10.53), [133]	Laos	140, (−0.12), [15]
Norway	2, (55.04), [163]	Tobago		Congo	141, (−0.008), [22]
USA	3, (88.28), [173]	Hungary	47, (14.05), [139]	Sudan	142, (−0.41), [9]
Japan	4, (65.19), [170]	Venezuela	48, (7.71), [124]	Togo	143, (0.16), [41]
Belgium	5, (87.46), [172]	Panama	49, (4.82), [115]	Nepal	144, (−0.037), [19]
Sweden	6, (62.24), [168]	Mexico	50, (6.31), [118]	Bhutan	145, (0.06), [34]
Australia	7, (53.97), [162]	St. Kitts	51, (2.5), [90]	Nigeria	146,(0.54), [55]
Netherlands	8, (48.74), [160]	and Nevis		Madagascar	147, (−1.1), [5]
Iceland	9, (24.3), [151]	Grenada	52, (0.62), [57]	Yemen	148, (0.53), [54]
UK	10, (59.1), [166]	Dominica	53, (0.558), [56]	Mauritania	149, (−0.15), [14]
France	11, (39.58), [157]	Estonia	54, (17.44), [144]	Bangladesh	150, (0.62), [58]
Switzerland	12, (59.58), [167]	Croatia	55, (8.56), [128]	Zambia	151, (0.92), [64]
Finland	13, (129.11), [174]	Malaysia	56,(15.02), [141]	Haiti	152, (0.22), [48]
Germany	14, (50.01), [161]	Colombia	57, (4.81), [114]	Senegal	153, (0.09), [38]
Denmark	15, (64.12), [169]	Cuba	58, (1.25), [69]	Cote d'Ivorie	154, (0.76), [61]
Austria	16, (46.48), [159]	Mauritius	59, (5.75), [117]	Benin	155, (0.06), [35]
Luxembourg	17, (55.09), [164]	Belarus	60, (2.34), [86]	Tanzania	156, (0.26), [50]
New Zealand	18, (13.4), [137]	Fiji	61, (4.25), [107]	Djibouti	157, (0.23), [49]
Italy	19, (33.47), [155]	Lithuania	62, (3.83), [103]	Uganda	158, (0.03), [30]
Ireland	20, (32.64), [154]	Bulgaria	63, (3.51), [101]	Malawi	159, (.009), [26]
Spain	21, (28.87), [152]	Surinam	64, (2.01), [82]	Angola	160, (0.16), [42]
Singapore	22, (42.99), [158]	Libya	65, (2.37), [87]	Guinea	161,(−0.04), [18]
Israel	23, (30.42), [153]	Seychelles	66, (2.17), [83]	Chad	162, (−0.028), [20]
Hong Kong	24, (67.17), [171]	Thailand	67, (9.68), [131]	Gambia	163,(0.1), [39]
Brunei	25, (6.85), [121]	Romania	68, (4.23), [106]	Rwanda	164, (−0.02), [21]
Cyprus	26, (13.69), [138]	Lebanon	69, (8.34), [126]	Central	165, (0.69), [36]
Greece	27, (15.45), [142]	W. Samoa	70, (0.96), [66]	African	
Portugal	28, (20.58), [147]	Russian	71, (9.23), [129]	Republic	
Barbados	29, (7.38), [123]	Federation		Mali	166, (−0.08), [16]
South Korea	30, (34.29), [156]	Ecuador	72, (1.89), [80]	Eritrea	167, (4.3), [108]
Bahamas	31, (4.42), [109]	Macedonia	73, (4.45), [110]	Guinea-	168, (0.064), [33]
Malta	32, (20.07), [146]	Latvia	74, (3.93), [105]	Bissau	
Slovenia	33, (17.53), [145]	St Vincent	75, (0.19), [45]	Mozambique	169, (0.0058), [24]
Chile	34, (8.45), [127]	Kazakhstan	76, (2.56), [91]	Burundi	170, (0.03),[31]
Kuwait	35, (17.3), [143]	Philippines	77, (2.63), [92]	Burkina Faso	171, (0.006),[25]
Czech	36, (22.85), [149]	Saudi Arabia	78, (7.33), [122]	Ethiopia	172, (0.009), [27]
Republic		Brazil	79, (7.76), [125]	Niger	173, (0.034), [29]
Bahrain	37, (13.29), [136]	Peru	80, (2.41), [88]	Sierra Leone	174, (0.16), [44]
Antigua	38, (2.95), [95]	St Lucia	81, (3.86), [104]	Mean	157
Argentina	39, (9.4), [130]	Jamaica	82, (5.27), [116]		
Uruguay	40, (6.38), [119]	Belize	83, (1.26), [70]		
Qatar	41, (21.18), [148]	Paraguay	84, (1.84), [79]		
Slovakia	42, (10.4), [132]	Georgia	85, (−0.32), [12]		
UAE	43, (23.44), [150]	Turkey	86, (6.84), [120]		
Poland	44, (14.14), [140]	Armenia	87, (−0.45), [8]		
Costa Rica	45, (3.07), [97]	Dominican	88, (2.85), [94]		
Mean	23	Republic			
		Oman	89, (2.49), [89]		
		Sri Lanka	90, (1.4), [74]		
		Ukraine	91, (3.39), [99]		
		Uzbekistan	92, (−1.55), [3]		
		Maldives	93, (1.2), [67]		

Table 6.3 Continued

HHD countries[a]		MHD countries[b]		LHD countries[c]	
Country	HDIR (EDI) [EDIR]	Country	HDIR (EDI) [EDIR]	Country	HDIR (EDI) [EDIR]
		Jordan	94, (4.6), [111]		
		Turkmenistan	96, (−1.99), [1]		
		Krgyzstan	97, (−1.17), [4]		
		China	98, (10.86), [134]		
		Guyana	99, (−0.24), [13]		
		Albania	100, (2.34), [85]		
		South Africa	101, (11.9), [135]		
		Tunisia	102, (3.61), [102]		
		Azerbaijan	103, (1.42), [75]		
		Moldova	104, (1.22), [68]		
		Indonesia	105,(4.63), [112]		
		Cape Verde	106, (−0.48), [7]		
		El Salvador	107, (3.5), [100]		
		Tajikistan	108, (−1.62), [2]		
		Algeria	109, (2.84), [93]		
		Vietnam	110, (4.69), [113]		
		Syria	111, (0.94), [65]		
		Bolivia	112, (1.27), [71]		
		Swaziland	113, (−0.81), [6]		
		Honduras	114, (1.43), [77]		
		Namibia	115, (0.06), [132]		
		Vanuatu	116, (0.08), [37]		
		Guatemala	117, (1.99), [81]		
		Solomon Island	118, (0.16), [43]		
		Mongolia	119, (1.4), [73]		
		Egypt	120, (1.42), [76]		
		Nicaragua	121, (0.019), [28]		
		Botswana	122, (0.48), [53]		
		Sao Tome	123, (−0.36), [11]		
		Gabon	124, (1.44), [78]		
		Iraq	125, (2.18), [84]		
		Morocco	126, (1.27), [72]		
		Lesotho	127, (0.65), [59]		
		Myanmar	128, (0.2), [46]		
		Papua New Guinea	129, (0.31) [51]		
		Zimbabwe	130, (0.66), [60]		
		Equatorial Guinea	131,(0.148), [40]		
		India	132, (3.04), [96]		
		Ghana	133 (0.2), [47]		
		Cameroon	134, (0.34), [52]		
		Congo	135, (0.77), [62]		
		Kenya	136, (0.820, [63]		
		Cambodia	137,(−0.002), [23]		
		Pakistan	138 (−0.36), [10]		
		Comoros	139,(−0.07), [17]		
		Mean	92.5		

Notes

a Correlation (HDIR and EDIR) for high HDI countries: −0.72
b Correlation (HDIR and EDIR) for medium HDI countries: −0.55
c Correlation (HDIR and EDIR) for low HDI countries: −0.08.

The aggregative picture conceals specific details that give rise to certain apparent anomalies. For example, Finland is not usually considered to be the environmentally worst country because the standard notion of degradation ignores factors such as paper consumption. The average paper consumption for HHD countries is 92.4 metric tons. Finland consumes almost two and a half times this amount. By contrast, the average for MHD countries is 5.1 metric tons, and for LHD countries, it is only 0.4 metric tons. Similarly, the share of world CO_2 emission for the US alone is over 22 per cent. These differentials are concealed by PCI and HDI.

To test the nature of the relation between environmental degradation and HDI, we run sets of regressions and find that the following cubic relation is a good fit.[21]

$$\text{EDI}_i = \beta_0 + \beta_1 \text{HDIR}_i + \beta_2(\text{HDIR}_i)^2 + \beta_3(\text{HDIR}_i)^3 + \varepsilon_i \tag{6.8}$$

Plotting levels of EDI_i against HDIR_i[22] and creating a predicted cubic trend line, we obtain an adjusted R^2 of 0.764. Furthermore, all coefficients are highly significant with β_0 equal to 72.5, β_1 equal to -2.1, β_2 equal to 0.0195 and β_3 equal to $-5.7668\text{E-}05$. This pattern indicates a negatively sloped cubic GEKC with a characteristic inverted N-shape. The first 50 countries account for almost the entire area under the cubic curve. Between the ranks 50 and 100, the cubic fit dips marginally into the negative quadrant. Thereafter, it rises marginally above the axis before plummeting below the axis again as shown in Figure 6.1.

To explore the foundations of this GEKC, we consider the decomposition of the predicted EDI obtained from the cubic function given in equation (6.8). First, we run a regression of EDI on HDIR for HHD countries. The fit is satisfactory with an adjusted R^2 of 0.6 and with F and t statistics significant at less than 1 per cent. The coefficient on HDIR is -1.54 indicating that, with higher levels of

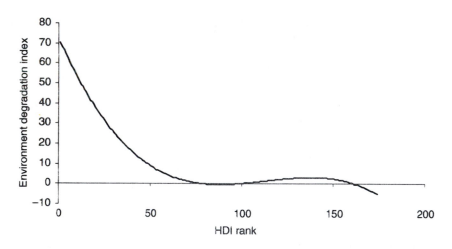

Figure 6.1 The inverse Global Environmental Kuznets Curve.

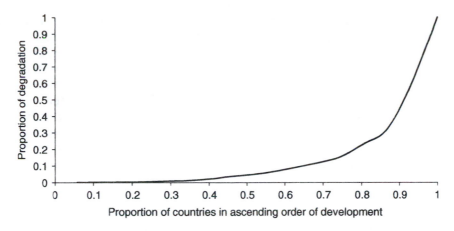

Figure 6.2 The distribution of environmental degradation.

development and lower values of HDIR, there is a significant rise in EDI. A regression of EDI on HDIR for MHD countries shows a less satisfactory fit with adjusted R^2 falling to 0.20 although the F and t statistics are still significant. The coefficient on HDIR is much smaller at -0.12 indicating a mild cumulative contribution of these countries. A final regression is run for the case of LHD countries and the fit is poor with a negative adjusted R^2 and F and t statistics insignificant even at the 10 per cent level. The cumulative contribution of these countries is relatively small.

To study the distribution of environmental degradation we construct a Lorenz curve[23] based on EDI. The proportion of the number of countries in ascending order of environmental degradation was plotted against the cumulative proportion of EDI. The countries were grouped into 17 groups of 10 countries each, except for the last group with only four countries. In each class, the proportion of EDI was cumulated. A large proportion of the total environmental degradation originates from the richer countries. Just 22 countries in the HHD class accounted for over 50 per cent of environmental degradation. As many as 131 countries belonging to the LHD and MHD classes accounted for only 23.4 per cent of total environmental degradation. The results are shown in Figure 6.2.

Conclusions: EKC and GEM

This chapter argues that the existing EKC methodology is inappropriate for understanding the link between economic development and environmental degradation. In this literature, there is no consensus about the empirical basis for the GED. The two contending views attempt to verify whether or not an inverted U-shaped EKC exists. Our PCA methodology emphasises the level of environmental degradation and relates this to a better measure of economic development. We establish empirically an inverted N-shaped GEKC.

This chapter also considers the distribution of environmental degradation among countries. We find extreme inequalities in the contribution of low, medium and high HDI country groups to GED with the low group effectively ameliorating GED and just 22 of the HHD group accounting for more than 50 per cent of it. The US alone has a highly disproportionate influence on all environmental degradation indicators. Hence, any design of a regulatory mechanism for GEM must recognise these distributional effects. Thus, this chapter provides a framework for assessing the current state of environmental degradation, its distribution worldwide and policy implications for a global agency, for example, the World Environmental Organization, interested in monitoring environmental degradation and its geographical distribution. Furthermore, the chapter establishes the contributions of countries with different levels of human development to environmental degradation and assists in assigning liability. The contention that GED is essentially caused by a certain type of development characteristic of high HDI countries is consistent with our results. Any comprehensive international environmental agreement must recognise this intrinsic relationship.

7 A critique of the environmental sustainability index

Introduction

A central issue in the context of the environment is that of its sustainability. As would be expected there is a plethora of definitions of the concept of sustainability. In Chapter 5 we have argued that any applicability of the notion of sustainability has ultimately got to be universal and refer to the indefinite future.

Once these broad contours are accepted the need for a measure of sustainability arises. Obviously such a measure must be general enough to cover various dimensions of the environment. This necessitates the development of an index that encapsulates both the current state of the environment as well as its potential to provide support for future human activity and should cover all the countries in the world. Such a measure is necessary for making international and intertemporal comparisons. This would reduce the ambiguity about the role of different countries, regions and income classes in efforts for GEM. Furthermore, it would provide an indicator of the progress that various countries make in the environmental arena and ultimately, transfers to developing countries could become contingent on this index just as financial transfers are currently contingent upon the attainment of specific macroeconomic and fiscal targets.

The 2002 ESI is a significant effort in this direction. It has been developed by collaboration of the World Economic Forum, Geneva, Center for International Earth Science Information Network, Columbia University, and Yale Center for Environmental Law and Policy, New Haven and is a measure of the overall progress towards environmental sustainability developed for 142 countries. It has aroused considerable interest even at the level of the scholarly popular press (see *The Economist*, 16 March 2002). The ESI is based upon a set of 68 basic indicators. These are then aggregated to construct 20 core indicators (Annex I of the *ESI 2002 Report*). These include: air quality, water quantity, water quality, biodiversity, land, reducing air pollution, reducing water stress, reducing ecosystem stress, reducing waste and consumption pressures, reducing population growth, basic human sustenance, environmental health, science and technology, capacity for debate, environmental governance, private sector responsiveness, eco-efficiency, participation in international collaborative efforts, reducing GHG emissions and reducing trans-boundary environmental pressures. A number of methods are used to capture each of these variables and their effect is classified according to their coverage, recentness and relevance. The process of ESI construction then aggregates the 20 core indicators into five broad indicators of sustainability. These broad indicators are: (i) environmental system; (ii) reducing environmental stress; (iii) reducing human vulnerability; (iv) social and institutional capacity component and (v) global stewardship. These indicators are then collapsed into a single ESI. The basic structure of the ESI index is described in Figure 7.1.

The ESI could presumably be a tool in environmental debate and, in the future, such a measure has the potential of seriously impacting domestic and international policy analysis. Hence, it is important that there be widespread acceptance of the structure and methodology of the ESI. Surely the construction of an index is an evolving process and periodic evaluation of this methodology would be useful. It needs to be compared with other such indices. The ESI report provides a review of some of the other existing indices of sustainability.[1]

The present chapter seeks to critically evaluate the structure and methodology of the ESI. There are two guiding concerns in doing so. First, a broad distinction has to be made between differing standpoints in relation to sustainability. Second, sustainability has to be studied within a causal framework.

Sustainability can be discussed as per at least three distinct standpoints:

1   environmental degradation
2   effects of degradation
3   environmental management.

Clearly the first dimension affects the second. The third must be designed so as to affect the former two. A causal and an impacted variable should not be clubbed into one grand index. However, this is precisely what the ESI does.

Our critique of the ESI methodology operates at two levels. At a *philosophical level* we question (i) the classification of variables; (ii) the coding of variables and

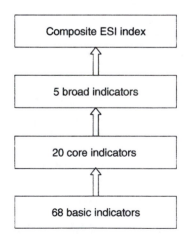

Figure 7.1 Structure of the ESI – 2002.

(iii) the specification (type) of the variables. At an *empirical level* at least three methodological problems arise: (i) aggregation problem; (ii) problem of cause and effect and (iii) weighting problems. We discuss these problems now.

Classification of variables

The classification of variables raises several questions. First, it is not clear why variables like urban NO_2 and SO_2 concentration should be a part of the 'environmental system' whereas NO_2 or SO_2 emissions per populated land area should be a part of 'reducing environmental stress'. Had these variables been defined as percentage drops there would have been some justification, but they have been not. Only two variables signifying change have been included in the methodology: one on forest cover, and the other most surprisingly, 'percentage change in projected population between 2001 and 2050'. How can a future (projected) rate of growth reduce present environmental stress? Moreover, the population variable does not match with the remaining variables. The variable 'proportion of undernourished in total population' cannot be directly related to environmental degradation.

The divide between 'social and institutional capacity' and 'global stewardship' is artificial. For instance, the source of GHG, CFC and SO_2 export is domestic. Better domestic management by each country is the only way to curb these gases. There is no way to separately curb trans-boundary pollution while not reducing domestic pollution concurrently. Also, it is not clear why CO_2-related variables are included *only* in global stewardship and excluded from indicators for environmental stress (which apparently signifies the domestic effects of pollution as opposed to the global effects). Does it imply that CO_2 is not harmful for domestic residents and adversely affects only the 'global environment' by sidestepping the local environment?

The coding of variables

A particularly serious lapse relates to the 'code' of the variables. For instance, in the core indicator, 'basic human sustenance', two variables are included, namely, proportion of undernourished in total population and percentage of population with access to improved drinking water. The problem with the 'code' is that if the index is low it favours the former variable and if it is high it favours the latter.

An important principle in the formation of an index is that the sum total of the variable must yield an interpretation that is unidirectional, that is, the 'code' must be the same. Once the index is aggregated such differences would not be known to users but would continue to have serious implications for analysis.

There is a similar problem with the broad indicator – environmental governance. The greater the 'percentage of area under protected status' the better, presumably, is governance. However, if the subsidy is on 'energy use' and 'commercial fishing' does it still amount to better governance?

Specification of variables

If the intention of the ESI is to be (as is stated to be the case) a 'near-complete' and an 'almost correct' index, then much more needs to be said about its coverage and correctness. For instance, under 'environmental governance' certain variables that have been included are either antiquated or politically incorrect. The variables that emphasise protected areas lay stress on the so-called 'fence and forget' approach but ignore recent understanding on the subject of forest management. Fundamental changes in thinking about forest management have not been reflected in the ESI approach. In real terms, a significant (though small) part of forest management is coming under co-operative management of and by the local populations (mainly tribal). This method is not only more politically correct but also more appropriate because, in large parts of the world, the thorniest problem in environmental management is the reconciliation of the interest of people and nature. Co-operative management tries to put this reconciliation into practice. The dynamics of management have evolved to 'joint-management', that is, private, co-operative and government and the literature on forest management has worked out the optimal shares of the three components of management (Gjertsen and Barrett 2001).

The broad category called 'social and institutional capacity' is incomplete and, at least in parts, politically incorrect since it ignores gender issues. The greatest inequity in forest management is in respect of gender. The indicator called 'Private Sector Responsiveness' has a corporate bias. It is biased towards industry and against agriculture/forestry. It is also biased towards corporate governance against people's governance. There is an advanced system of management of common lands, agriculture and forests called 'Heritage Parks' (Henderson 1993). This approach is *avante garde*. It envisages a private sector initiative but not necessarily through 'corporates'. The indicator is incomplete also because it does not consider the role of NGOs. There are vast tracts of countryside where the corporates cannot reach. NGOs have made inroads in some areas where there is deadlock between the government and the 'people'.

The aforementioned analysis although far from being complete, makes it clear that the variables included in five broad indicators need to be re-examined from the point of view of coverage, correctness, unbiasedness and above all, uniformity of 'code'. Also it is clear that five categories are not tenable. The three broad indicators, environmental system, stress and vulnerability, need to be coalesced together and sorted into two indices: environmental degradation and degradation effect. Both these indicators need to be supplemented appropriately by drawing certain variables (on 'global environment') from 'global stewardship'. The remaining 'stewardship' variables can be merged with social and institutional capacity, to form an indicator called 'environmental management'.

Hence, there are only these three logical categories of broad indicators. Any other division is not tenable. Further, these three indicators cannot be collapsed into one index since there is a causal chain amongst the three indicators. As things stand, if a country has a high index of sustainability the implication is that it has a high degree of degradation, severe degrader effects and better management as well!

Problems of methodology

There are serious problems in respect of methodology. These involve (i) inter-correlation amongst variables – cause and effect; (ii) use of equal weights – ignoring PCA (for a brief overview of PCA see Chapter 4); (iii) ignoring outliers – truncation; (iv) correlation with other variables; (v) ambiguity of the index (changing the sign); and (vi) relevance index (implicit weights). We now briefly discuss these problems.

Inter-correlation

Data reduction methods in general and PCA in particular are important methodological advancements having great utility in the area of developing indices. There are many real world situations where a large number of observable variables represent a single phenomenon. Very often these variables may not only be correlated but causally linked (with feedback) as well. For instance, excessive paper consumption would result in deforestation, which would cause a fall in water resources and a growth in CO_2 levels, which would then cause global warming, soil degradation and denudation, which would adversely affect biodiversity and so on. In such linkages it is not possible to separate cause and effect. PCA methodology is specifically designed to deal with such a situation.

However, one of the main reasons put forward by the ESI methodology to reject the use of PCA is that the correlation amongst indicators is low (0.05) (*ESI 2002 Report*, p. 47).

The problem appears to be the level at which the correlation has been measured. At the level of the 20 core indicators the data has already been processed to a considerable extent since the extreme values have been truncated and the code problem remains because of which after aggregation of individual variables at the level of indicators the correlation may be ironed-out. Moreover, an ambiguous procedure of switching the numerator has been followed for obtaining the Z-scores.

Equal weights

The use of equal weights can be criticised on several counts. First, if only three separate indices were to be formed (degradation, effects and management) and if all 68 variables were to be apportioned by ensuring the proper code, the inter-correlations would have shown-up. Second, if arbitrary procedures were not adopted, this trend would have been more prominent. Third, the use of PCA under such circumstance would have given different results. Fourth, the 'relevance' attached to each of the variables negates the argument that 'in our judgment there was no firm basis for applying differential weights given the current state of scientific understanding' (p. 47).

Another argument advanced for rejecting PCA was that 'the principal component (did not) have any sensible interpretations' (*ESI 2002 Report*, p. 47). However, this might have happened because of their choice, code, grouping and treatment of variables. Also, where results are not interpretable the procedure of rotation can be used in PCA methodology – an aspect that has been ignored in the construction of the ESI.

Ignoring outliers

A serious problem with the methodology is that the outliers of the variables were trimmed. Observed values above 97.5 percentile and below 2.5 percentile were reset. No convincing rationale is offered for this. A meaningful and attractive part of PCA methodology is that it identifies and distinguishes them from influential observation. This is very relevant for environmental analysis, given the wide diversity of environmental impact. Removing outliers unnecessarily irons out the variation.

Correlation with other drivers

The main *ESI Report* uses the correlation between ESI and other indicators like measures of democratic institutions, control of corruption and civil liberties. The justification for doing so is

> recognising that per capita income does not alone *determine* the ESI or its constituent indicators, it becomes important to try to identify other factors which, when combined with per capita income, help to explain the observed variation in environmental outcomes.
>
> (*ESI 2002 Report*, p. 22)

Further, it is said that, 'a number of variables have significant correlation with ESI, making them plausible drivers of environmental sustainability'.

However, some of these variables are already a part of ESI and for *determining* the *drivers* of environmental sustainability a causal framework as well as the EKC literature exist.[2] Such an important question cannot be decided on the basis of some *ad hoc* correlations.

Ambiguity

Apart from the ambiguity caused by the code of variables an *ad hoc* procedure was used which would have compounded the ambiguity. This is reflected in the following statement made in the context of calculating Z-scores. 'For variables in which high observed values correspond to low values of environmental sustainability, we reversed the terms in the numerator to preserve this ordinal relationship' (*ESI 2002 Report*, p. 46).

Table 7.1 Weight structure for five broad indicators

Indicator	Rank	Relevance index
Environmental system	1	5.15
Reducing stress	2	4.53
Global stewardship	3	3.61
Social and institutional capacity component	4	3.40
Human vulnerability	5	3.0

Relevance index

Although the methodology avoids using differential weights, it implicitly believes in one. In table A.1.1, in Annex 1 of the *ESI Report*, there is a column named 'relevance'. Here the authors of the Index have implicitly specified qualitative weights for each of the 68 variables. All these variables are grouped into 20 core indicators, which are then combined into five broad indicators. We have assigned a numerical weight from 1 to 7 for the qualitative weights specified. This range of weights depends on the nature of comments about relevance. The weight is 1 for low and goes up to 7 for extremely high. A weighted average of such weight has been calculated for each of the five broad indicators. Table 7.1 shows the ordering amongst them.

In light of this, when ESI has an implicit weighting system, why did they not use differential weights? Furthermore, ESI implies that each of these indicators may hold different levels of importance for different users. In such a situation merely continuing with the five indicators cannot be rationalised.

Hence, it can be said that ESI suffers from both conceptual as well as empirical problems. Before the index can be used for policy analysis and popularised it is necessary to thoroughly rework the entire index with the help of standard methodology like PCA instead of *ad hoc* procedures. More importantly, we need to develop a clearer understanding of the concept of environmental sustainability and its constituents. We now advance an alternative methodology for the construction of such an index.

Data, methodology and results

A basic criticism of the ESI methodology is that it does not use PCA. Their own justification is in terms of the low correlation amongst variables.[3] The very nature of many of the variables is such that, many of them are closely related, if not causally related. It is quite telling that, out of 45 correlation coefficients $((10 \times 10) - 10$ (own correlation)/2), only 16 are not significant, at the 5 per cent level. The remaining variables are highly correlated and have statistically significant correlation coefficients. Thus around two-thirds of the variables are correlated (see Table 7.2).

Table 7.2 Correlation matrix

		1	2	3	4	5	6	7	8	9	10
Correlation	VOCKM	1.00	0.29	−0.05	0.03	0.91	0.24	0.25	0.37	0.06	0.43
	SO$_2$KM	0.29	1.00	0.08	0.24	0.36	0.14	0.61	0.32	0.17	0.49
	PRTMAM	−0.05	0.08	1.00	0.50	0.02	0.27	0.11	0.03	−0.07	0.15
	PRTBRD	0.03	0.24	0.50	1.00	0.04	0.08	0.13	0.28	0.16	0.08
	NO$_X$KM	0.91	0.36	0.02	0.04	1.00	0.29	0.32	0.48	0.13	0.45
	FERTHA	0.24	0.14	0.27	0.08	0.29	1.00	0.17	0.29	0.00	0.45
	COALKM	0.25	0.61	0.11	0.13	0.32	0.17	1.00	0.42	0.13	0.72
	CO$_2$PC	0.37	0.32	0.03	0.28	0.48	0.29	0.42	1.00	0.52	0.42
	CO$_2$GDP	0.06	0.17	−0.07	0.16	0.13	0.00	0.13	0.52	1.00	0.03
	CARSKM	0.43	0.49	0.15	0.08	0.45	0.45	0.72	0.42	0.03	1.00
Level of significance (one-tailed)	VOCKM	1.00									
	SO$_2$KM	0.00	1.00								
	PRTMAM	**0.29**	**0.17**	1.00							
	PRTBRD	**0.37**	0.00	0.00	1.00						
	NO$_X$KM	0.00	0.00	**0.42**	**0.30**	1.00					
	FERTHA	0.00	0.04	0.00	**0.16**	0.00	1.00				
	COALKM	0.00	0.00	**0.09**	**0.06**	0.00	0.02	1.00			
	CO$_2$PC	0.00	0.00	**0.35**	0.00	0.00	0.00	0.00	1.00		
	CO$_2$GDP	**0.23**	0.02	**0.21**	0.03	**0.07**	**0.50**	**0.06**	0.00	1.00	
	CARSKM	0.00	0.00	0.04	**0.17**	0.00	0.00	0.00	0.00	**0.36**	1.00

Note
Only 16 correlation coefficients (in bold print) are *not* significant at 5% level. All the rest are highly statistically significant.

It is fairly well-known that if variables are correlated then PCA is ideally suited for such a situation. This is further confirmed even in cases where there are a large number of variables. The ESI is based on 68 variables. However, since

> Principal Component Analysis (PCA), is a statistical technique that linearly transforms an original (*large*) set of variables into a substantially smaller set of uncorrelated variables, that *represents most of the information* in the original set of variables[4] (emphasis added) the use of PCA is justified.

Environmental variables are usually closely related. By working with a large number of variables, the computation of the ESI is prone to the vagaries of the accumulation or compounding of reporting or measurement errors. The data on environmental variables is highly prone to such errors. The ESI document is itself replete with such allusions. While many other controversial methods have been used, PCA has been consciously avoided.

The environmental variables at the global level are also prone to have non-normal or skewed distributions. Here again PCA has an advantage. It does not need the normality assumption. While observing worldwide data the variance is likely to be very high. Here again PCA has the advantage that it does not have to explain the correlation (or covariance) amongst the largest possible ('fully specified') set of variables. It is very parsimonious because it uses the least number of variables to explain the full contours of a widely spread-out phenomenon by accounting for the maximum possible variance.

It is also economical because it minimises the effort and time while achieving similar results. It reduces the cost of data collection. This is relevant especially, if the authors of ESI want it to be a model index for emulation. It can be sustained only if it is economical. Especially, if governments of poor countries are expected to collect bulky data from their own resources, the cost of collection becomes very relevant. These governments would either be dependent on donors, who are rich countries or institutions, for funds for such purposes, which may have to be diverted from other developmental purposes or would 'cut corners' because of which data coverage, reliability and quality would suffer.

There are set procedures for scientifically selecting these variables from amongst many (see Jolliffe 1986; McAbe 1984). The chosen variables are known as 'principal variables'. There are certain measures that can be used for judging the utility (explanatory power) of such variables. Define total variation explained

$$(TVE) = n_r + \sum_{i \in d} R^2_{i,r} \tag{7.1}$$

where the set d consists of all variables; n_r is the number of retained variables and $R^2_{i,r}$ stands for the squared multiple correlation of the ith discarded variable with the r retained variables obtained by regressing each of the discarded variables on the four retained variables. The number of retained variables is added because each of the retained variables explains its own variation (variance $= 1$). The measure $R^2_{i,r}$ is summed over the discarded variables because it represents the variation in the discarded variables explained by the retained variables. Now, the ratio of TVE to total variation is a measure of the explanatory power. The measure of total variation is $d \times 1 = d$ since the total variation can be 100 per cent if all variables are included.

Another advantage with PCA is that, unlike factor analysis, it does not have to assume any underlying hypothetical factors. Yet it is possible to have a meaningful interpretation with the help of select variables. It only reduces the redundancy of data. The method of rotation allows better interpretation while explaining the same amount of variance. For instance, it allows us to pick up one air quality variable out of many, one biodiversity variable amongst many and so on. A range of variables can be represented by a few.

We reduced the number of variables using three procedures: (i) by eliminating some variables that have a 'code' problem or are not very relevant; (ii) by sorting the variables into 'environmental degradation variables', 'degradation effect variables' and 'environmental management variables', which reduces the number in each category to around 15 and (iii) by using PCA to achieve data reduction.

In the first stage variables were chosen on the basis of the following five criteria: (i) uniformity of code; (ii) high coverage; (iii) representativeness of each aspect of the environment; (iv) ease of interpretations and (e) relevance.

On this basis the following ten variables were selected:

VOCKM – VOCs per populated land area.
SO_2KM – SO_2 emissions per populated land area.
PRTMAM – Percentage of mammals threatened.
PRTBRD – Percentage of birds threatened.
NO_xKM – NO_x emissions per populated land area.
FERTHA – Fertiliser consumption per hectare of arable land.
COALKM – Coal consumption per populated land area.
CO_2PC – CO_2 emissions per capita.
CO_2GDP – CO_2 emissions per \$ GDP.
CARSKM – Vehicles per populated land area.

We have applied Varimax Rotation Criterion (Kaiser 1958) and have accordingly retained four variables.

1   VOCKM – representing air quality.
2   COALKM – representing depletion of resource.
3   PRTMAM – representing biodiversity
4   CO_2GDP – representing global pollution.

The explanatory power of these four variables is given by using the formula in equation (7.1) and stands at

$$4 + 2.735 = 6.735/10 \quad \text{or} \quad 67.35\%$$

The component scores of these variables that have been used for building the EDI are given in Table 7.3.

Finally, the EDI was constructed on the basis of component scores. The ranks were established on the basis of ascending value of EDI. This was done to make the ESI and EDI comparable. The logic is, that a low value of EDI corresponds to a more sustainable environment, which can be represented by a higher value of the ESI. This makes the code of both comparable. Then the relative ranks of the 2002 ESI and our EDI were compared (see Table 7.4).

Ideally, the rank correlation coefficient should have been (+) unity. This would have endorsed that there is no flaw in the estimation of 2002 ESI. However, the rank correlation coefficient was only 0.1067 and the Z-value was only 1.2. Hence, the rank correlation was not significantly different from zero. A test using the Z-value confirms that the rank correlation is (statistically significantly) below +(1) unity.

There are wide differences in the ranks of many countries giving anomalous results. For instance, Australia has a difference of (−) 119 in rank – ESI minus EDI. This means that it is highly sustainable and extremely degrading – both simultaneously! Only very few countries retain the ranks. On the other hand Guinea-Bissau is hardly degrading but almost unsustainable! This is true of most poor countries. Most of the rich countries have extremely high vehicular traffic

Table 7.3 Component score coefficient matrix

	Component			
	1	*2*	*3*	*4*
VOCKM	−0.135	*0.478*	−0.070	−0.014
SO$_2$KM	0.405	−0.141	−0.045	0.040
PRTMAM	−0.050	0.003	*0.577*	−0.130
PRTBRD	−0.067	−0.075	0.486	0.214
NO$_X$KM	−0.113	0.454	−0.045	0.031
FERTHA	−0.039	0.251	0.261	−0.186
COALKM	*0.503*	−0.174	−0.078	−0.037
CO$_2$PC	0.000	0.096	0.039	0.416
CO$_2$GDP	−0.074	−0.087	−0.050	*0.643*
CARSKM	0.365	0.046	−0.002	−0.176

Source: Extraction method PCA. Rotation method: Varimax with Kaiser normalisation.

Note
Component scores of retained variables in bold italics.

Table 7.4 Relative ranks of the 2002 ESI and EDI

ESI rank	EDI rank	EDI	Country	Diff. in rank
59	1	0.624	Mozambique	58
75	2	1.558	El Salvador	73
127	3	2.017	Giunea-Bissau	124
52	4	2.617	Nicaragua	48
67	5	2.859	Gautemala	62
103	6	2.871	Gambia	97
95	7	2.900	Benin	88
39	8	3.065	Moldova	31
24	9	3.110	Albania	15
25	10	3.134	Paraguay	15
82	11	3.305	Malawi	71
101	12	3.504	Burkina Faso	89
105	13	3.597	Togo	92
98	14	3.840	Guinea	84
115	15	3.892	Burundi	100
46	16	4.024	Zimbabwe	30
47	17	4.234	Honduras	30
81	18	4.349	Senegal	63
9	19	4.359	Costa Rica	−10
76	20	4.515	Uganda	56
10	21	4.526	Latvia	−11
69	22	4.568	Zambia	47
65	23	4.669	Ghana	42
6	24	4.845	Uruguay	−18
43	25	4.993	Cent. Afr. Rep.	18
111	26	5.036	Angola	85
134	27	5.366	Sierra Leone	107
123	28	5.585	Niger	95
119	29	5.645	Rwanda	90
36	30	5.660	Gabon	6
109	31	5.723	Zaire	78
85	32	5.926	Mali	53
21	33	5.958	Bolivia	−12
93	34	5.965	Cameroon	59
40	35	5.982	Congo	5
121	36	6.007	Trin. and Tobago	85
108	37	6.034	Ivory Coast	71
27	38	6.045	Lithuania	−11
17	39	6.138	Panama	−22
49	40	6.152	Byelarus	9
102	41	6.160	Sudan	61
130	42	6.208	Liberia	88
56	43	6.240	Kyrgyzstan	13
107	44	6.328	Syria	63
5	45	6.492	Switzerland	−40
29	46	6.629	Peru	−17
132	47	6.649	Somalia	85
38	48	6.672	Armenia	−10
15	49	6.704	Argentina	−34
1	50	7.295	Finland	−49

Table 7.4 Continued

ESI rank	EDI rank	EDI	Country	Diff. in rank
18	51	7.350	Estonia	−33
32	52	7.669	Colombia	−20
48	53	7.675	Venezuela	−5
26	54	7.724	Namibia	−28
96	55	7.813	Chad	41
142	56	8.008	Kuwait	86
110	57	8.070	Tajikistan	53
41	58	8.251	Ecuador	−17
53	59	8.326	Jordan	−6
113	60	8.328	Ethiopia	53
112	61	8.402	Pakistan	51
133	62	8.441	Nigeria	71
4	63	8.654	Canada	−59
3	64	8.667	Sweden	−61
12	65	8.713	Croatia	−53
80	66	8.854	Tanzania	14
90	67	9.055	Myanmar	23
7	68	9.109	Austria	−61
13	69	9.188	Botswana	−56
42	70	9.282	Mongolia	−28
11	71	9.326	Hungary	−60
88	72	9.360	Khazakstan	16
61	73	9.404	Tunisia	−12
118	74	9.455	Uzbekistan	44
14	75	9.485	Slovakia	−61
54	76	9.498	Thailand	−22
138	77	9.519	Saudi Arabia	61
32	78	9.641	Laos	−46
23	79	9.779	Slovenia	−56
73	80	9.821	Morocco	−7
99	81	9.821	Nepal	18
89	82	9.859	Kenya	7
45	83	9.890	USA	−38
57	84	10.208	Bosnia	−27
92	85	10.252	Mexico	7
62	86	10.360	Turkey	−24
139	87	10.579	Iraq	52
106	88	10.589	Lebanon	18
70	89	10.633	Algeria	−19
131	90	11.128	Turkmenistan	41
126	91	11.230	Mauritania	35
97	92	11.231	Cambodia	5
68	93	11.235	Malaysia	−25
120	94	11.463	Oman	26
104	95	11.481	Iran	9
2	96	11.716	Norway	−94
60	97	11.774	Greece	−37
94	98	11.820	Vietnam	−4
31	99	11.891	Denmark	−68
74	100	12.046	Egypt	−26

(*continued*)

Table 7.4 Continued

ESI rank	EDI rank	EDI	Country	Diff. in rank
84	101	12.068	Italy	−17
114	102	12.289	Azerbaijan	12
20	103	12.435	Brazil	−83
83	104	12.449	Macedonia	−21
30	105	12.648	Bhutan	−75
72	106	12.797	Russia	−34
64	107	13.007	Czech. Rep.	−43
37	108	13.502	Ireland	−71
86	109	13.860	Bangladesh	−23
55	110	13.894	Srilanka	−55
33	111	14.007	France	−78
66	112	14.389	Romania	−46
77	113	14.409	South Africa	−36
35	114	14.662	Chile	−79
71	115	14.664	Bulgaria	−44
122	116	14.783	Jamaica	6
129	117	14.967	China	12
63	118	15.084	Israel	−55
141	119	15.130	UAE	22
136	120	15.390	Ukraine	16
51	121	15.501	Papua N.G.	−70
87	122	16.944	Poland	−35
140	123	17.255	N. Korea	17
28	124	17.548	Portugal	−96
124	125	17.653	Libya	−1
50	126	17.942	Germany	−76
44	127	19.041	Spain	−83
116	128	19.185	India	−12
100	129	19.266	Indonesia	−29
34	130	19.546	Netherlands	−96
117	131	19.989	Phillipines	−14
78	132	20.177	Japan	−54
128	133	20.992	Madagascar	−5
125	134	21.043	Belgium	−9
16	135	21.420	Australia	−119
58	136	21.777	Cuba	−78
91	137	22.519	UK	−46
135	138	24.916	South Korea	−3
79	139	31.121	Domin. Rep.	−60
8	140	35.798	Iceland	−132
19	141	47.413	New Zealand	−122
137	142	77.264	Haiti	−5

Notes
The Spearman rank correlation between ESI (based on ESI index in descending order) and ED ranks (based on ascending order) is given below:
Spearman's rank correlation coefficient = 0.106.
Standard error = 0.084.
Z-value = **1.268**.
Hence, rank correlation coefficient is not significant at 5% level.

and pollution and are by the EDI highly degrading but are fairly sustainable by the count of their ESI.

Conclusions

This chapter has argued that the basic design of the ESI leaves much to be desired. It has conceptual problems in its visualisation of environmental degradation and sustainability. The choice of variables as well as the statistical methodology of compiling the index is also found to be wanting. We proposed an alternative methodology using PCA and argued that this is an improvement upon the ESI methodology. Given the likely use of aggregate environmental indexes in future environmental management, the critique advanced in this chapter is of considerable significance.

8 A consumption-based human development index and the Global Environmental Kuznets Curve

Introduction

Chapter 6 has explored, in some depth, the relationship between environmental degradation and economic development. It has argued that the standard approach embodied in the EKC relationship, purported to be an inverted U-shaped curve between select pollutants and PCI is flawed. Some commentators argue that the EKC supports the contention that so long as developing countries' PCIs are below the threshold of PCI where the EKC turns back, their economic growth would only increase GED. Since developed countries' PCIs lie beyond the peak of the EKC, further economic growth in these countries would only lower GED. Hence the global environment would be benefited by developing countries sacrificing growth and developed countries enhancing their growth. This argument, would thus achieve global intertemporal efficiency by fostering global spatial inequity.

As argued in Chapter 5 our contention is that 'the applicability of the notion of sustainability has ultimately got to be *universal and refer to the indefinite future*' and must be related to consumption. Further as Jha and Whalley (2001) have argued, the notion of what constitutes environmental degradation varies between developed and developing countries. The EKC literature has, by and large, focused primarily on emissions since these are the most important concern for developed countries whereas developing countries may be more concerned about land degradation. Any comprehensive view on the links between environmental degradation and economic development must then study (an appropriately weighted) aggregate of relevant environmental degraders. Furthermore, Jha and Whalley (2001) argue, the EKC for any given country is tenuous, at best. In addition, there has been little effort in the extant literature to relate PCI (or some other broad measure of economic development) to a composite index of environmental degradation in a cross section of countries. In Chapter 6 we report estimates of a GEKC, for 174 countries using a more complete measure of economic development than PCI – the HDI ranks of countries – and relate these to a composite measure of the levels of environmental degradation (encapsulated in a composite in EDI) for these countries. We establish that this GEKC assumes a cubic form with developed countries contributing the lion's share of GED.

This chapter takes up an important focus of this book, namely, that environmental degradation should be related to consumption. In this sense we identify 'excessive' consumption and the percolation of such consumption patterns as an important contributor to GED. We attempt to shift the focus in the growth–environment debate towards consumption as a part of a complete model that explains the relationship between development and GED.

Existing consumption-based approaches

While it is common to relate environmental degradation to PCI some studies have argued that factors related to production could be important reasons behind environmental degradation (Grossman 1995; Grossman and Krueger 1995, 1994; Panayotou 1997; Radetzki 1992).[1] Nonetheless, other studies (e.g. Ehrlich and Holdren 1971) have attempted to relate environmental degradation to consumption. This literature works with the Ehrlich identity:

$$I \equiv PAT$$

where I is environmental impact, P is population, A is affluence and T is technology. Ekins and Jacob (1995) and Dietz and Rosa (1994) have rephrased this identity by

$$I \equiv PCT$$

where C is consumption.

Other authors (Amalric 1995; Ekins and Jacob 1995; Raskin 1995) have emphasised the role of the composition of consumption. On balance the IPAT literature provides the basic reference point for consumption-based approaches. The broader question that is being asked is whether environmental degradation is anthropogenic or natural.

In contrast, production-based approaches emphasise scale, composition and technique of production (Grossman and Krueger 1995; Panayotou 1997). The scale of production is responsible for reducing the per unit energy use. As national income rises the share of agriculture in national income is likely to fall, and that of industry, and later, services go up. It is claimed that this transition is associated with the emergence of an inverted U-shaped pattern in terms of the corresponding pollution levels. Along with economic development would come better techniques of production, which would result in lower pollution per unit of output.

There are reasons to believe that the analysis of environmental degradation in terms of consumption-based approaches can be seen as being similar to production-based approaches. The scale of production is related to the size of the market and hence to population. As the composition of the national income shifts from (subsistence-based) agriculture to manufacturing and then up to services there could be an initial rise in consumption levels due to 'pent-up' demand being released and a subsequent fall. The parallel between technique and technology is straightforward. Hence, the parallels to scale, composition and techniques can be seen as population, consumption and technology, which are the broad planks of the IPAT framework.

Although there is a parallel between the two approaches the production approach suffers from certain problems, the most fundamental of which is that demand for production activity is a derived demand (Daly 1996; Duchin 1998; Rees 1995). Further, Ekins (1997) argues that, if the shift in production patterns has not been accompanied by a shift in consumption patterns two conclusions would follow. First, environmental effects due to the composition effect are being displaced from one country to the other rather than being reduced. Second, the best means of reducing environmental impacts will not be available to the latest developing countries, because there will be no countries coming-up behind them to which environmentally intensive activities can be transferred.

Furthermore, production-based approaches do not capture the degradation that is caused directly by consumption, for example, as production and disposal of waste, vehicular pollution, excessive withdrawal of water resources, final consumption of energy and paper, etc. Taking income as a proxy for production is also problematic. While consumption may be a derivative of income, and may be closely related to it, there is reason to believe that consumption may nonetheless be a better measure than income in relation to the impact on environmental degradation. Now consider the problem of measuring pollution intensity across countries. The chosen measures could be either:

$$I_{pi} = \frac{E_i}{NI_i} \quad \text{or} \quad X_i = \frac{E_i}{C_i}$$

where X_i = consumption pollution intensity in the ith country, C_i = consumption level of the ith country and I_{pi} = the income–pollution intensity in the ith country with E_i = emissions of the ith country and NI_i = national income of the ith country.

Now, if the propensity of consumption in the jth country is half of that of the ith country and if consumption level replaces NI in the denominator then

$$\frac{X_j}{X_i} = 2$$

whereas

$$\frac{I_{pi}}{I_{pj}} = 1$$

This illustrates the point that income-based measures may tend to unduly narrow differentials where they exist.

When using the consumption approach Hawken (1995) and Rees (1990) have termed waste as a problem of 'non-consumption'. However, there is a measurement problem if such an approach is taken to its logical conclusion. For instance, if energy intensity is being measured one may write

$$C = C_a + C_w$$

where C_a = actual consumption and C_w = waste during consumption and

$$N_p = \frac{V}{NI}$$

$$N_c = \frac{V}{C}$$

$$N_a = \frac{V}{C_a}$$

where V = energy use; N_p = production-based measure of energy intensity; N_c = total consumption-based measure of energy intensity; N_a = actual consumption-based measure of energy intensity.

The relationship between the three measures is

$$N_p < N_c < N_a$$

This would clearly create problems when measuring the performance across countries since the level of both consumption as well as waste would differ. Further, these dimensions cannot be mechanically subsumed within production.

In the context of international trade, Divan and Shafik (1992) and Pearce and Warford (1993) have emphasised that the North can improve local environmental quality at the cost of global pollution due to the 'debunking' technologies that they possess (Pollution Haven Hypothesis). To this must be added the fact that if consumption and disposal patterns were taken into account, the global pollution inequalities would get accentuated because in the North high levels of consumption (C) can continue at the cost of C_w being transferred to the South. Therefore, a consumption-based approach to the EKC whose interest is in ascertaining the levels of GED and, more importantly, the distribution of degradation across the globe is preferable.

More recently, Rothman (1998) provides a useful review and meticulously charts the relationship between consumption and GDP and establishes an inverted-U (EKC-type) pattern in the case of certain commodities. It must be pointed out that EKC does not imply that the consumption pattern has an inverted-U shape – only that environmental degradation has an inverted-U shape when plotted against PCI. The contribution of Rothman lies in raising the question, 'Is it possible to go further to more explicitly and completely link a measure of environmental impact to consumption?' On the other hand, Suri and Chapman (1998) have concentrated on 'energy consumption itself, as a chief source of a number of environmental problems'. Their model begins by estimating pollution as:

$$P_{ij} = a_{ij}E_i$$

where a_{ij} = emission/unit energy (emission coefficient); E_i = energy consumption; P_{ij} = pollutant j from energy source i.

Since high energy intensity also generally implies high pollution intensity, the two terms are used interchangeably. Their final model uses GDP:

$$\log E_i \text{ per capita} = f(GDP, GDP^2)$$

Hence they neither directly measure pollution (let alone environmental degradation, which is a broader concept) nor do they introduce consumption *per se* as an explanatory variable. Their subsequent models include only manufacturing and trade-related variables as explanatory variables. But nothing is done to modify the dependent variable – energy consumption. Effectively, then, there is no study that estimates the behaviour of environmental degradation against consumption. The present chapter purports to fill this void.

Methodology and data

Our *modus operandi* for arriving at a better understanding of the links between environmental degradation and consumption is as follows. Along the lines of Chapter 6 we use the method of PCA to construct an EDI for each country. We then identify outliers and influential observations between both the environmental and consumption-related variables. Canonical discriminant analysis is used to classify development classes along environmental lines. We then estimate a simultaneous equation model to model the pattern of causation between PCI, consumption and environmental degradation. Finally, we present an alternative consumption-based HDI to UNDP's income-based HDI. We then compare the ranking of countries according to the consumption-based HDI ranks with their ranking according to their EDI.

Two sets of data drawn from the HDR (UNDP 2000)[2] are used in the analysis. One relates to the environment and the other to developmental variables. For the formation of a composite index that would enable the estimation of a GEKC for 174 countries, we used cross-sectional data used in the HDR. The HDR contains data on the following environmental variables.

1   internal renewable water resources per capita (cubic meters/year);
2   annual fresh water withdrawals per capita (100 cubic meters);
3   annual fresh water withdrawals as a percentage of water resources;
4   average annual rate of deforestation (per cent);
5   printing and writing paper consumed per 1000 persons;
6   total CO_2 emission (million metric tons);
7   share of world total CO_2 (per cent);
8   per capita CO_2 emissions (metric ton);
9   SO_2 emissions per capita (kilograms).

Construction of the EDI

Data on SO_2 was scanty so it was dropped. Internal renewable water resources per capita are very large in comparison to the other variables. Hence this variable was dropped. For a similar reason the variable 'total CO_2 emissions' was also dropped. Thus, we are left with six variables. They are:

1   PCFWW – annual per capita fresh water withdrawals.
2   CENTFWW – annual fresh water withdrawals as a percentage of water resources.

3   PAPCPM – printing and writing paper consumed per capita.
4    $PCCO_2$ – per capita CO_2 emission.
5   CO_2SH – share of world total CO_2.
6   DEFOR – rate of deforestation.

Surely, there are additional indicators of GED such as biodiversity, waste and soil degradation, but paucity of comparable data prohibits us from using these variables. The selected variables were expressed as ratios or as per capita measures, in order to minimise scale problems.[3] In certain cases, DEFOR was negative implying reforestation, for this and other reasons DEFOR was dropped. Data gaps (there were very few) were filled with help of substitute means based on values for neighbouring countries.[4]

The 174 countries covered by the HDR were classified into three classes according to the following criteria:

1   HDI ≥ 0.8 – high human development. This included countries with HDI rank (HDIR) from 1 to 45.
2   HDI 0.5–0.799 – medium human development. This included countries with HDIR from 46 to 139.
3   HDI < 0.5 – low human development which include countries with HDIR from 140 to 174.

The HDR 2000 contains certain developmental variables related to consumption. We use the following to understand the underlying developmental causal factors.

1   Per Capita Consumption (CONS).
2   GDP per capita in PPP $ (GDPPC$).
3   Energy consumption per capita (ENERGY).
4   Value of international trade (exports plus imports) (TRADEV).
5   Rate of urbanisation (URBAN).

If the objective is a simple summary of the information contained in the raw data, the use of component scores is desirable. It is possible to represent the components exactly from the combination of raw variables. The scores are obtained by combining the raw variables with weights that are proportional to their component loadings. In our case the component scores have been used for determining the weight of each of the raw variables in constructing a composite EDI for the *i*th country and, similarly, for other countries. As more and more components are extracted, the measure of the explanatory power would increase. However, this would defeat the purpose of reducing the dimensionality. It is necessary to strike a balance between parsimony and explanatory power.

Both the unrotated and rotated solutions explain exactly the same amount of variation in the variables. The choice between them hinges upon their respective interpretative power. Once the number of retained principal components is determined and the rotated component scores obtained, we have the choice of using the principal components as such or selecting a subset of variables from the larger set of variables.

We were able to narrow down the number of variables from six to four.[5] However, the principal components were themselves not directly used. We discard two variables, namely, the second (CENTFWW) and the sixth (DEFOR), and define the EDI

$$EDI_i = \sum_{j=1}^{5} w_j \cdot x_{ji}$$

for the ith country. Here w_j is the jth component score; x_{ji} is the value of the jth variable for the ith country; and $j = 1, 3, 4$ and 5.

Then GED is given by:

$$GED = \sum_{i=1}^{174} EDI_i$$

Identifying outliers and influential observations

Principal Component Analysis allows identification of outlying observations. To accomplish this we plot the two most significant components and identify the countries lying beyond reasonable limits. An outlier (in a relative sense) would significantly differ from the norm, in comparison with its neighbours. This is done separately for each of the development classes. A distinguishing feature is that while all influential observations are outliers, all outliers are not influential observations. The difference lies in the fact that influential observations have a significant impact on the component scores. The methodology involves the elimination of each suspect observation and re-estimation of the component scores. If the ratio of the original score to the new score remains the same then the particular country is not an influential observation. However, if the sign changes and this ratio is different from unity the particular country is to be treated as an influential observation, that is, its absence leads to radical changes in the overall component scores.

Canonical discriminant analysis

There could be three factors causally linked to GED. They are:

1   Human development that is broad-based and includes economic as well as social factors.
2   Consumption that is moulded by economic and cultural factors that adjunct to economic factors.
3   Geophysical factors that can be gauged by the common agro-climatic regions.

We classified the set of 174 countries, on which data are available in HDR 2000, into three classes by Canonical Discriminant Analysis according to the criteria laid down in HDR, that is, on the basis of the level of the HD index. The null hypothesis is that countries responsible for environmental degradation can be classified on the basis of consumption-related causes. The alternative is that the classification should be based on geophysical causes and not consumption-related factors. Thus, we classified the same set of countries using two criteria: (i) on the basis of environmental degradation variable according to HDI and (ii) by consumption-related variables according to HDI. If the null hypothesis were correct, the classification by environmental variables and that by consumption-related variables would coincide. On the other hand, if geophysical causes were behind degradation then the classification would have to be on a geographical basis.

Causal framework of GED

Since causal factors are so intertwined it is necessary to establish a causative framework, so as to separate the influence of the individual factors. To accomplish this we construct a simultaneous equations model. Our purpose is three-fold.

1 To explain the income generating factors (some of which are cultural).
2 To estimate a global consumption function based on income.
3 To predict the GEKC using consumption.

In the earlier analysis it was shown that consumption patterns that evolve in rich countries determine the nature of demand and its relationship with technology (the PCC and the TCC analysis in Chapter 2). The pattern and the level of consumption are enabled by income. Our maintained hypotheses are that on the one hand, the 'type' of economic development, established by rich countries, that leads to a certain pattern of income generation, has percolated down to poor countries; and, on the other hand, their consumption patterns have been imbibed by poor countries, as well.

We use the following three-equation framework for establishing the nexus between the 'type' of economic development, the patterns of (over) consumption and the patterns of GED. Given below is the simultaneous equation model, using cross-section data across 174 countries:

$$GDPPC = a_0 + a_1 * ENERGY + a_2 * TRADEV + a_3 * URBAN + U_1 \quad (8.1)$$

$$Consumption = b_0 + b_1 * GDPPC + U_2 \quad (8.2)$$

$$EDI = c_0 + c_1 * (HDIR) + c_1 * (HDIR)^2 + c_1 (HDIR)^3 + U_3 \quad (8.3)$$

We use two-stage least squares (2SLS) to estimate this set of equations.

Construction of the consumption-based HDI

Our alternative consumption-based HDI is based on three indicators:

1 Life expectancy at birth.
2 Educational attainment (with two-third weightage for primary education).
3 Standard of living measured by real GDPPC in PPP $.

Each variable has a minimum and maximum range.

10   Life expectancy: 25–85.
11   Educational attainment: 0–100 per cent.
12   Standard of living: (PPP $) 100–40,000.

The general formula for computing each component is:

$$\text{Index } (X_i) = \frac{\text{Actual } X_i \text{ value } - \text{ minimum } X_i \text{ value}}{\text{Maximum } X_i \text{ value } - \text{ minimum } X_i \text{ value}}$$

Income is taken to be a proxy for living standard. However, unlimited income may not be necessary to achieve a respectable level of human development. Therefore, over the years the HDI team developed a complex formula to discount income above a threshold level. Apart from the question of what that level should be, the problem with this procedure was that it discounted higher incomes excessively, as indicated by Anand and Sen (1999). These authors advocate more moderate discounting as in:

$$W(y) = \frac{\log y - \log y_{min}}{\log y_{max} - \log y_{min}}$$

The justification for this is that this formula does not need a threshold nor does it penalise middle-income countries unduly.

Clearly the approach involving discounting has a normative intent since it scales extremely high values. An implication is that even if developing countries do not attain such high values of income they will still benefit and, according to this calculus, the gap between their realised income and the high incomes of the developed countries would be narrower than would have been the case if such discounting had been eschewed. However, if no discounting is used the HDI would reflect how things *stand*, which is a positive approach. As a consequence of following this approach the actual gaps between the levels of income in developed countries and those attainable by developing countries would be revealed. Thus, this approach would reveal the true inequalities of income. Once such inequalities are revealed their consequence for environmental degradation would also become relevant.

A measure of the inequalities in consumption-related variables and environmental degradation variables can be gauged from Tables 8.1 to 8.3. While the proportions may differ the parallelism is striking.

Table 8.1 is based on of the mean values of the respective developmental and environmental variables in proportion (low: medium: high) to HDI classes. Thus, the construction of the HDI as it stands conceals more than it reveals.

We propose a consumption-based HDI which can ultimately be used for estimating a GEKC based on a new measure of HDI. Our methodology is as follows: First, the income component has been netted out from the existing HDI.

Table 8.1 Inequality in consumption and environmental degradation across HDI classes

Developmental status	Low : middle : high	Environmental	Low : middle : high
Consumption	1 : 3 : 14	Water consumption	1 : 5 :7
GDP (per capita)	1 : 4 : 18	Paper consumption	1 : 21 : 240
Energy consumption	1 : 15 : 77	CO_2 (per capita)	1 : 6 : 23
Trade	1 : 10 : 200	CO_2 Share	1 : 30 : 60
Urbanisation	1 : 2 : 3		

Table 8.2 Basic statistics – environmental degradation

	PCFWW	CENTFW	PAPCM	PCCO₂	CO₂SHA	DEFOR
High HDI						
Mean	7.2	107.9	59.66	11.09	1.09	−0.1
Std. dev.	4.0	445.1	51.1	9.16	3.36	0.74
CV	0.55	4.12	0.85	0.82	3.08	−6.97
Medium HDI						
Mean	7.08	80.29	4.21	3.03	0.46	0.73
Std. dev.	8.93	315.3	5.57	3.24	1.65	1.51
CV	1.26	3.92	1.32	1.07	3.58	2.05
Low HDI						
Mean	1.56	15.02	0.22	0.56	0.017	0.73
Std. dev.	3.09	68.8	0.38	1.87	0.05	0.64
CV	1.97	4.58	1.69	3.35	3.31	0.87

Table 8.3 Basic statistics – consumption patterns

	CONS	GDPPC$	ENERGY	TRADEV	URBAN
High					
Mean	13,801.29	18,477	7735.67	231.396	76.207
Std. dev.	4616.399	6349.3	5249.08	383.481	16.508
CV	0.33449	0.3436	0.67856	1.65725	0.2166
Medium					
Mean	3299.79	4120.5	1494.79	26.4361	51.92
Std. dev.	1645.595	2245.2	1385.27	55.2395	18.437
CV	0.498697	0.5449	0.92674	2.08955	0.3551
Low					
Mean	979.1671	1095	95	2.81571	28.989
Std. dev.	325.2334	392.37	128.742	4.45418	15.192
CV	0.332153	0.3583	1.35518	1.5819	0.5241

Per capita real consumption has been derived from real GDP in PPP $ and added back to the net value. The gross value so obtained has then been averaged using equal weights as is done with the original index. Countries in various developmental classes have then been ranked according to the new consumption-based HDI.

Results

The distributions over the first two components of environmental variables are given in Figures 8.1–8.3. While there may be some others that are outliers we have chosen the following six countries. Reasons for excluding these are indicated.

1   USA – outlier and large developed market economy.
2   Russia – vast country, an outlier and a non-market, declining economy.
3   China – outlier, vast, populous and non-market developing economy.
4   Finland – outlier (though) small and developed market economy.
5   Japan – small market economy, developed and populous, and an outlier.
6   India – large, populous, mixed developing economy, not a significant outlier.

The component scores were worked out after eliminating each of these countries, seriatim. The results are not reported for want of space. However, the broad conclusion is that the old to new scores remain within 10 per cent of each other in all cases except the US. In the case of the US the deviation is around 40 per cent on an average across all environmental variables. In fact the sign on certain variables changes and, in the case of certain individual variables, the change is nearly 100 per cent. Therefore, only US is an influential observation. In fact, it is overwhelmingly influential. While some other countries are outliers they are not

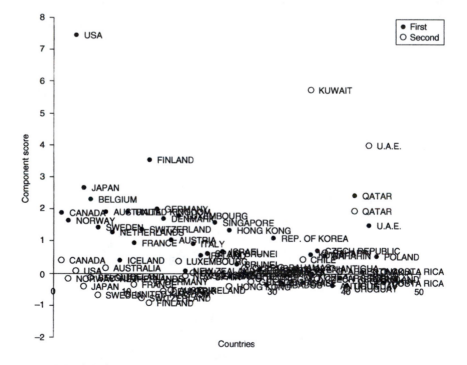

Figure 8.1 High-development environmental outliers.

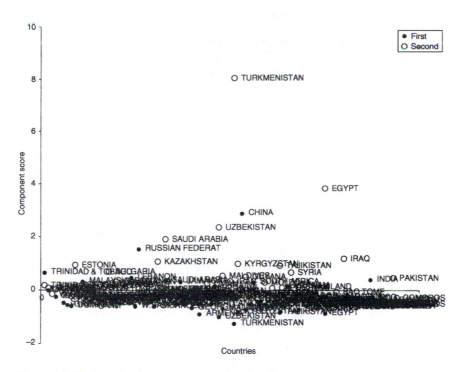

Figure 8.2 Medium-development environmental outliers.

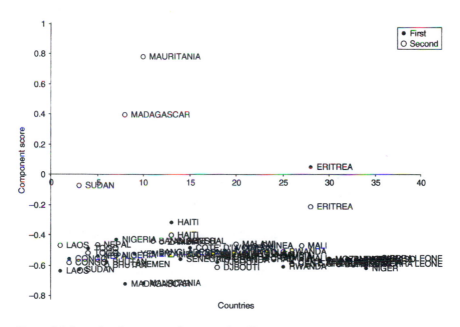

Figure 8.3 Low-development environmental outliers.

influential. Another significant result is that in both cases – environmental and consumption-related variable – the low developmental class has virtually no outlier. Their contribution to the environmental degradation is uniformly low. Finally, there is a striking similarity between the two lists of outliers. With some exceptions it can be said the outliers are the same (Figures 8.4–8.6). This provides a preliminary basis for believing that primarily it is consumption that is the 'cause' for environmental degradation.

In the discriminant analysis we used Box's *M*-test for testing for the equality of population co-variance matrices. These were found to be unequal. *F*-tests with levels of significance between 5 and 10 per cent were used to include or exclude variables. On this basis we retained variables 1, 3, 4 and 5 amongst environmental variables. The eigenvalues justified extraction of two linear discriminant functions. The prior probabilities were taken to be equal since there was no other information. These results hold good for both classifications.[6] Finally, both classifications proved that the basis of environmental degradation was not geophysical. In the case of environmental variables the classification was 70.1 per cent true (Table 8.6). In the case of classification by consumption-related variables it was beyond 81 per cent (Table 8.7). In the classification that emerges, as a result of the discriminant analysis, countries that have been classified together have little in common in geophysical terms. Hence, it can be concluded that human development, consumption and environmental degradation are all

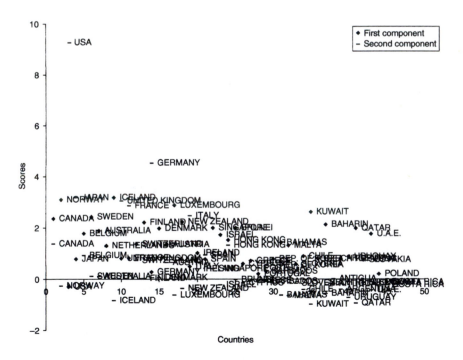

Figure 8.4 High-development countries – consumption outliers.

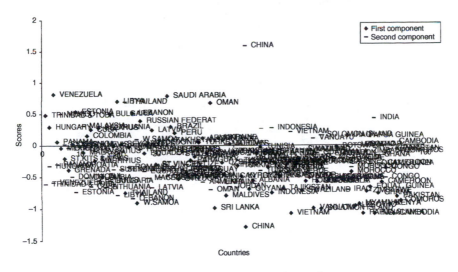

Figure 8.5 Medium-development countries – consumption outliers.

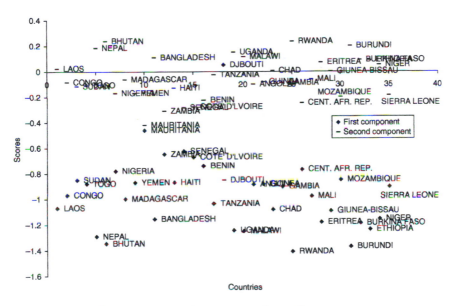

Figure 8.6 Low-development countries – consumption outliers.

positively related. The country groupings are the same for all the three. Thus, urbanised, open, high-income and high energy-use economies are clearly associated with a high degree of environmental degradation. Detailed results appear in Tables 8.4–8.8.

Table 8.4 Component score coefficient matrix of environmental variables

	Component			
	1	*2*	*3*	*4*
PCFWW	.301	.392	−.111	.459
CENTFW	.243	.532	.354	−.131
PAPCPM	.299	−.451	.066	−.319
PCCO2	.383	−.062	.264	−.506
CO2SHA	.237	−.362	.301	.791
DEFOR	−.270	.011	.905	.016

Note: Extraction method: principal component analysis.

Table 8.5 Classification function coefficients of environmental variables

	Class		
	1	*2*	*3*
PCFWW	.120	.164	5.292E-02
PAPCPM	8.845E-02	7.363E-03	5.964E-04
PCCO$_2$	.380	8.749E-02	1.792E-02
DEFOR	.181	.747	.575
(Constant)	−6.270	−2.104	−1.356

Note: Fisher's linear discriminant functions.

Table 8.6 Classification results of environmental variables

		Predicted group membership				Total
		Class	*1*	*2*	*3*	
Original	Count	1	34	10	1	45
		2	2	57	35	94
		3	0	4	31	35
	percentage	1	75.6	22.2	2.2	100.0
		2	2.1	60.6	37.2	100.0
		3	.0	11.4	88.6	100.0

Note: 70.1% of original grouped cases correctly classified.

If this premise is admitted we can address the question of the structure of causality. How does this causality work out? There are three stages to analyse this. First, an economy with high-energy use that is open to international trade and urbanised has the potential to generate high incomes (equation (8.4) and Table 8.9). All coefficients are significant and the $\bar{R}^2$ is 0.87.

Table 8.7 Classification results of developmental variables

		Predicted group membership				Total
		Class	1	2	3	
Original	Count	1	40	5	0	45
		2	0	69	25	94
		3	0	3	32	35
	percentage	1	88.9	11.1	.0	100.0
		2	.0	73.4	26.6	100.0
		3	.0	8.6	91.4	100.0

Note: 81.0% of original grouped cases correctly classified.

Table 8.8 Classification function coefficients of developmental variables

	Class		
	1	2	3
CONS	1.438E-03	3.540E-04	1.048E-04
GDPPC	6.447E-04	−9.956E-05	−1.352E-04
TRADEV	−7.931E-03	−1.906E-03	−3.554E-04
URBAN	.160	.169	.103
(Constant)	−22.148	−5.841	−2.570

Note: Fisher's linear discriminant functions.

Income generation function

$$GDPPC = 9569 + 0.57 * ENERGY$$
$$+ 5.37 * TRADEV + 42.24 * URBAN + U_1 \qquad (8.4)$$

(Intercept for medium HDI class: 926 and low HDI class: (−) 199)

All equations have been tested for functional form. Also slope and intercept dummies have been tried out in equations (8.4) and (8.5). Only the first equation shows significant intercept dummies. Low-development countries have a negative intercept indicating that their income generating potential is low in absolute terms. Second, we also estimated a global consumption function:

Global consumption function

$$Consumption = 315.52^{a} + 0.725 * GDPPC + U_2 \qquad (8.5)$$

(*a* not significant)

Table 8.9 Predicted GDP per capita PPP $

Regression statistics

Multiple R	0.9353
R^2	0.874786
Adjusted R^2	0.87106
Standard error	2752.602
Observations	174

ANOVA

	df	SS	MS	F	Significance F
Regression	5	8.89E+09	1.78E+09	234.7414	7.75E-74
Residual	168	1.27E+09	7576816		
Total	173	1.02E+10			

	Coefficients	Standard error	t Stat	P-value	Lower 95%	Upper 95%
Intercept	9569.035	1065.806	8.978215	5.38E-16	7464.936	11673.13
ENERGY	0.574461	0.07791	7.373341	7.23E-12	0.420651	0.72827
TRADEV	5.377281	1.070506	5.023122	1.29E-06	3.263904	7.490658
URBAN	42.24545	12.73208	3.318031	0.001111	17.10995	67.38094
DMHDI	−8642.79	714.0057	−12.1046	1.19E-24	−10052.4	−7233.21
DLHDI	−9768.41	950.6086	−10.276	1.59E-19	−11645.1	−7891.74

Table 8.10 Global consumption function

Regression statistics

Multiple R	0.92
R^2	0.85
Adjusted R^2	0.85
Standard error	2153.68
Observations	174

ANOVA

	df	SS	MS	F
Regression	1	4666307113	4666307113	1006.027886
Residual	172	797795801.2	4638347.681	Significance F
Total	173	5464102914		8.98378E-74

	Coefficients	Standard error	t Stat	P-value
Intercept	315.53	232.12	1.36	0.17
PreGDPC	0.72	0.02	31.72	8.98E-74

The estimated equation reveals that high income leads to high consumption (see Table 8.10) (GDPPC is significant and the $\overline{R}^2$ is 0.853). The estimated global consumption function reveals that (i) it is in accordance with the long-term consumption function and does not have an intercept, and (ii) it is possible that even low-income countries have imbibed the consumption patterns of rich countries. This could be on account of openness, globalisation and modernisation. All these reflect a certain 'type of development'.

Finally, predicted consumption enters in the form of a new consumption-based HDI and affects environmental degradation. It is captured in the last equation (see Table 8.11). (All coefficients are significant and $\overline{R}^2$ is 0.77.) This is the consumption-based GEKC now written explicitly as equation (8.6).

Consumption-based GEKC

$$EDI = 73.21 - 2.15 * (HDIR) + 0.02 * (HDIR)^2 - 6.05 * (HDIR)^3 \quad (8.6)$$

The cubic equation shows that high-development countries dominate the GEKC. The low and medium countries hardly contribute to environmental degradation. The GEKC certainly does not have an inverted-U shape. Most importantly, the structure of causality is clear. A certain type of development leads to high incomes and consequent high consumption. This results in environmental degradation. The cause of entropy is high consumption. Unsustainable levels of consumption have been reached amongst high-development countries. The GEKC is plotted in Figure 8.7.

A cubic representation for the GEKC appears to be the most appropriate with high-consumption countries contributing excessively to GED and middle-consumption countries slightly less. Low-consumption countries are contributing

Table 8.11 Consumption-based GEKC

Regression statistics

Multiple R	0.878615244
R^2	0.771964746
Adjusted R^2	0.767940595
Standard error	9.733421524
Observations	174

ANOVA

	Df	SS	MS	F
Regression	3	54522.46217	18174.15406	191.8329218
Residual	170	16105.71408	94.73949457	Significance F
Total	173	70628.17625		2.4762E-54

	Coefficients	Standard error	t Stat	P-value
Intercept	73.20980166	3.016326333	24.27118076	4.01446E-57
HDIR_C	−2.154849616	0.148842285	−14.47740218	1.81519E-31
HDIR_C2	0.020315142	0.001973325	10.29487898	1.26734E-19
HDIR_C3	−6.05419E-05	7.41349E-06	−8.166457921	6.88054E-14

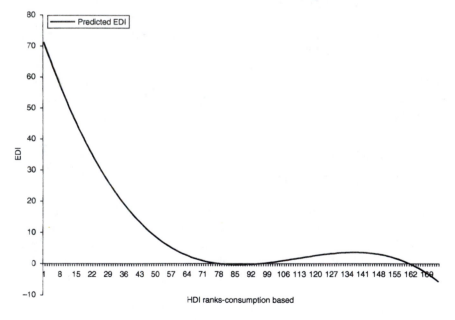

Figure 8.7 Global consumption-based GEKC.

Table 8.12 High-development countries – consumption-based HDI ranks

Country	EVN1345	HDIR_C	EDIR	DIFFR
Finland	129.11	8	1	−7
USA	88.28	1	2	1
Belgium	87.46	12	3	−9
Hong Kong	67.17	21	4	−17
Japan	65.19	7	5	−2
Denmark	64.12	18	6	−12
Sweden	62.24	4	7	3
Switzerland	59.59	17	8	−9
United Kingdom	59.06	9	9	0
Canada	57.57	2	10	8
Luxembourg	55.09	14	11	−3
Norway	55.04	3	12	9
Australia	53.97	11	13	2
Germany	50.01	6	14	8
Netherlands	48.74	13	15	2
Austria	46.47	20	16	−4
Singapore	42.99	22	17	−5
France	39.58	10	18	8
Rep. of Korea	34.29	25	19	−6
Italy	33.47	16	20	4
Ireland	32.64	24	21	−3
Israel	30.43	23	22	−1
Spain	28.87	19	23	4
Iceland	24.31	5	24	19
UAE	23.44	43	25	−18
Czech Republic	22.85	29	26	−3
Qatar	21.18	40	27	−13
Portugal	20.58	41	28	−13
Malta	20.07	28	29	1
Slovenia	17.52	32	30	−2
Estonia	17.44	47	31	−16
Kuwait	17.30	26	32	6
Greece	15.46	27	33	6
Malaysia	15.03	77	34	−43
Poland	14.14	39	35	−4
Hungary	14.06	51	36	−15
Cyprus	13.69	31	37	6
New Zealand	13.40	15	38	23
Baharin	13.29	30	39	9
South Africa	11.93	109	40	−69
China	10.86	92	41	−51
Trinidad and Toba	10.53	49	42	−7
Slovakia	10.40	34	43	9
Thailand	9.68	95	44	−51
Argentina	9.40	38	45	7
	Mean difference in EDI and HDI ranks			−5.83
	Correlation between EDI and HDI ranks			0.71

Table 8.13 Medium-development countries – consumption-based HDI ranks

Country	EVN 1345	HDIR_C	EDIR	DIFFR	Country	EVN 1345	HDIR_C	EDIR	DIFFR
Russian Federat	9.23	50	46	-4	Guatemala	1.99	123	94	-29
Croatia	8.56	56	47	-9	Equador	1.89	81	95	14
Chile	8.44	37	48	11	Paraguay	1.84	86	96	10
Lebanon	8.33	75	49	-26	Gabon	1.43	135	97	-38
Brazil	7.76	87	50	-37	Honduras	1.43	113	98	-15
Venezuela	7.71	55	51	-4	Egypt	1.42	120	99	-21
Barbados	7.38	35	52	17	Azerbaijan	1.41	67	100	33
Saudi Arabia	7.33	89	53	-36	Sri Lanka	1.40	91	101	10
Brunei	6.85	42	54	12	Mongolia	1.40	107	102	-5
Turkey	6.84	97	55	-42	Morocco	1.27	126	103	-23
Uruguay	6.37	36	56	20	Bolivia	1.27	112	104	-8
Mexico	6.31	60	57	-3	Belize	1.26	93	105	12
Mauritius	5.75	98	58	-40	Cuba	1.25	48	106	58
Jamaica	5.27	71	59	-12	Moldova	1.22	78	107	29
Panama	4.82	63	60	-3	Maldives	1.20	100	108	8
Colombia	4.81	72	61	-11	W. Samoa	0.96	84	109	25
Vietnam	4.69	104	62	-42	Syria	0.94	111	110	-1
Indonesia	4.62	110	63	-47	Zambia	0.92	149	111	-38
Jordan	4.60	90	64	-26	Kenya	0.82	134	112	-22
Macedonia	4.45	59	65	6	Congo	0.77	130	113	-17
Bahamas	4.42	33	66	33	Cote' D'Ivoire	0.76	158	114	-44
Eritrea	4.36	168	67	-101	Zimbabwe	0.66	131	115	-16
Fiji	4.25	69	68	-1	Lesotho	0.64	125	116	-9
Romania	4.22	65	69	4	Bangladesh	0.62	150	117	-33

Country				
Latvia	3.93	64	70	6
St. Lucia	3.86	99	71	−28
Lithuania	3.83	52	72	20
Tunisia	3.61	108	73	−35
Bulgaria	3.51	46	74	28
El Salvador	3.50	106	75	−31
Ukraine	3.39	53	76	23
Iran	3.26	103	77	−26
Costa Rica	3.07	44	78	34
India	3.04	127	79	−48
Antigua	2.95	45	80	35
Dominican Repub	2.85	96	81	−15
Algeria	2.84	114	82	−32
Phillippines	2.63	73	83	10
Kazakhstan	2.56	62	84	22
St. Kits and Nevis	2.50	79	85	6
Oman	2.49	101	86	−15
Peru	2.41	80	87	7
Libya	2.37	70	88	18
Belarus	2.34	57	89	32
Albania	2.33	88	90	2
IRAQ	2.18	124	91	−33
Seychelles	2.17	94	92	−2
Suriname	2.01	68	93	25

Country				
Grenada	0.62	66	118	52
Dominica	0.55	54	119	65
Nigeria	0.54	142	120	−22
Yemen	0.53	143	121	−22
Botswana	0.48	133	122	−11
Cameroon	0.34	136	123	−13
Papua Guinea	0.31	132	124	−8
Tanzania	0.26	147	125	−22
Djibouti	0.23	153	126	−27
Haiti	0.22	154	127	−27
Ghana	0.20	129	128	−1
Myamnar	0.20	119	129	10
St. Vincent	0.19	82	130	48
Sierra Leone	0.16	172	131	−41
Solomon Island	0.16	118	132	14
Angola	0.16	163	133	−30
Togo	0.15	148	134	−14
Equat. Guinea	0.14	128	135	7
Gambia	0.10	164	136	−28
Senegal	0.09	157	137	−20
Vanuatu	0.08	121	138	17
Cent. Afr. Rep.	0.06	165	139	−26
Mean difference in EDI and HDI ranks				−4.2
Correlation between EDI and HDI ranks				0.68

Table 8.14 Low-development countries – consumption-based HDI ranks

Country	EVN1345	HDIR_C	EDIR	DIFFR
Benin	0.01	155	140	−15
Bhutan	0.12	151	141	−10
Guinea-Bissau	0.54	169	142	−27
Namibia	0.53	122	143	21
Uganda	1.11	162	144	−18
Burundi	0.40	170	145	−25
Niger	0.03	173	146	−27
Nicaragua	0.26	115	147	32
Ethiopia	0.15	171	148	−23
Malawi	0.92	156	149	−7
Burkina Faso	0.62	174	150	−24
Mozambique	0.06	167	151	−16
Cambodia	0.15	137	152	15
Congo	0.23	140	153	13
Rwanda	0.22	159	154	−5
Chad	0.06	160	155	−5
Nepal	0.01	146	156	10
Guinea	0.09	166	157	−9
Comoros	0.76	139	158	19
Mali	0.02	161	159	−2
Laos	0.03	141	160	19
Mauritania	0.08	152	161	9
Guyana	0.03	102	162	60
Georgia	0.16	58	163	105
Sao Tome	0.10	116	164	48
Pakistan	0.06	138	165	27
Sudan	0.03	145	166	21
Armenia	0.00	61	167	106
Cape Verde	4.36	105	168	63
Swaziland	0.06	117	169	52
Madagascar	0.03	144	170	26
Kyrgyzstan	0.009	83	171	88
Uzbekistan	0.16	76	172	96
Tajikistan	0.03	85	173	88
Turkmenistan	0.006	74	174	100
	Mean difference in EDI and HDI ranks			23
	Correlation between EDI and HDI ranks			−0.68

insignificantly, or even negatively, to GED. This is broadly in agreement with the results on the income-based GEKC reported in Chapter 6.

Our final formal analysis consists of comparing consumption-based HDI ranks with EDI ranks. If a country has a larger HDI number it indicates a lower rank and, hence, lower potential for degradation. If it has a larger EDI number it has lower potential for degradation. Therefore, a low EDI rank coupled with high HDI rank is desirable. This implies that negative correlation is desirable between HDIR and EDIR. The formula difference in ranks for comparison is

(EDIR − HDIR). It would be desirable to have this difference as positive. Observing results for this across the development classes is quite revealing. The high-development class has an average (defined as (Σ(EDIR − HDIR)/number of countries) of around (−) 5.8). The Spearman's rank correlation between EDIR and HDIR is 0.713 and, hence, high. Medium-class countries have an average of (−) 4.2 and a rank correlation coefficient of 0.68, which is only slightly lower. The low-development class has an average of (+) 23 and a rank correlation coefficient of (−) 0.68. Thus, their performance is the best! Detailed results are reported in Tables 8.12–8.14.

Conclusions

The two main contributions of this chapter are building a consumption-based HDI and estimating a GEKC based on consumption. The consumption-based HDI only further confirms the fact that rich countries are responsible for GED. A simultaneous equations model explains the causal structure that is responsible for GED. Further, with canonical discriminant analysis it has been shown that GED does not have a geophysical basis but an anthropogenic basis. As part of the system of equations a global consumption function has been estimated, which shows the alarming fact that poor countries have already imbibed the consumption patterns of rich countries. In net, this chapter shows that a certain 'type of development' that characterises high-income countries is primarily responsible for GED.

9 Political economy of global environmental governance

Introduction

The analysis in this book has emphasised the role of consumption in GED. It has emphasised that a broad-based consumption switch, difficult as it may be to put into practice, may play a significant role in reducing GED. An important question at this juncture is the design of an institutional mechanism that may help ameliorate global environmental problems. This chapter is addressed to this issue. Our emphasis, throughout, is on the stake that developing countries have in the redressal of GED and the underpinnings of global policy that would help in this effort.

Our argument in this book has been that fundamental to the containment of GED in order to ensure sustainable growth is the need to internalise the global externalities associated with GED. This would be the case even if we confine ourselves to global environmental problems. It is clear, to begin with, that global environmental problems in the final analysis arise out of local phenomena. Hence, local environmental externalities (and their internalisation) cannot be ignored, even if the concern were about the global environment. A strategy to attain a globally sustainable environment must address the local environmental problems of developing countries.

A common perspective of developing countries in regard to environmental problems could emerge on account of common socio-economic characteristics more immediately than common environmental concerns. This may be because of three factors: (i) their geo-climatic conditions vary considerably; (ii) each country may face specific environmental problems; and (iii) such countries in any case need to be persuaded to follow the global environmental agenda rather than the their narrowly defined specific environmental agendas. A common perspective amongst some developing countries could emerge on account of their common economic characteristics, for example, capital deficiency, paucity of information and technology, primary exports, adverse balance of payments and overpopulation.

The main global environmental problems have been identified as deforestation, land degradation, pollution of the atmosphere, and marine and fresh water bodies, depletion of the ozone layer and climatic warming induced by GHGs. Global warming, in particular, is seen to be the most important reason for environmental degradation. The effects of climatic warming are storm and flood frequencies, imbalances in plant and animal distributions and disequilibrium in glacier and ice-sheet dynamics and changes in sea levels.

Given that decisions about global environmental problems will have to be made by nation-states voluntary internalisation rather than command and control will have to be the primary means of addressing these environmental issues. The current global institutional structure seems incapable of addressing this problem. In this chapter we first address the barriers to such internalisation. The third section discusses the lack of internalisation of GED as an institutional failure whereas the fourch section advances the institution of a World Environmental Organization (WEO) as a mechanism to dealing with this institutional failure. The outline of some institutional mechanisms to underpin the WEO is discussed in section titled 'Institutional mechanisms to underpin the WEO'. The section 'Other roles of the WEO' considers some non-global roles that the WEO could pursue. The last section is 'Conclusion'.

Barriers to internalisation: locally and globally

The discussion in this book has emphasised that incomplete internalisation – at the local, trans-boundary and international levels – is perhaps the single most important contributor to environmental problems. In view of the high costs associated with the lack of such internalisation it is pertinent to inquire into the reasons why such internalisation is not forthcoming.

A complex set of reasons is behind the lack of progress towards internal internalisation in the developing countries of the region. These include weak and ill-defined property rights over resources, inefficient enforcement (Prasad 2004), large transactions costs, poor technology of surveillance and poor governance. Further, the experience of the developing countries in this regard is quite different from those of developed countries. Developing countries have often been thought of as following the development experience of the developed countries with a compressed lag. OECD countries have grown over some 200 years and transformed from primary agricultural to primarily high-technology service providers. Developing countries are following this experience at varying speeds and in different ways, but the transition time is clearly shorter. Korea, for instance, may have transformed itself from a country with lower-income per capita than India in the mid-1950s to a lower-income OECD country in 40 years. However, whereas the OECD countries during their years of rapid industrialisation could follow a policy of 'grow now and clean up later', the developing countries of today are under considerable strain to clean up. These pressures come from donor governments, international organisations and developed country NGOs, and sometimes carry the threat of punitive action. At the height of OECD country industrial revolutions, effectively no environmental controls were in place.

Thus, developing countries are subject to the twin pressures of having to raise PCIs rapidly and yet clean up during the process. What should be their response?

Following developed country experience would seem to indicate adopting few environmental controls, and that with income growth environmental quality will improve. Indeed, a great fear is that attempts to heighten environmental regulation will only serve to slow growth, and hence slow eventual achievement of higher environmental quality through growth. On the other hand, given problems of compliance one can argue that perhaps developing countries have no choice but to follow the older developed country industrial revolution experience of largely benign neglect.

Furthermore, the developing countries of today continue to be hit with shocks the likes of which the current developed countries did not experience during the peak of their industrialisation. The time periods involved are compacted, and hence the flow of environmental damage per year during industrialisation is larger. The current developed countries simply did not experience population growth rates of 3 per cent per year plus massive growth in urban vehicle densities, or other elements contributing to today's environmental ills in the developing world. Not only is the process more compact, the severity of damage time adjusted probably exceeds that experienced in the OECD 100 years ago. Further, many of the developed countries of today had access to a steady stream of foreign savings from their colonies, which the current developing countries (many of them former colonies) do not have. Further, even though abatement technologies exist access to them is limited because of cost and governance considerations.

As a consequence, the process of internalisation of (domestic) environmental external effects has gone much further in developed OECD economies. For instance, in the OECD countries we observe a strong decoupling of emissions of local air pollutants from economic growth. OECD countries have also achieved a strong decoupling between energy use and economic growth over the past 20 years, with the economy growing by 17 per cent between 1980 and 1998 and energy use falling by about the same percentage. Water and resource use continued to grow but at a rate slower than GDP growth, reflecting a weak decoupling of the two. Thus, decoupling of emissions in OECD countries and generally the developed countries has been accomplished through a combination of technological change and a strong environmental policy. The latter consists of 'greening' of fiscal policy, removing subsidies to environmentally harmful activities and the use of economic instruments to internalise environmental cost. For example, a number of EU policy initiatives – the Broad Economic Policy Guidelines 2001, among others – have promoted a gradual but steady and credible change in the level and structure of the tax rates until external costs are fully reflected in prices. Such initiatives are attempting to cope with most of the fundamental structural problem in all developed countries: the unsustainable patterns of production and consumption. In the energy markets these guidelines aim to uses taxes and other market-based instruments to rebalance prices in favour of reusable energy sources and technologies. Other EU initiatives in this direction are the European Climate Change Programme (ECCP), the directive establishing an EU framework for emissions trading, and the Integrated Product Policy (IPP) – all of which aim at realigning price relations and stimulating investments in new technologies that promote sustainable development. Member States are encouraged to improve market functioning by addressing market failures such as externalities through 'increased use of market-based systems in pursuit of environmental objectives as they provide flexibility to industry to reduce pollution in a cost-effective way, as well as encourage technological innovations' (UNEP 2003, p. 326). The tax instruments are promoted as the most efficient means of decoupling economic growth from pollution, as they alter price relations and thereby also drive changes in technology and consumer behaviour (preference) that lie behind the growth–environmental relationship. As exemplified by the energy and transport sectors, the EU decoupling policy consists of demand management through full cost pricing and development of more environmentally friendly alternatives by promoting technological innovations. The United Nations Economic Commission for Europe has repeatedly called upon its members to raise the prices of various energy sources to their full economic costs and adapt economic instruments to internalise the costs to human health and the environment associated with energy production and consumption. The aim is to decouple emissions from energy use and energy use from economic growth.

Commensurate progress in these areas in the case of developing or transition countries has been lacking, although some progress has been achieved. Thus, since 1990 all economies in transition have made efforts to restructure their energy and transport sectors along market principles and to raise energy prices closer to economic and international levels. However, because of the political sensitivity of energy pricing and the lagging reforms in many transition economies, a gap of 20–85 per cent continues to persist between energy prices in economies in transition. For example, electricity prices for households in Eastern Europe are only 50 per cent of those of the EU; for industrial consumers, electricity prices are closer to their economic and international levels, being 20 per cent lower than those of the EU. Subsidies on electricity for agriculture continue to be extremely high in India (Jha and Thapa 2003) and many other countries.

Although gains from internalisation (at the international level) are jointly shared and are substantial, why are custodians of assets not able to agree to manage and conserve assets in return for payment by those who benefit from such practices? From the viewpoint of the developing countries, given the large cost estimates for their environmental problems, it is likely that these countries may want to pursue a much more activist environmental policy. However, given the greater cost of local degradation issues, such efforts will have a dominant focus on local degradation over pollution – particularly international pollution. International external effects are more likely to be emphasised in any international environmental co-operation and not in domestic policy. To make such co-operation more attractive to the developing countries of the region, concessions would have to be made to enable them to address their domestic environmental concerns – in particular, environmental degradation. In fact, an enlightened international environmental policy would link the issue of support for domestic internalisation policies in developing countries to co-operation in international environmental agreements such as those on GHGs.

Several other factors contribute to the observed lack of internalisation at the international level. First, it is difficult to put together negotiations between groups with an interest in the management practices used for environmental resources. For instance, governments may agree to conserve forests but may find it difficult to pursue this if most encroachments into forests are made by the poor. Similarly, in OECD countries there may be a willingness to pay for environmental protection in poorer countries, but any attempt to estimate this (by survey methods, for instance) will be subject to free riding. The benefits from environmental protection abroad are a public good which is hard to finance through voluntary action. A related problem is that individual countries can free ride on the environmental quality improvement by other countries. Hence some countries may hold back from multilateral negotiation in which they need to pay a price to achieve environmental quality improvements that others will benefit from. This has been emphasised by Barrett (1994). Environmental enforcement also has an important time-inconsistency dimension. OECD countries may strike deals with countries to meet environmental targets such as forest cover or species populations over a number of years. But if payment for these concessions takes place immediately, more money could potentially be repeatedly requested for environmental compliance. On the other hand, if payment is postponed until the end of the agreement, countries that conserve environmental assets have no assurance of getting paid.

Lack of internalisation as an institutional failure

This lack of internalisation denotes an institutional failure. In fact the international institutional architecture reflected in the present global environmental regime, and some 35 years in evolution, does not take as its starting point the design of mechanisms that seek to achieve internalisation of environmental externalities across countries. No agency attempting to achieve Coase's internalising deals across countries recognises the many problems in deal-making to improve environmental quality. The modern economics literature shows why private negotiation cannot easily complete the deals needed for international environmental internalisation, why intermediary agencies are needed, why scientific standard-driven arrangements produce only low-level environmental outcomes – in short, why a new global or at least regional agency for the environment is needed.

Progress in these areas has been scanty and faltering. International environmental negotiations in the region are still in their infancy. In fact the present global economic institutions still reflect their 1940s origins and focus primarily on trade and finance as the dominant economic linkages between countries, rather than physical linkages.

The central global environmental problem is the relative lack of internalisation of cross-border and global externalities. We need an institutional form that seeks to achieve internalisation internationally, and one that does this by facilitating Coasian deals based on the perceived interests of the participants. At least since Coase (1960) it is known that bargaining between the parties to an externality would serve to achieve internalisation – no Pigou-type tax was needed.

Coase argued that the issue of who should pay the additional costs of internalisation was a matter of property rights – who has the rights to what? Bargaining between the parties to an externality would serve to internalise it, with payments of compensation for damage to those having the legal rights to pursue redress and payment to induce reduction of damage by those parties having no such rights. Economic analysis is silent on the issue of who should have such rights. Also in the presence of an externality, bargaining (or Coasian deals) may already have been entered into and imposition of taxes or other measures could actually worsen the allocation of resources. Coase's discussion was largely centred upon narrowly defined externalities. In the case of global externalities the number of people affected is in the millions and the transaction costs of such bargaining (which Coase approximated to zero) are likely to be large. In fact we have seen some of the reasons why such bargaining may be hard to put in place. However, there is need for an international mechanism to facilitate such bargaining on this large scale. Other ancillary functions that need to be addressed are allowing for verification of completion of contracts and acting as a financial guarantor. While the WTO is cast within a bargaining framework, it is restricted since no cash is involved and the rules of the WTO Charter (via GATT 1994) constrain bargaining (such as the MFN rule).

The prospects of internalisation – the WEO

The growing consciousness about global environmental problems around the world has led to a patchwork quilt of over 200 multilateral environmental agreements (MEAs) between various groups of nations. These agreements range from non-binding ones to ones with binding commitments on instruments and emission levels, from regional to global agreements and from property rights type agreements to joint emission reduction. Most reflect a LCD outcome of a narrow area negotiation without side payments for those adversely affected. Most treaties reflect environmental concerns of developed, rather than developing countries; there are few if any inter-developing country treaties. Some have provision for positive and negative sanctions. The problem areas covered are quite diverse and include global and transnational pollutants, process and product standards and biodiversity. The sovereign states remain units of signing or negotiations, although often environmental concerns transcend nation-states boundaries, or also often apply to undefined jurisdictions (such as international waters or airspace).

It is striking to note that many of the MEA have features that directly or indirectly contradict existing international agreements on trade and capital flows. The WTO itself admits this in a document prepared for the High Level Symposium on Trade and the Environment (WTO 1999, p. 7) wherein it states that 'Lack of coordination (between trade and environmental agreements) has, in the past, contributed to the negotiation of conflicting agreements in trade and environment fora.' However, the document argues that MEA remain the best vehicle for resolving trans-boundary and global environmental problems. Two points need to be mentioned here. First, the existing patchwork quilt of MEA does not exploit cross-MEA interdependencies. Furthermore, the existing MEA do not reflect *bargaining opportunities*, wherein some side payments to some parties could have been used in exchange for enhanced bargaining opportunities and greater compliance. The failure to include such opportunities can be attributed to a generalised 'prisoners' dilemma' phenomenon, since who pays and who benefits might not fully coincide. Another notable feature of many environmental agreements is the almost universal lack of *issue linkages* such as linking trade sanctions and environmental sanctions[1] or linking trade and environmental concessions. It is clear that there is a role for an international institution that would address these shortcomings.[2]

The economic interdependence of nations and global nature of trade and capital flows gave rise to institutions such as IMF, World Bank and later the WTO, whose design addressed some of the interdependencies and coordination tasks involved in rationalising trade and capital flows. However, since these institutions evolved in an era when environmental interdependencies were not seen as important, there were hardly any provisions to handle global environmental concerns. Recent rounds of negotiations of the GATT put in provisions, which permitted actions of nations to depart from free trade principles on the basis of environmental and other concerns.[3] However, there is some disquiet about this, particularly among developing countries, who view the imposition of such requirements as another way of imposing non-tariff barriers on their exports and are wary of international institutions dictating policy to sovereign states.

An awareness of 'environmental interdependence' among nations is relatively recent, and, therefore, addressing this interdependence may call for new institutional design. This is what we call the WEO. Various forms of the WEO proposals ranging from merely a meeting place and a clearing house to a strong body which formulates and enforces rules and policies, have been explored by Whalley and Zissimos (2002a). These range from WEO-1 (the weakest version with the WEO acting as mere facilitator) to WEO-3 (the most interventionist).[4]

We argue in this book that central to any strategy to meaningfully lower GED must be efforts to internalise external effects resulting from global environmental interdependence. An institutional response to facilitating such internalisation could centre around a WEO. The concept of a WEO has found mention and has been discussed in various forums, for example, the WTO Director-General Renalto Ruggiero expressed his support for such a mechanism in March 1999.[5] The formation of a WEO is itself speculation as of now. An immediate concern of this chapter is an assessment of how developing countries will react to such a proposal and what will it take to get them involved in this process.

The stance of developing countries towards a WEO will necessarily be affected by the perceived needs, costs and benefits of forming and joining such an organisation. Much will also depend on the how the agenda for the formation of WEO is framed. Therefore, in any analysis of the prospects for a WEO it would not be proper to presume a 'uniform' or non-differentiated developing country view on environmental problems and their management and global environmental concerns. For example, developing countries might perceive that the WEO might be construed to pursue a 'northern agenda' and, hence, might resist its formation. But, at the same time, developing countries, by virtue of their immense diversity, have varying environmental assets and priorities. Could knowledge of these be coalesced into the formation of a response that might be termed the 'southern agenda'?

A differentiated developing country view

In a special issue of *The World Economy* in 2002, a number of authors spelt out the contours of the possible form of a WEO. Jha *et al.* conduct such an analysis for the case of Asian developing countries (ADCs). Some of their conclusions apply more generally to developing countries. One of the principal conclusions of that analysis is that if the WEO is to carry credibility and hence be able to garner support within developing countries, it must be seen to be addressing some local environmental problems that are of more immediate concerns to the developing countries concerned (e.g. soil degradation) than those that are global in nature (say CO_2 emissions).

Degradation of their environments has led to a reduction in the economic potential of many developing countries. This has supplemented concern about degradation of the environment. Taking the ADC as an example, the most pressing environmental concerns are the consequences of economic growth, of urbanisation and the pressure of population growth. The issues of soil degradation, deforestation and inadequate arrangement for potable water are common to all countries. Other issues such as air and water pollution are environmental problems in urban areas. Desertification is of prime concern in some parts of the region (see Table 9.1). Developing country priorities are clearly in favour of economic development and alleviation of mass poverty over environment. Such a priority has obviously been more pressing at the end of the twentieth century when it is well recognised that the problem of poverty could indeed be solved within a few decades with rapid economic growth accompanied by some redistributive measures. As elsewhere in the world, growth could further degrade the environment. The costs of air and water pollution could be large in the absence of adoption of clean (and costly) technology. In the absence of easy availability of technologies that would mitigate the harmful environmental impact of current economic growth, this leads to a dilemma in preferences for developing countries: environmental preservation vs. economic development and poverty alleviation.

Apart from having different environmental priorities from developed countries, developing countries also face a second-stage trade-off. How would they spend the limited resources available on the environment? Would they expend these funds on their local environmental problems or keep them for global problems? The general perception at present in developing countries is to view several local environmental problems as more urgent than the ones causing global damages. This appears to be a natural process to them for even the developed world turned attention to global problems after solving their local problems. A survey conducted by Asian Development Bank and Harvard Institute of International Development (ADB 1997) reports that among environmental issues ranked in order of importance by Asian environmental policy-makers, air and water pollution, fresh water depletion, solid waste and soil erosion ranked much higher than global issues of climate change and biodiversity loss (Table 9.2). This shows that pressing concerns are indeed local rather than global.[6]

Notwithstanding this the effect on developing countries of international environmental problems such as CO_2 emission, deforestation and biodiversity loss is likely to be high and increase over time. But these global bads are not currently high on their list of priorities. Rapid economic growth and the environmental problems that have been associated with it seem more important. There is also the perception

Table 9.1 Key environmental issues confronting the Asia-Pacific

Land	• Land degradation • Desertification • Land use change
Forests	• Forest degradation • Deforestation
Biodiversity	• Habitat loss • Forest loss and degradation • Alien species
Fresh water	• Water scarcity • Pollution
Coastal and marine	• Degradation of coastal and marine resources • Pollution due to mining and coastal development
Atmosphere	• Air quality • Ozone depletion • GHG emissions and climate change
Urban areas	• Air pollution • Waste management • Water supply and sanitation
Disasters	• Floods • Droughts • Volcanoes • Earthquakes

Source: UNEP, *Global Environmental Outlook*, 2003, London and Sterling, VA, USA.

Table 9.2 Ranking of environmental priorities of ADCs

1	Water pollution and fresh water depletion	2	Air pollution
3	Deforestation	4	Solid waste
5	Soil erosion	6	Biodiversity loss
7	Wildlife loss	8	Fish depletion
9	Desertification	10	Climate change

Source: ADB (1997).

that since the OECD countries have turned their attention to global environmental problems only after attaining high levels of consumption per capita and solved most of their domestic environmental problems and, are in any case, primarily responsible for global environmental problems. However, this view may not persist for long. It is becoming increasingly clear that 'global environmental problems' are assuming difficult proportions in developing countries as well. CO_2 emissions continue to grow at ever increasing rates in developing countries. Deforestation is contributing to soil erosion and, therefore, to a difficult future food situation. The loss of biodiversity will lead to a loss of employment opportunities and so on.

It appears, therefore, that notwithstanding first appearances there exists a window of opportunity to get the developing countries interested in a proposal for a WEO, especially if it addresses domestic concerns as well. It also appear to be the case that this would be best possible through a mix of making some proposals of the WEO relevant to the interests of developing countries and giving them economic incentives to join in. These might include for example, mechanisms to underpin and reinforce domestic environmental policies and management. We comment on these possibilities in the next section.

Developing country response to the WEO

We now discuss several factors that we think will determine the developing country stance towards the WEO. These factors would be related to the form of the WEO. A weak version of the WEO that merely acts as a clearing house for deals on (say) cash transfers from rich countries to developing countries in exchange for the latter promising and delivering increased protection to their forests and biodiversity and other assets would be agreements between two willing partners and the WEO would do no more than facilitating them. Clearly, such an arrangement would not be objected to by the developing countries.[7] Given the scale of global environmental problems, and the fact that developing countries need strong incentives for exercising restraint in the environmental area, it probably would be the case that these types of environmental deals, by themselves, would not be able to make much of a dent on global environmental problems. In particular, issue linkage and the internalising of externalities from one such deal to another may not be optimally achieved within such an arrangement.[8] A stronger version of the WEO would, on the other hand, be more effective in addressing pressing global environmental problems. In this context, we argue that there are several reasons (discussed below) why developing country enthusiasm for a stronger version of the WEO might be less. It would then be apparent that if the proposal for such a version of the WEO is to succeed it must address these concerns. The possible contours of the design of a WEO that might satisfactorily address these concerns are then discussed.

Any proposal for a version of the WEO that goes beyond being merely a clearing house for deals between willing parties, would have to address the following reasons for lack of adequate support from developing countries. Only when these are satisfactorily addressed can one hope to make sufficient progress in this direction.

Most environmental problems of developing countries would fall in the category of local, or at best, bilateral problems. These include urban congestion and air pollution from industrial effluents and vehicle emissions; soil erosion; overgrasing; desertification; water pollution from raw sewage and runoff of agricultural pesticides since tap water is not potable in many countries; huge and rapidly growing population overstraining natural resources. Even in the relatively affluent east Asian economies, urban congestion[9] and air pollution remain as pressing concerns. Thus, global concerns such as CO_2, deforestation, ozone and biodiversity do not seem to have manifested themselves as much in these countries. Thus their enthusiasm about a WEO purely focused on global issues, seen as a primarily OECD concern is expected to be muted. If, however, some of the local concerns are also bundled in the WEO agenda, this agenda is likely to garner some support within the developing world.

In dealing with a developing country response the WEO would also have to address the fact that developing countries span climatically tropical to temperate zones and a large range of income and resource conditions. Thus, it would be incorrect to attribute an undifferentiated and homogenous developing country view on the WEO. In the organisation of a WEO, room would have to be found to accommodate different points of view and the notion of a WEO would have to be found relevant by countries with very different environmental problems and conflicting interests (e.g. in international trade) in the global arena.

In operational terms this means that the WEO, if its primary focus were on global environmental issues, would have to accommodate the legitimate environmental/economic concerns of a very differentiated continent. Thus, issue linkage in the area of trade and environmental negotiations, for example, would have to be quite detailed and encompass many products and services if it is to appeal to developing countries.

Addressing the perceived environmental problems of developing countries through a WEO is made more complex by the fact that many of these environmental problems are really failures of policy operative in other sectors. For example, subsidies in the use of fertilisers and pesticides lead to problems of soil degradation and salinity due to excessive use. Similarly, water subsidies lead to depletion of the water table and desertification. Fuel subsidies, especially on diesel, lead to over-use and traffic-related problems. Policies and laws regarding management and ownership of forests, land, water and fisheries have led to very severe manifestations of the problem of the commons. Many laws have a colonial legacy, wherein the government had the sole rights to the produce of the forests and fisheries, and to that extent their management suffered from inadequate personnel, lax implementation of laws, and a generally anti-people stance. In fact, it would not be too much of an exaggeration to suggest that some of the major environmental problems of developing countries need to be tackled not as environmental problems but as problems of wrong pricing, tariff and tax policies, failure of urban planning and so on.[10] Hence, if the WEO is to be seen to be relevant to the environmental problems of the developing world it would have to address the reasons for these policy failures.

Ideally these problems should be dealt with at their point of origin. This may require harmonisation of tax and subsidy policies, better urban planning with relative prices of goods reflecting environmental priorities and relative scarcities through say full marginal cost pricing and so on. The pursuit of such policies might entail some hardships most notably for the poor in the short run. It should be remembered that, in many developing countries, direct tampering with the price mechanism is one of the most significant ways of redistributing incomes. Examples include food subsidies for the poor and input subsidies to farmers. These policies would require funds in the short run and may involve some costs (e.g. when subsidies are reduced) especially for poorer sections of society. If the WEO is to carry credibility, it must be seen to be addressing some environmental problems that are of more immediate concern than, say, CO_2 emissions. In other words, it must find some way of making the aforementioned transition in tax/pricing and other policies relatively easy. As price and tax reforms take place and subsidies are reduced the poor would get adversely affected in the short run. Redressing these may require transfer of technology and expertise, credit on easy terms, help in the design and targeting of direct subsidies to the poor to replace tampering with the price mechanism and so on. Since it is being argued that the design of a successful WEO would involve cash transfers to developing countries in lieu of their lowering CO_2 emissions or deforestation rates, these transfers could ideally be tied to the price and tax reforms of the type discussed above. Such a policy package would involve reduction of global and local environmental problems as well as increased efficiency through price and tax reforms as well as more effective redistribution in favour of the poor in developing countries.[11]

There is a general perception among many developing countries that provisions of Uruguay round of GATT (which had an unprecedented bigger agenda than mere tariff reductions as in earlier GATT rounds), and which allowed departures from free trade principles were applied asymmetrically to developing countries. In particular the environmentally motivated exceptions, which earlier GATT rulings had either declared illegal or outside its jurisdictions, were being applied and amounted to de facto non-tariff barriers (NTBs).[12]

A case in point is Article XX, although to date there is not much evidence that it has been applied substantially against developing countries. Article XX defines environmental exceptions to GATT principles, as (quoted directly):

> Subject to the requirement that such measures are not applied in a manner which would constitute a means of arbitrary or unjustifiable discrimination between countries where the same conditions prevail, or a disguised restriction on international trade, nothing in this Agreement shall be construed to prevent the adoption or enforcement by any contracting party of measures:
>
> '(b) necessary to protect human, animal or plant life or health; . . .
> (g) relating to the conservation of exhaustible natural resources if such measures are made effective in conjunction with restrictions on domestic production or consumption.'

Developing countries are aware that Article XX under GATT and its subsequent inclusion in the WTO charter allows a country to depart from the principle of free trade to protect domestic human, animal and plant life, health and safety. Ambiguities in its meaning have led to considerable pressure from the developed countries to bring the environment more directly into the WTO's agenda. They have advanced the following reasons in support of this. First, there is the argument that discrimination against products that harm the environment should be allowed. Second, it is argued that the use of low environmental standards to improve a country's competitive advantage constitutes eco-dumping amounting to unfair trade practices and should be prohibited. Third, there is the argument that if trade restrictions are imposed to enforce environmental goals, these trade restrictions should not be challenged under multilateral rules.

Since developing countries perceive themselves at the receiving end of GATT XX, they feel that inclusion of environmental concerns into GATT/WTO has served the cause of the developed countries largely. The stakes in arriving at workable solutions to global environmental problems are very high. If these solutions are to work through the WEO then this organisation must carry the conviction that it will not be used for partisan purposes by the developed countries.[13] Since the developing countries have most of the environmental assets, their active participation would be essential for success in the area of reduction of global environmental problems. Hence, the need for the credibility of the WEO.

The Trade-Related Intellectual Property Rights (TRIPS) Agreement has become an especially important bone of contention. For example, with respect to technology transfer, patents increase the difficulty as well as the costs of obtaining new technologies. Such technologies may be required either due to changes agreed under certain MEA (such as the Montreal Protocol) or to meet environmental requirements in export markets. Further, there has been an increasing concern for the conservation and sustainable use of biodiversity. The rapid progress in the area of biotechnology has meant that greater importance is attached (by the richer countries) to easy access to genetic resources. Developing countries are the depositories of such resources. They may view the patenting agreements on genetic processes initiated by the richer countries as infringements upon their natural resources if sufficient compensation is not given to them.

The matter of precedent

In light of the arguments in the previous section, skepticism about WEO would appear to grow if one were to judge matters on the basis of the precedents set by earlier MEAs. Some of the MEAs had provisions of 'aid in exchange for compliance'. A notable example is that of the Montreal Protocol. The Montreal Protocol on substances that deplete the ozone layer is an international agreement that has been in force since 1 January 1989, binding more than 70 countries to a timetable for phasing out the production and consumption of controlled substances known to damage the earth's ozone layer. Developing countries whose per capita consumption of the CFCs remains below 0.3 kg (the so-called Article 5 countries), are granted a grace period of 10 years for phasing these out. For a developing country such as India, almost 75 per cent of its production is for exports, mainly to LDCs. The growing use of refrigerants, and an expanding middle class (estimated to be around 200 million) means that even domestic demand for CFC using products is increasing. There does not seem to be any large-scale switch over to ODS substitutes, especially in refrigeration and air conditioning. Unlike OECD countries there is also no evidence of pressure from consumers on producers of refrigeration appliances to switch to 'greener' technologies. The so-called 'positive incentives' of the Montreal Protocol, that is, technology transfer and aid has not been forthcoming in a big way. Hence, developing countries would be wary of yet another environmental agreement, even if it is a mega agreement, unless such an arrangement is sensitive to the constrains faced by these countries and is seen to be relevant to the developmental and environmental priorities of these countries.

It is apparent that, from the viewpoint of the developing countries, the inclusion of an environmental clause, a labour and social clause and technical barriers to trade under the GATT rules are all applied to protecting the interests of OECD countries and used to justify non-tariff barriers against developing countries. Furthermore, there are hardly any provisions for positive sanctions as a reward for greater compliance. For example, granting of most-preferred-nation status or preferential access for export markets is not automatically granted, but negative sanctions are put into effect automatically and immediately. For developing countries, which are dependent on exports of textiles, leather and timber products, a trade-environment linkage with both positive and negative sanctions is important. If the WEO takes on the responsibility of implementing these sanctions, and is authorised to coordinate with WTO, its chances of acceptance by the developing countries would be enhanced.

Problems of implementation

A significant part of success in the environmental initiatives has come because of the pressure of 'user groups'. Examples include Greenpeace, eco labelling in Germany because of peer group pressure and so on. At the present point in time, the pressure for an organisation to deal with global environmental problems comes essentially from groups within the OECD and some developing country NGOs. Since the benefits of initiatives in this regard will accrue throughout the world, it is important that public opinion be built in its favour in developing countries as well. There will have to be considerable education of the public in this regard in these countries, moreover any proposed WEO must establish its credibility as an organisation genuinely interested in the problems and welfare of the people in developing countries.

This problem for the WEO may be made somewhat easier by the fact that, once the developing countries sign on, adhering to the terms of the WEO would become an international commitment for them. This would add pressure on developing country governments to comply. In addition if the WEO can align itself with NGOs within developing countries it can help monitor progress made by governments in regard to adhering to international standards set as well as making progress in ameliorating domestic environmental problems. This could be one way of keeping a check on progress made on the domestic environment front by recalcitrant developing country governments.[14]

In sum, then, it appears that in the case of developing countries it would be difficult to separate the environmental and development agendas. An organisation like the WEO would have to be relevant in addressing this indivisibility if it is to be successful. It has to recognise that there are costs and benefits of developing countries joining an international environmental protection programme.

Institutional mechanisms to underpin the WEO

The rationale for WEO appears to be elusive because the implications of GED and the need for GEM are not as apparent to prospective member States, as was the case in other international organisations such as the WTO. In the latter case, the problem might have been that of a clash of interests (say, in agriculture between the developed and the developing countries), but the identity of gainers and losers is rarely in doubt. The gains from the WEO, however, would largely be in the form of global public goods (preservation of global environment) whereas developing countries see the costs to them (in terms of forgone economic growth to meet environmental targets) as being too high. Voluntary provision of public goods – whether these are local or global – is often inadequate. The essential challenge is to ensure that the developing countries – their governments as well as their peoples – are clear that they would be compensated to an extent sufficient to make up for this gap between perceived benefit and actual cost.

An important problem in pushing forward the WEO agenda is that the materialisation of a rationale in the mind-set of the states is inhibited by the apparent lack of *quid pro quo*. On the other hand, these very states could easily misconstrue the WEO as an impingement on the sovereignty of the nation-states and this would militate against the establishment of WEO. On the other hand, such contacts of the WEO with NGOs will enhance the support for WEO within the population of the developing countries.

Hence, in the agenda the foremost priority must be afforded to understanding and publicising the rationale for a WEO. More importantly there is a need to work out a strategy for making the idea of the WEO acceptable, especially amongst the NGOs, without which it may not become a reality. In this regard, nation-states would have to be convinced by the argument that the rationale pivots on the idea of 'social contract'. Such a nation-state should willingly accept the requisite curbs on its sovereignty in return for the 'social good' of GEM.

The NGOs are an important link in the WEO mechanism. Acceptance of the WEO by NGOs would be greater if the organisation is projected as a body that would strive for the benefit of individual member States, rather than fashion itself exclusively as a policing body or as an arbiter, whose concern is limited only to trans-boundary environmental issues.

Member States and NGOs would be convinced only if the intention of the WEO is to move from the global to the regional, to the domestic and finally to the local level, both in terms of issues and in terms of the personnel being involved. The justification for the WEO to adopt such an approach can then be sought in the cause of global environmental problems.

The case for the WEO crucially depends upon the magnitude of the visible areas of environmental degradation. Developing countries can expect developed countries to expedite the formation of the WEO if there are large areas of common concern among developed and developing countries. If this was true, an international compensation approach to GEM could find favour with the developed countries. It appears that the identifiable global environmental concerns common to most developed countries would include, in diminishing order of importance, pollution, global warming, deforestation, biodiversity and over-exploitation of natural resources. Such convergence of concerns does not obtain in the case of developing countries. The existing institutions and global and regional environmental treaties have failed in (i) using side payment mechanisms for internalising cross-border externalities; (ii) using issue linkage that is, non-environmental incentives along with environmental negotiations and (iii) have not used global mechanisms to underpin and reinforce domestic policies on the environment. Any design of the WEO needs to address these deficiencies explicitly.

Well-designed transfer mechanisms can guarantee that no country refuses to sign a WEO agreement because the loss of net benefit of not signing the agreement. However, it is not sufficient to guarantee net gains by transfers to induce the participants to sign an international agreement. Incentives to free ride must also be offset to make the agreement stable. For the agreement to be effective it would need to be stable which, in turn, would require that there is no incentive for either the developed or developing countries to leave the WEO. Such an arrangement would be self-enforcing. The presence of asymmetries across countries and the incentive to free ride makes it difficult for self-enforcing treaties to exist. In any case, more than one instrument needs to be used to tackle multiple objectives. Hence, the need for issue linkage agreements in addition to transfers.

Importance of incentives

An upshot of the above arguments is that the WEO must be based on the following principles, if it has any serious chance of acceptance:

1 It must be voluntary.
2 There must be incentives not only to join, but also to stay.
3 There must be a mechanism for binding commitments from all the signatories. This is related to the issue of enforcement of the charter of WEO.
4 There must be a good monitoring mechanism, even in the absence of conflicts.

Issue linkage

The analysis aforementioned seems to give the impression that adjustment to global environmental standards (say in CO_2 emission) are implemented all at once and also that a more demanding versions of the WEO is in place. It might well be the case that these calculations may somewhat exaggerate the inducement needed by developing countries to participate in the WEO. The following arguments can be made in support of this.

1   Once some major countries have joined, there will be pressures on others to join. These pressures could be of several forms – both positive as well as negative. First, the members of WEO can apply pressure through trade and other means on the countries outside the purview of the WEO in order to induce them to join. If the members of the WEO are in a dominant position, then, an initial estimate of the viability of the WEO should not require the design of mechanisms whereby *all* or even *most* countries in Asia are induced to join. As a matter of fact if large countries such as China, India, ASEAN, Brazil, South Africa and others join, it is hard to see how the remaining developing countries can stay out of the WEO.
2   Second, countries outside the WEO would be identified as those that are responsible for continuation of any global environmental crisis. This would imply moral and international pressure on them to reconsider.
3   Third, one can argue that the establishment of a WEO would be preceded by an enunciation of a global and common responsibility of nation-states and peoples to protect the global environment. It could also be argued that given the fact that the developing countries are in the most disadvantageous position with regard to the environment growth trade-off, their obligations within the WEO would have to be interpreted liberally. For example, they could be given more time to comply with global environmental standards or they could be given pollution quotas on a more liberal basis and these quotas could be made tradable across time.
4   Furthermore, most countries would suffer in the long run to some extent by global environmental problems such as carbon emissions. Thus, there would, in general, be a cost of not joining a coalition aimed at preserving global environment. A country would resort to long-term free riding only when the benefit–cost ratio of remaining outside a coalition is higher compared to that for joining it.

An opportunity exists now, for some developing countries to exploit their relative bargaining strengths in environmental treaties. This is because the bulk of the 'environmental assets' of the world, in terms of forest cover (sinks for CO_2 emissions) and biodiversity lie within the sovereign boundaries of these nations, whereas the pressing concern for a global treaty comes from the OECD countries. Second, the developing countries can demand side payments to compensate them for (i) preservation of environmental assets; (ii) slower economic growth and welfare loss resulting from their complying with global environmental practices. Finally, an opportunity also exists for using environmental leverage for other concessions including those for tackling local environmental problems.[15]

An implication of these arguments is that the developing countries are expected to effect changes in their environmental policies so as to arrest further deterioration in the global environment. This would naturally imply that they would expect some compensation from developed countries as *quid pro quo* for following the agenda of advanced countries rather than seeking to further their own economic interests (Jha *et al.* 2002; Newell and Whalley 1998). The following mechanism could be used as such *quid pro quo*.

Transfer of technology

If a developing country restricts its wood exports with a view to protect the environment, it would expect compensation. This compensation could be in the form of technology transfers that would enable production of wood substitutes. Such transfers should include 'information' and advanced-country technology as well as help in adapting to the new technology. As it stands, the pressure on land and natural resources so great that any further restriction on forest exploitation (which is labour-intensive) would slow down employment and income growth.

Trade

This is perhaps the most significant area suitable for inducement. The data in Table 9.3 indicate that tariff levels in OECD countries for developing country exports are still high. A broad-based OECD tariff reduction plan could yield substantial gains to developing countries if the volume of trade (the base) is large and growing fast.

Two points then become relevant at this stage. First, has the phenomenon of tariff escalation (higher tariffs as we go downstream in the chain of production) in the past hurt developing country exports of processed goods so much that trade patterns are biased so overwhelmingly towards primary goods? Second, if yes, has the Uruguay Round been able to make a dent on this problem? If yes, then is there sufficient scope for further post-Uruguay tariff reduction for processed goods, which might give adequate compensation to LDCs for cutting down on carbon emissions?

The evidence seems to suggest that most post-Uruguay Round nominal tariffs do not seem to constitute a major constraint against the further processing and exports of LDC commodities in the aggregate. As a matter of fact, only five commodity processing chains display applied tariff rates of 10 per cent or above for the post-Uruguay Round duty. The highest incidence of applied tariffs affected tobacco products, followed by sulphur and manganese, fruits and cocoa. For 31 major categories the post-Uruguay Round tariff is less than 5 per cent. It is also worth noting that focusing exclusively on the structure of MFN tariff rates may give a misleading picture. Import duties have declined significantly once account

Table 9.3 MFN average tariff rates (for imports from developing countries)

Product group	USA		EU		Japan		Canada	
	A	B	A	B	A	B	A	B
Agricultural products (non-tropical)	9.1	7.0	23.5	16.8	19.5	14.9	7.6	4.9
Agricultural products (tropical)	2.1	1.2	17.4	10.0	17.4	10.9	1.2	0.6
Other tropical products	3.2	1.4	3.0	1.5	4.5	1.9	7.2	3.6
Natural resource based products	2.6	2.0	6.0	4.8	3.8	2.2	3.3	1.9
Textiles and clothing	18.7	16.9	11.9	10.1	11.7	7.9	22.1	15.6
Leather and footwear	9.6	9.1	9.1	7.8	13.3	11.5	19.8	15.0
Other industrial products#	3.3	1.7	3.5	2.0	3.9	2.3	6.8	3.1
All imports#	7.6	5.5	9.8	6.9	7.4	4.7	12.4	7.4

Source: UNCTAD (1994): Trade and Development Report, 1994.

Notes
A = pre-Uruguay Round; B = post-Uruguay Round; # excluding fuel.

is taken of the preferences LDCs receive in OECD markets through GSP, CBI, Lome Convention and other schemes.

However, the above applies only to nominal tariffs. As is well known, even with low nominal tariffs at the end product stage in a vertical production change, the effective rate of protection may be quite high. Estimates of this for the OECD country imports from LDCs need to be collected to assess the possibility of tariff reduction being enough of an inducement for LDCs to join in and stay in a WEO.

It might well be argued that under the aegis of the WTO tariff concessions would be available anyway. Hence, the WEO would have to go beyond this, in particular to non-tariff barriers. At present, it may be argued, under the WTO regulations environmental and other arguments are being used as *de facto* NTBs. It might well be important for the WEO to develop a standardised approach to NTBs and balance genuine social and other concerns of developed countries with the need to provide an incentive to developing countries to use reductions in NTBs as an inducement for complying with regulations of the WEO concerning global externalities.[16]

Another possible area of compensation is the reduction of NTBs to international trade, which are pervasive in almost all countries. NTB consist of all barriers to international trade except tariffs and take a wide range of forms ranging from import quotas, licensing of import/export, anti-dumping and countervailing duties, sanctions and voluntary export restraints to less familiar ones like preference procurement of domestic goods, customs valuation and clearance procedures, copyrights and intellectual property rights. At a broader level, at times any non-tariff policy that has a distortionary or discretionary impact on trade and foreign investment could be classified under NTB; for example, immigration policy, foreign investment policy, employment and social security policy and even industrial and taxation policy. There might also be informal barriers associated with administrative procedures, market structures and social institutions.

Table 9.4 lists some of the major categories of NTBs and Table 9.5 give the frequency ratios calculated as product categories that were subject to NTB expressed as a percentage of total number of product categories in corresponding group. Import coverage ratio is calculated by determining the value of imports subject to NTB as a percentage of total imports. The NTBs covered in this table

Table 9.4 Categories of NTBs

I	*Quantitative restrictions and similar specifications*
1	Import quotas
2	Export limitations
3	Licensing
4	Voluntary export restraint
5	Exchange and other financial control
6	Prohibition
7	Domestic content and mixing requirement
8	Countertrade
II	*Non-tariff charges and related policies*
1	Variable levies
2	Advance deposit requirements
3	Anti-dumping duties
4	Countervailing duties
5	Border tax adjustments
III	*Government participation in trade, restrictive practices and more general government policies*
1	Subsidies and other aid
2	Government procurement policies
3	State trading government monopolies and exclusive franchises
4	Government industrial policy and regional development measures
5	Government financed research and development and other technology policies
6	National system of taxation and social insurance
7	Macroeconomic policies
8	Competition policies
9	Foreign investment policies
10	Foreign corruption policies
11	Immigration policies
IV	*Customs procedures and administrative practices*
1	Customs valuation procedure
2	Customs classification procedures
3	Customs clearance procedures
V	*Technical barriers to trade*
1	Health, sanitary regulations and quality standards
2	Safety and industrial standards and regulations
3	Packaging and labelling regulations including trademarks
4	Advertising and media regulations

Source: Compiled from Deardorff and Stern (1998).

Table 9.5 Frequency ratio of NTBs in 1993

	USA		EU		Japan		Canada	
	Frequency ratio	Import ratio	Frequency ratio	Import ratio	Frequency ratio	Import ratio	Frequency ratio	Import ratio
All NTBs	22.9	17.0	23.7	11.1	7.7	8.0	11.0	4.5
Quantitative restrictions	18.1	10.2	17.2	7.1	6.7	2.8	6.8	1.7
a Export restraints	13.1	10.1	13.9	5.6	0.3	0.2	5.8	1.4
b Non-automatic licensing	0.0	0.0	3.5	1.7	5.7	1.0	0.2	0.0
Price control measures	10.8	7.3	8.4	3.5	0.3	0.8	1.4	0.8

Source: OECD (1995) as quoted by Deardorff and Stern (1998).

Table 9.6 Frequency ratio of NTBs by commodity groups 1993

	USA	EU	Japan	Canada
Agriculture and allied products	3.6	14.9	5.2	4.1
Mining and quarrying	2.3	3.5	0.4	0.7
Manufacturing	24.7	22.8	7.4	8.8
Food, beverage and tobacco	12.1	44.2	6.7	11.4
Textiles and apparel	69.9	76.8	21.4	41.5
Wood and wood products	0.6	0.0	0.0	3.2
Paper and paper products	1.3	0.4	0.0	1.2
Chemicals	5.8	5.1	0.7	0.3
Non-metallic mineral products	5.3	0.2	0.0	0.4
Basic-metal industries	57.1	19.0	0.9	4.6
Fabricated metal products	13.8	2.3	0.0	1.4
Other manufacturing	1.1	2.0	0.0	1.2
All products	23.0	22.1	7.1	8.3

Source: OECD (1995) as quoted by Deardorff and Stern (1998).

include price control measures, finance measures, automatic licensing measures, quantity control measures and monopolistic measures. Table 9.5 covers only what has been called 'core' NTBs, that is, all NTBs except finance measures and monopolistic measures. The magnitudes of NTBs are large. NTBs, in one form or another, are present in about 23 per cent of commodities in the US and the EU. The proportions of imports affected by NTBs are 17 per cent for the US and 11 per cent for the EU. NTBs are not as wide in Japan and Canada with only about 8 and 5 per cent of respective total imports getting affected. Table 9.6 quantifies NTBs by commodity groups.

This opens up the possibility of the WEO exploring the possibility of using phased reductions in NTB to elicit support. To begin with, it could attempt to develop a unified approach to NTB. It could delineate what could and what could not be construed as a NTB and could define the conditions under which a country would be allowed to impose NTB and how trade-offs between phased reductions in NTB and in CO_2 emissions, for example, could be exploited.

Investment: including concessional aid, debt reductions and debt for nature swaps

Another possibility is to tie reductions in international debt obligations of developing countries to their record of compliance with respect to international environment agreements. As Table 9.7 indicates since many of the poorest countries of the world remain severely indebted, there is some room for this policy initiative and the burden of the debt across country groups is depicted in Table 9.8. However, a programme of debt forgiveness could involve problems of moral hazard as countries that can count on debt reductions through the process of international environment negotiations, may pursue imprudent monetary and fiscal policies. Similarly, it is hard to see what can be built into the international environment negotiations to stimulate FDI flows into countries that are complying with international environment standards. It seems to be the case that targeting tariff and non-tariff barriers to developing country exports, cash paid as side payments, technology transfer and aid in ameliorating the domestic environment problems of developing countries offer the best hope for negotiations on a WEO and building goodwill towards it among the population of the developing countries.

There is only limited scope for debt for nature swap arrangements; see Jha and Schatan (2001).

Immigration

Consequent upon slower growth and employment. There could be international compensation in the form of easier immigration laws in developed countries.

International liquidity consequent upon decline in exports

The import capacity would be limited, especially that of essential imports like food, oil, fertiliser, etc. These would have to be compensated by provision of international liquidity.

Spagnolo (1996) has argued that when international policy issues are linked together then there is room for positive gains in the case of some linked negotiations, but not all. Clearly, this would be possible when the government's objective function is separable in the various targets since the slack in one policy objective can be transferred to another. When policy objectives are substitutes for each other in the government's objective function (say trade and environment policies) then even when no slack is present linkage might be helpful. However, this would not be the case when policy objectives are complementary (e.g. monetary and fiscal policies).

Table 9.7 Total debt to GDP (%)

Country group	1990	1991	1992	1993	1994	1995	1996
East Asia and Pacific	36.89932	38.28007	38.11479	40.17203	38.85905	36.0517	
Europe and Central Asia	18.00662	20.45733	23.36708	32.50427	40.52218	39.64382	36.78164
Latin America and Caribbean	46.14925	48.62495	46.32624	45.41109	42.44345	44.30765	41.75519
LCDs: UN classification	106.4029	113.7377	120.8909	122.5361	138.9471	124.1492	
Low and middle income	36.27835	39.06413	39.8574	43.29321	44.45842	43.06545	40.13449
Low income, excl. China and India	96.8545	99.77182	98.11534	110.1275	120.2106	110.8527	97.82672
Low income	46.82225	49.98172	49.92799	52.741	49.24651	42.90714	
Lower-middle income	33.10009	35.78096	38.79028	44.86296	51.3713	49.37133	45.60467
Middle income	32.9192	35.5828	36.56216	40.16756	42.75343	43.25117	40.64118
South Asia	38.25524	44.57315	47.39076	46.03295	44.40202	39.45561	35.37688
Sub-Saharan Africa	69.86659	72.33762	70.5595	80.68004	90.73497	87.19169	82.14916

Source: World Bank.

Table 9.8 Burden of the public debt across country-groups

World	Total debt as percentage of GDP (2000)	Interest payment on public debt as percentage of GDP (2000)
Low income	—	—
Middle income	33.2	10.3
Lower-middle income	51.3	11.6
Upper-middle income	26.7	7.8
Low and middle income	—	11.8
East Asia and Pacific	52.3	13.9
Europe and Central Asia	42.4	9.5
Latin America and Caribbean	—	11.5
Middle East and N. Africa	—	12.2
South Asia	77.3	35.4
Sub-Saharan Africa	—	—
High income	55.3	7.5
Europe EMU	60.2	14.3

Source: World Development Indicators (2003).

Bargaining in trade and environment negotiations could be linked so that it would be possible for developing countries to extract trade concessions from developed countries in exchange for environmental concessions from the former, say reducing the rate of deforestation. Similarly, developed countries can reward compliance with environmental standards in negotiations on international trade.[17]

Clearly one important area of issue linkage is with respect to exports from developing countries. Export expansion is becoming an increasingly important factor for growth in ADC. Hence, a tying in of tariff concessions to performance on the global environment front would be one way of inducing participation by developing countries.

The quantum of trade concessions would be an important ingredient of any package designed to ensure developing country support for a WEO. How much tariff concessions would actually be needed would depend upon the form that the WEO might take (Whalley and Zissimos 2002a). A WEO that performs only the minimal role for coordinating all international environmental agreements may not be difficult to agree to. However, such an organisation would have only limited effect. If the WEO is to be at all able act as a conduit for ameliorating global environmental problems, it will have to make trade and environmental linkages in a manner designed to address the concerns of developing countries.

Other roles of the WEO

Global concerns need not necessarily be restricted to trans-boundary issues since many a time, local issues await solutions because of the lack of information. This becomes especially telling when solutions exist and are being practiced in similar situations in other regions of the globe. Typically, such situations should be addressed by the WEO, could be endowed with information regarding such solutions, being practiced elsewhere in the world.

If such solutions are not adopted, even though they exist, they must be seen as forgone opportunities and should be treated as 'social costs' by the States. Although it may not be a direct 'social bad' like trans-boundary pollution, it involves an implicit cost. A 'social benefit' could flow if the WEO facilitates such a solution by emulation, as the following instance shows.

The Central African Republic could not afford management of the rich rain forest adjacent to a National Park. It had leased out the forest to a French sawmill company for the sake of revenue that would partly go towards maintaining the National Park. The sawmill company indulged in indiscriminate felling under the pretext of 'culling'. It is common knowledge that this would lead to the intensification of the flood–drought cycle, siltation, loss of arable land and hence, lead to domestic environmental degradation and global ecological imbalance.

To the relief of the Central African Republican, in the early 1990s, the German Republic took over 2000 odd square kilometres of the forest on lease. They 'adopted' the forest, merged it into the National Park and rehabilitated the local personnel of the sawmill (which was shut-down), in the National Park. Through this act the local region benefited and, automatically, the objective of GEM was furthered. However, the German government had many problems in actually negotiating and effecting the arrangements, especially, on account of the need for making capital payments to a foreign government.

This is typically an area in which the WEO has a role to play – both directly and indirectly. Directly, it could have helped both the governments in the negotiations and arrangements. Indirectly, in a similar situation that might exist in another country, the WEO could, perhaps, suggest such a solution to the host country and might find a willing 'sponsor-country', which would 'adopt' such a forest area. Such a conception of the role of WEO furthers the thinking that it 'should play a more activist role'.

Further the design of the WEO could incorporate certain precautionary elements. This has two aspects. One, the possibility of learning 'lessons' from human rights activists and two, etching out a role for the NGOs. The first proposal here is that, like the 'human rights watch' of the Country Chapters of the Amnesty International, a 'WEO Environment Watch' could be formed with similar Country Chapters. The specialty of these chapters would be that the personnel of one country would keep a watch on another country, through a swap arrangement, under the aegis of the WEO. This would become a 'Global Environmental Watch', while not losing sight of the common cause of GED, namely, the rooted environmental problems in each country.

The second proposal is that the WEO can appoint the personnel or organisations of local NGOs (registered with them) as 'Ombudsmen', in case proposals for environmental protection, conservation, control or deterrent action emerge as a result of such a 'Watch'. Such 'Ombudsmen' should, ideally, have diplomatic immunity, like UN inspectors. All this would involve the establishment of new international principles in an area that is hitherto untouched.

The example of the rehabilitation of the 'Doon' valley, situated in the Shivalik hills, in north India, is illustrative of such possibilities. The valley, which at one time was an environmental preserve, became a victim of urbanisation and indiscriminate industrialisation. After sustained protests mining, quarrying and harmful industries have been banned in the valley. This holds lessons for areas elsewhere.

Trans-boundary or local?

Having said earlier, it would be proper to review some possible situations in which the WEO can step in. A distinction needs to be made between purely bilateral trans-boundary issues and regional issues. Such issues could be resolved through third-party mediation (with the WEO as the third party). Inter-country river water disputes are good examples of this.

Alternately, the WEO can, in fact, stand as guarantor with some international financial body and raise soft loans for ensuring the necessary financial support to the relatively poor country, so that it can also provide the necessary protection to the flora and fauna. A third solution could be that the WEO raises an 'Aid Fund', for this purpose, which is financed by other member countries and multilateral agencies.

Regional issues

Certain problems are regional and hence, are not the concern of an individual country. Examples include over-exploitation of marine resources in the economic zones, oil slicks caused by rigs and sea-borne vessels in international waters, disposal of nuclear or other wastes, etc. This would need surveillance and general supervision. Since the WEO could not maintain a navy, it would have to rely on other countries.

Here, it would be possible to link such a surveillance mechanism with incentives. The coast guards of various countries could bid for the contract of undertaking the task of surveillance. The country can earn foreign exchange in the process. Alternately, a task force with representation from all littoral States, can be formed, which could be run on the lines of a UN peace-keeping force. Sometimes a combination of all these solutions might have to be used simultaneously.

For some of the aforementioned purposes, as well as, for ascertaining the forest cover and for other geophysical and meteorological surveys that are necessary for GEM, the WEO might require satellite surveillance. Multilateral international agreements, protocols and checks and balances would have to be worked out and agreed upon, especially if the purpose of the WEO is not to be misunderstood as being one of strategic surveillance.

The earlier issues and examples make it amply clear that there are certain areas where both market and non-market solutions may not coexist. Where they do coexist, admittedly, the level of development and the ethos may influence the choice between the two. It may also be true that developed countries adopt policies that work by incentives rather than by 'fiat'. However, where both market and non-market solutions do not coexist, the issue is not just whether market solutions should be encouraged but also to see what best can be done with the help of non-market solutions, if that is second best.

Demarcation of roles

An important aspect of this problem is the need to demarcate the spheres of different international bodies. We list below some examples of the differences between the WEO and existing international bodies.

- while the World Wildlife Fund is responsible for protection of endangered species the WEO would be responsible for trans-boundary issues like the preservation of biospheres that are located across borders and for remedying the effects of environmental disturbances on animals;
- while the World Bank might decide to extend financial support to projects such as reforestation the WEO would identify, recommend and prioritises the projects;
- while the ICJ would arbitrate in situations where existing international law is being violated the WEO would frame new laws in relation to the environment and would refer cases that it cannot solve by its own intervention and bilateral persuasion. Moreover, the WEO may have to work, in some instances, towards upholding fair principles rather than merely enforcing laws.

Conclusions

Trans-boundary and international environmental problems are a pressing concern for the global community and call for innovative institutional design to address them. Whereas the developed countries value the international environment highly they realise that some of the solutions must originate within the geographic boundaries of developing countries. However, developing countries do not appear to have these problems high on their agendas at least at first glance. The more important appear to be economic growth and domestic environmental concerns. However, it is also true that not addressing global environmental problems could hurt, in specific areas, developing country economic growth and their domestic environmental problems. But, the fundamental fact of the indivisibility of the growth and environmental agendas in the developing countries has to be faced.

Since the developed countries seem to consider global environmental problems as an emergent issue and since some developing countries will soon become major contributors to this problem, it would be necessary to have the foresight to conclude a treaty at an early date. This would mean that developing countries would have to be persuaded and provided enough incentives to enter into international environmental negotiations and remain committed to this process.

The chapter has argued that since developing countries have considerable environmental assets, they should probably look for linking slowing down the depletion of these assets to other areas of linkage to the developed countries. In particular, this would include international trade, transfer of technology and, perhaps, direct transfers. Since this linkage would be very wide ranging, it would be necessary to exploit any positive external effects that might flow from some treaties and avoid duplication and conflicts in others. It makes sense, therefore, to have a WEO to coordinate these efforts.

But what version of a WEO is to be opted for is, at this point in time, an open question. Clearly a mild version of a WEO that brings all environmental treaties under one umbrella, provides technical know-how and facilitates negotiations would be innocuous enough and, therefore, acceptable. However, such a WEO would also not be very effective in controlling the problem of global externalities, assuming that this problem is of an emergent nature. Stronger versions of a WEO would not be acceptable to many developing countries unless issue linkage of the sort discussed here becomes a reality. Before that is achieved, given the past experience of developing countries with MEA, the WEO would have to build considerable credibility as an organisation that is truly interested in global environmental problems, is sensitive to the needs of developing countries and is not acting as a mechanism for imposing the will of the developed countries on developing countries.

The task of controlling global external effects is complex, not the least because this has to be accomplished by voluntary action of nation-states. A properly designed WEO could be a central element of a successful strategy to place the generation of global external effects on a sustainable path. This chapter has espoused the developing country point of view on this and substantiated the window of opportunity that exists at present. It is another matter that this window may start closing sooner rather than later – but that is an issue beyond the scope of this chapter, indeed this book.

10 Issues in global environmental management

Introduction

In Chapter 9 the discussion concentrated largely on the form of GEM (although there was some discussion on the function also). The emphasis was on the political economy of the form of GEM. In this chapter we are more concerned with the basic principles, the functions and the priorities of GEM. At the outset we would like to clarify our reasons for our preference for the term 'GEM'.

The prevalent terms used in extant literature[1] are global governance and global environmental mechanism (GEME). The former usage is meant to imply global environmental governance (GEG). However, the evolution of the term global governance does not adequately reflect this intention. The spirit of the term global governance should place an emphasis on participatory processes and governance structures that assume the involvement of stakeholders, such as businesses and NGOs.[2] Therefore, it has to do with form rather than function. The terminology[3] 'GEM' implies an instrument or device that is more often than not semi-automatic. Moreover, it does not necessarily assume the existence of a single institution. A mechanism could be a system or an arrangement.

Esty and Ivanova (2002) describe GEM as follows:

> (GEME) could emerge in various ways, driven by functional needs. Its core capacities might include: (1) provision of adequate information and analysis to characterize problems, track trends, and identify interests; (2) creation of a 'policy space' for environmental negotiation and bargaining; and (3) sustained build up of capacity for addressing issues of agreed-upon concern and significance. A Global Environmental Mechanism could build upon the expertise of existing institutions and create new mechanisms where key functions were deemed to be non-existent or inadequate.
>
> (p. 5)

Relation between global governance, GEM and GEME

What is the relationship between the three concepts – GEG, GEM and GEME? The term GEM implies a function. Governance necessarily refers to form and mechanism refers to a (semi-automatic) device or system. The polemics of the debate outlined in Chapter 9 mystifies the fact that our primary interest in this book is in GEM and that management refers to the function, role and priorities.

Global governance refers to a system-wide structure that both facilitates and constrains the behaviour of actors in interdependent relationships in the absence of an overarching political authority. The global international system is the best example of this. Traditionally, governance has been associated with 'governing', or with political authority, institutions and, ultimately, control. Governance in this particular sense denotes formal political and legal institutions that aim to coordinate and control interdependent social relations and that have the ability to enforce decisions. However, authors like James Rosenau have also used 'governance' to denote the regulation of interdependent relations in the absence of overarching political authority, such as in the international system. Thomas G. Weiss, director of the Ralph Bunche Institute for International Studies at the Graduate Center (CUNY) and editor (2000–05) of the journal *Global Governance: A Review of Multilateralism and International Organizations*, defines 'global governance' as 'collective efforts to identify, understand, or address worldwide problems that go beyond the capacity of individual states to solve'.

The underlying fact is that global governance is a descriptive, not normative, concept. Global governance is not a normative term denoting good or bad practice. It is a descriptive term, referring to concrete co-operative problem-solving arrangements. They may be formal, taking the shape of laws or formally constituted institutions to manage collective affairs by a variety of actors (such as state authorities, intergovernmental organisations, NGOs, private sector entities and other actors, and individuals). But these may also be informal (as in the case of practices or guidelines) or temporary units (as in the case of coalitions).

Thus, global governance may be defined as 'the complex of formal and informal institutions, mechanisms, relationships and processes between and among states, markets, citizens and organisations, both inter- and non-governmental,[4] through which collective interests on the global plane are articulated, rights and obligations are established and differences are mediated'.[5]

The fact that global governance is not a normative term is of utmost importance to our study. Our concern in this chapter is to summarise the existing positive aspect of environmental management and to point out towards the normative questions, which in our opinion are crucial to the whole debate.

The foundation for global governance

'Our Global Neighborhood', a report of the Commission on global governance was the first document to speak of global governance. The Commission consists of 28 individuals, carefully selected because of their prominence, influence and their ability to effect the implementation of the recommendations. Although not an official body of the UN, the Commission was endorsed by the UN Secretary General and funded through two trust funds of the United Nations Development

Program (UNDP), nine national governments, and several foundations, including the MacArthur Foundation[6] the Ford Foundation and the Carnegie Corporation.

The Commission on Global Governance (1995) report was released in preparation for a World Conference on Global Governance, in 1998, at which official world governance treaties were expected to be adopted for implementation by the year 2000. The Commission was based on the foundation for global governance and incorporated the belief that the world is now ready to accept a 'global civic ethic' based on 'a set of core values that can unite people of all cultural, political, religious or philosophical backgrounds'. This belief is reinforced by another belief: 'that governance should be underpinned by democracy at all levels and ultimately by the rule of enforceable law'.

The core value of 'justice and equity' is the basis for sweeping changes in the UN as proposed by the Commission.

> The Commission has determined that: 'Although people are born into widely unequal economic and social circumstances, great disparities in their conditions or life chances are an affront to the human sense of justice. A broader commitment to equity and justice is basic to more purposeful action to reduce disparities and bring about a more balanced distribution of opportunities around the world. A commitment to equity everywhere is the only secure foundation for a more humane world order... Equity needs to be respected as well in relationships between the present and future generations. The principle of intergenerational equity underlies the strategy of sustainable development.
>
> (Commission on Global Governance, pp. 7–8)

The above summary of the foundation of global governance raises many issues. First, the term global governance is taken to mean GEG. We feel that while there may be some common areas between general governance and environmental governance it needs to be understood that a separate approach is needed for GEG. Second, the enunciation of the 'foundations' in terms of such general principles as 'equity and justice' does well for general governance but not for environmental governance. Even where such principles are talked of their purpose is 'to reduce disparities and bring about a more balanced distribution of opportunities around the world'. Our concern about disparity is not to do with 'opportunity' but with the consequences of disparity for the environment. Third, in the case of the environment what we need is a foundation that is based on principles of sustainability. The interpretation of the equity principle according to our understanding has to include intragenerational equity (spatial equity). The reference to 'disparity' in the above document does in no way relate to environmental sustainability.

UNEP governing council

Since the reform of the international institutions was not a topic for the Rio Summit it is becoming clear that those institutions in their current form are unable to address sustainable development. The UNEP Governing Council agreed during its session in February 2001 to set-up a Ministerial working group, the main task of which was to examine environmental governance issues.

Given the planetary ecological crisis, it has been argued for some time that a substantial reform of the system of international institutions could assist more effective global environmental policies. An overwhelming amount of policy guidance in the field of sustainable development, including a large number of legally binding agreements, has been produced since 1990. Priority should be given to the implementation of and compliance to these agreements. Whatever comes out of such a reform could also serve as the advocate of further development of international environmental standards. Several suggestions have been made to that regard for the reform of the CSD and the reform of UNEP.

It was felt by the Council that genuine, effective and equitable participation of civil society organisations from all regions in international environmental governance is a pre-condition for sustainable development. Further, it should also be ensured that all countries are able to participate effectively and that a holistic concept of sustainable development is fostered. An institutional reform that would weaken the position of civil society and/or developing countries in international environmental governance would not be worth achieving.

The current system of international environmental governance

International environmental governance carries with it the inherent problem that its central aim must be to provide public goods without coercive authority. Thus:

> The difficulty of pursuing environmental governance at the global scale is made greater by the obvious fact that there is no global government – no central institution with authority sufficient to craft strong environmental protections at the international level and to insist on compliance. In its absence, a looser system of global environmental governance has emerged. The current system reflects the strengths and dysfunctions of global politics, and shows the difficulty of inspiring effective cooperation among the fractious community of nations – even on environmental matters that all agree require common action.
>
> (World Resources 2002–2004, p. 138)

The current system of international environmental governance consists of three basic elements. One component is a collection of intergovernmental organisations, such as the United Nations Environment Programme (UNEP), UNDP and other specialised UN agencies and commissions that are responsible for coordinating policy on the environment at the international level. These organisations, controlled by UN member nations, are charged with formulating an international agenda that will protect the environment and promote sustainable development. A variety of other international organisations, such as the World Bank and the World Trade Organization (WTO), also play important roles in global environmental decision-making.

A second element of the international environmental governance system is the framework of international environmental law that has evolved over the last century or so. This takes the form of a web of environmental treaties, such as the Framework Convention on Climate Change or the recently negotiated Stockholm Convention on Persistent Organic Pollutants. These are legally binding agreements among countries to take joint action on different environmental problems, with each nation responsible for action within its own territory.

A third element consists of financing mechanisms – to build capacity to carry out treaty commitments, to supplement national efforts towards sustainable development in poorer countries, and to support the UN agencies and treaty secretariats that coordinate and carry out environmental efforts. Some of these mechanisms are more general, such as the system of dues and voluntary contributions that funds UN agencies, or the financing that the World Bank and other multilateral development banks provide for development activities with environmental components. Other financing mechanisms, such as the Global Environment Facility, are more specifically targeted to environmental activities.

Together, the three components of international environmental governance are supposed to set priorities and facilitate steps to protect the environment and further sustainable development. Most of these steps must be implemented by individual nations themselves. From legislation to regulation to enforcement, it is the actions taken by nations at the domestic level that ultimately count most for success at the global level. But international organisations like UNDP, UNEP and the World Bank also play major roles in implementation.

Bilateral aid agencies and civil society groups also participate in important ways, as does the private sector. Supplementing these elements is a continuing series of international environmental 'summits', such as the 2002 World Summit on Sustainable Development in Johannesburg and the Earth Summit in Rio de Janeiro in 1992. These large gatherings are intended to provide highly visible forums that advance global resolve on the environment.

The record of governance this loose global regime has compiled is decidedly mixed. On the positive side, the international community has clearly accepted the environment as a key topic in global affairs, crafting hundreds of environmental agreements that promise co-operation on topics as specific as protecting certain species of sea turtles and as broad as preventing harm to the global climate. Supporting this growing will towards sustainability has been a gradual expansion of the capacity to assess global environmental threats through monitoring and analysis that the international community accepts as scientifically valid, and therefore a neutral basis for understanding and negotiation. Although far from perfect, this analysis has begun to bring the principle of access to environmental information to life at the international level – an essential enabling condition for action.

However, the international environmental governance regime has fallen short in many respects. Even internal UN assessments have concluded that the system is fragmented, with a host of policy-making organisations, treaties, financing mechanisms and implementation projects whose efforts are often poorly coordinated and sometimes overlapping. Thus, there is a strong sense that 'current approaches to global environmental management and sustainability are...ineffective' (UNEP 2001, p. 19).

In many instances, international negotiations produce agreements with ambitious goals, but without realistic means of implementing or financing them. At a more fundamental level, divisions among countries and regions, often manifesting themselves as North–South divides in terms of environmental priorities and perceived responsibilities weaken international governance institutions. These weaknesses and divisions limit the capacity of the international community to respond to even the most pressing environmental problems and may be an important reason why the combined efforts of dozens of organisations, hundreds of treaties, thousands of international meetings and billions of dollars have failed, in most instances, to reduce environmental decline.

Principles to guide international governance reform

Many steps can, and must, be taken to improve the institutional framework for international environmental governance and mobilise new partners and practices for attaining global environmental goals. In the opinion of the UNEP, two principles should guide the reform of international environmental governance in general. First, environmental objectives can only be met if they are compatible with the broader goals of sustainable development, and especially with the overriding aim of eradicating or reducing poverty worldwide. Second, any reform efforts should be guided by the principles of The Rio Declaration – in particular, the common but differentiated responsibility principle and the precautionary approach.

If these are the principles of GEG, it must be pointed out that these latter principles are again general principles and do not arise out of environmental considerations. In the case of the former principles there is a need to specify as to what the 'broader goals of sustainable development' are. This cannot be understood without going into the analysis and measurement of GED. Our thrust is that such goals need to be first understood at a more fundamental level of undertaking to enable a dispassionate analysis of the global trends in environmental degradation. The tools that we have developed and used to measure these trends are essential to buttress such an understanding.

World federalist movement

The Institute for Global Policy recommends that protecting the world environment is a critical foundation of sustainable development. Two-thirds of the earth is beyond the territorial sovereignty of UN member states; it is truly the 'global commons'. The ocean of the world's atmosphere is equally borderless; and its pollution, warming and disintegration are transnational threats. The international community must govern the global commons. To avoid devastating exploitation of our common, indispensable global environment, the protection and preservation of the global commons must be placed under the governance of the UN. Accordingly, world federalist movement (WFM) advocates for the establishment of a WEO.

In order for environmental and social issues to be adequately addressed in the international legal order, they will have to be given equitable legal and institutional authority. WFM therefore believes that the solution is the creation of a WEO or a 'Sustainable Development Organization' that could counterbalance the powerful finance and trade institutions. A WEO would be a designated and empowered advocate for adequate response to environmental management and sustainable development, and thus provide a more balance, effective and accountable system of global governance.

A WEO and global environmental mechanism

The developing countries are arguing strongly against the creation of a new organisation that would deal only with environmental issues.[7] The US is also strongly against the creation of a new and expensive UN institution. The same reasoning is used to counter the idea to create a World Organisation on Sustainable Development by combining and strengthening UNEP and UNDP. The mistrust towards new organisations, the lack of financial support and the unclear mandate of such a 'world government' for sustainable development are major obstacles in the discussions.

Ultimately, the establishment of a WEO must be judged by how much it increases the power of international environmental agreements to be legally binding and enforceable. As NGOs like Friends of the Earth argue, it should be ensured that powerful actors like the WTO or International Financial Institutions, but also transnational corporations comply with sustainable development agreements, including agreements promoting sustainable agriculture and food security. Many NGOs demand that sustainable development agreements should override trade and investment rules.

Global environmental mechanism

Esty and Ivanova (2002) have distinguished four basic 'governance' options:

- do nothing;
- renew the status quo governance structure;
- launch a new global environmental organisation;
- develop a new governance approach: a global environmental mechanism.

They point out that one option for strengthening GEG focuses on creating a structure that can deliver the functions needed at the global level. These proponents of a GEME argue that no bureaucratic structure can build an internal organisation with the requisite knowledge and expertise to address the wide-ranging, dynamic and interconnected problems we now face (Esty and Ivanova 2002; GEMPAG 2002). Accordingly, they argue not only for a multi-tier but also a multi-dimensional governance structure.

Esty and Ivanova (2002) argue that, a GEME could emerge in various ways, driven by functional needs. The main idea that they project is that the GEME could build upon the expertise of existing institutions and create new mechanisms where key functions were deemed to be non-existent or inadequate. They further emphasise:

> Initial elements might comprise a global information clearinghouse with mechanisms for data collection, assessment, monitoring, and analysis; a global technology clearinghouse with mechanisms for technology transfer and identification and dissemination of best practices; and a bargaining forum, along the lines proposed by Whalley and Zissimos in this volume, to facilitate deals that improve environmental quality and reconcile the interests of different parties.
>
> (p. 6)

They recommend a gradualist approach. Thus,

> It could begin with 'the art of the possible' and gradually assemble the elements of an effective institutional structure as issues and mechanisms are identified and developed, building on a core set of functions such as information provision and a mechanism for dissemination of policy and technology strategies. A GEME could expand into more ambitious domains such as bargaining, tradeoffs, norm development, and dispute settlement as (and only if) the value of those activities is demonstrated. A GEME offers a new model of governance that is light, more virtual and networked, and potentially more entrepreneurial and efficient.
>
> (p. 6)

There are many problems with such a formulation. First, it has been pointed out that 'governance' is a descriptive concept and not a normative concept. Therefore, it is not concerned with what should be done. Second, 'building on a core set of functions' is in the realm of GEM. The first step in management is to define the functions and set the objectives. Third, to speak of a 'global information clearing house' as well as a 'bargaining forum' is somewhat ambiguous. These approaches are different. Fourth, while we also may recommend a gradualist approach but what is of utmost importance is the need for clear unambiguous thinking. Fifth, a mechanism cannot be a substitute for an institution. Finally, whether the mechanism needs to be 'light' or 'heavy'; 'real' or 'virtual'; and 'potentially efficient' or 'actually equitable', depends on the perception about the nature, degree, source and seriousness of the problem of GED.

Global environmental data and information

Esty and Ivanova (2002) rightly emphasise the need for a foundation for global-scale environmental decision-making to be based on a new and coordinated programme of global environmental data gathering and information sharing. Building on existing efforts, such an initiative might focus on ensuring that a core set of baseline environmental indicators (covering air, water and land) were tracked in every country in the world on a methodologically consistent and rigorous basis that would permit cross-country comparisons. Furthermore, individual countries or regional groupings might supplement the global data set with additional metrics addressing local priorities. Information systems could reveal new policy options and lead to better decision-making, improved performance and greater efficiency through reduced uncertainty, enhanced comparative analysis and greater ability to define points of policy leverage. Data that are comparable across countries also facilitate benchmarking and the identification of best practices, creating both a spur to lagging jurisdictions and a guide for all. A more 'measured' approach to environmental problem solving would not only enhance analysis and decision-making, it would make it easier to evaluate policy and programme performance, track on-the-ground progress in addressing pollution control and natural resource management challenges, and identify successful (and unsuccessful) efforts and approaches.

We are fully in agreement with the above described thrust towards data, information and analysis. However, the following crucial elements are missing:

1   The emphasis on methodological issues in measurement.
2   The need for a composite index of GED.
3   The importance of data reduction techniques.

The last point (on data reduction) is particularly important. The approach and methodology adopted in this book are important from the point of view of the cost and practicability of building up such a mechanism. If data reduction methods are adopted it would ensure that poor countries have to invest less in data collection and maintenance. For instance, many countries may not have the means to collect satellite data. Their priorities in data collection can be determined. The reliability of the process of data gathering and storing can be improved. For methodological improvement there could be a periodic sample check to see whether the commonalities in the data are valid. This would take care of the issue of intertemporal consistency of the data collection mechanism. In our view this is a very important policy issue that no one has raised.

A number of aspects of the problem of GED are not highlighted in the developments and proposals outlined above. First and foremost the problem and the conceptualisation of GED is highly empirical in nature. Therefore, the approach towards global environmental governance or mechanism, as may be the case depends on the understanding, conceptualisation and measurement of the problem of GED. Crucial questions exist and have been raised earlier in this book. What is the nature of GED? How is it measured? What is its relationship with local phenomenon? How to form an index of GED? And so on. These questions do not find a place in the developments and proposals above. The approach taken in this book articulates a clear notion of GED. Second, our understanding of the problem of GED is that it is serious. It needs to be dealt with a heavy hand. There is no scope for 'light' solutions. Third, the source of GED is clearly identified in the 'type of economic development' and 'consumption patterns' that are spreading globally, at the cost of the global environment and more particularly at the cost of poor countries. Fourth, we have shown that the inherent inequity is not just a moral problem but is the source of the GED. Therefore, the policy issue is not about attaining an efficient growth path, and having the necessary 'efficient mechanism' to do so, but to put into effect an equitable solution (both spatially and intergenerationally) so that an efficient growth path is reached. In other words, unless global inequalities in development and consumption are reduced, or minimised, in the path of global economic development, the 'global social environmental cost' cannot be minimised. We need to arrive at a 'socially efficient path of development' not an 'entrepreneurially efficient path', when the concern is the global environment.

Three crucial questions remain, in this context:

1   What is the global social cost?
2   What is the solution?
3   How to determine the functions of the GEM?

The global social cost has to be recognised, understood and measured. We have already, in many ways demonstrated how there are vast disparities between rich and poor countries in terms of developmental variables, consumption variables and environmental variables and as to how this has serious implications for GED. Conceptually, this can be treated as an implicit subsidy to the developed countries.

The economic concept of subsidy[8] is derived from the assumption that the market allocates resources more effectively than any other mechanism, and that a government payment to the producer of a particular good reduces the private cost of the good so that it no longer reflects the social cost – the output that must be foregone in order to make the good. The result is a distortion in the resource-allocating function of the market.

The assumption that the social cost of a good should be reflected in its price is also the basis in economic theory for opposing export subsidies: subsidies allow the natural advantages possessed by one country to be offset by an artificial advantage created by another. Further, since subsidies distort relative international trade prices that would have been determined otherwise by the principle of comparative advantage, they also reduce the advantages of specialisation in international trade.

Closely related to the economic concept of subsidy is the notion of implicit subsidy discussed above. An implicit subsidy arises when the production of a good creates a negative externality – a cost imposed on society by a good or activity which is not fully reflected in the market price, because those affected are not involved in the market transaction. Thus, some of the true costs of the good's production and consumption are not borne by the producer, who receives a subsidy from those who do bear those costs. Typically, this would apply to the global environmental costs incurred by poor countries at the cost of rich countries.

What is the solution? Can these externalities be internalised? At the national level, for implementing the concept of internalisation of costs, there are four general questions to be resolved – all of them involving political choices.

1   First, how can environmental and social costs be monetised; that is, how can they be valued in money terms?

2   The second and third questions relate to how the costs, once identified, are to be collected and distributed. Taxes accrue to the government treasury, but the revenues are rarely if ever reinvested in projects that correct the problem. Gasoline taxes, for example, in theory should be reinvested in public transportation but by the time the tax policy is enacted, the public transportation components tend to be whittled away during the political process.

3   Likewise, if the costs are internalised through prices in the private sector, they may be collected by the firms but rarely if ever are they reinvested in altering production patterns. Unless the price increase is so severe as to alter consumption patterns, little is actually changed. And the political will to do so is missing.

4   Finally, if there is sufficient political will, there is a question about a transition process. If implemented so as to truly change producer and consumer behaviour, marginal consumers and marginal producers are going to fall out of the system.

Even in the US, there are very many poor people who simply cannot afford to absorb cost increases of any kind. Further, there are many small- and medium-sized entrepreneurs who find it difficult to survive without some form of assistance. If such assistance is not forthcoming there will be increased poverty and unemployment, unless safety nets are devised and financed, and increased corporate concentration in production sectors is tackled. In the absence of such measures the problem of monopolistic pricing gets aggravated and firms with significant shares of a given market are able to determine their own prices often at levels which externalises ever more costs: the exact opposite of what we are trying to accomplish.

All of this is problematic enough at the national level. Each of these questions becomes even more complex when considered globally. Market shares determine the world price for many traded goods, whether national or corporate. Many commodities are priced by producer cartels via commodity agreements.

Conclusions

The discussion in this chapter has clarified that internalisation of global environmental costs is very difficult. The natural question is as what the solution could then be. Internalisation is *post facto*. The adage 'prevention is better than cure' is most apt in this situation. Thus, Abrego and Whalley (2002) argue that 'adaptation (or behavioural responses) to the damage associated with externalities, (is) a pervasive phenomenon and (has been) ignored in literature' (p. 1). Examples of such adaptation are individuals spending more time indoors to avoid UV exposure and switching travel time to avoid rush hours. In a similar vein as we have suggested in Chapter 4 of this book, behavioural changes can come about collectively. This may lead to environmentally sustainable behaviour through the proposed 'endogenous sustainability hypothesis'.

The functions of GEM cannot be predetermined, or assumed away, by arriving at the mechanism or governance structures before understanding the crucial issues that we have outlined above. Even if a consensus is not arrived at, at least, a common approach needs to be followed for attempting to arrive at this understanding. It is only after a reasonable understanding is reached that the functions can be determined. For instance, in our understanding the foremost function of any global mechanism or institution should be to recognise and measure the gross inequalities in GED and their source. The next function should be to look for solutions for a transfer of consumption from rich to poor countries, as a medium-term solution. The third most important function should be to evolve behavioural changes.

11 Summary and conclusions

Points of departure of this book

In this book we have laid out a new approach to environmental sustainability and have called it 'The Consumption Approach'. The extant approaches are 'The Structural Approach', 'The Production Approach' and so on. There was a need for a fresh approach because we found many questions were unanswered by the existing approaches. Not only have we enunciated a new approach but we have also provided a framework for the comparison of various approaches and a critique of the framework of extant approaches (Chapter 4).

We first observed (Chapter 1) that trends in development and the environment reveal great disparities that are often assumed to be inherent in the process of globalisation. The study of such disparities is, then, an important issue. At one level the response to this question is to explore the equity angle and examine issues relating to inequality and poverty. This broad approach that emphasises social and human development[1] has often been emphasised in the literature and the human development approach has been formalised in the form of HDIs and the corresponding index along with the ranks of countries have been published periodically. The intention of HDI is to evaluate human development and reward such progress through periodic revision of rankings.

Our approach is different in many ways. First, while we are concerned about equity issues and the human dimensions of development, our primary purpose for delving into the disparities in the process of globalisation is analytical. Our understanding is that global disparities lie at the root of aggravating GED. Second, while we use the HDI and HD ranks in our analysis and modelling, in the process we are able to expose how the HDI conceals the level of environmental performance of different countries and more so, different developmental classes (Chapter 6). Our methodology relates GED to global disparities through the use of HDRs.

Third, our approach is to illuminate how globalisation has set-in motion a process by which patterns of development as well as consumption are converging and are likely to set-in a process of environmental degradation for the indefinite future (Chapter 8). Moreover, an essential part of our approach is not merely to study the cause and analytical framework of GED, but to point out that there is an urgent need for GEM (Chapter 10), whose central theme would be to address these disparities as the basis of environmental degradation. An institution like the WEO has to evolve and come to terms with this reality. Mere tinkering with treaties, conventions and permits would not provide a satisfactory solution (Chapters 9 and 10).

Our analysis reveals (Chapters 1 and 2) that global environmental conditions have changed greatly during the recent past. Along with this have come immense changes in human conditions. The population of the planet has increased sharply, consumption levels in rich OECD countries remain high and high economic growth in some developing countries holds out promise for substantial increase in their consumption levels. As a consequence the environment has been heavily drawn upon to meet a multiplicity of human needs. In many areas, the state of the environment is much more fragile and degraded than it was in the 1970s.

Thus, we could categorise the world as consisting of four major divides (UNEP 2003):

1 The environmental divide. In many countries of the OECD environmental quality is high and may indeed have improved in recent times. In contrast, the environmental quality in many parts of the developing world has deteriorated sharply. With no institutional mechanism to internalise transnational externalities an emerging threat is the sustained degradation of the global environmental commons.

2 The policy divide. There is sharp inequality between developed and developing countries in regard to both policy design and policy implementation. Whereas some developed countries are adept at both many developing countries lack the institutional capacities to formulate let alone implement policies.

3 The vulnerability divide. As argued in Chapter 2, some countries are increasingly vulnerable to environmental change. In view of existing trends, the environmental outlook for the near future appears grim for many parts of the developing world.

4 The lifestyle divide. There are large gaps in lifestyles between the developed and developing worlds. The former houses just one-fifth of the world's population but accounts for 90 per cent of total consumption whereas poverty is widely prevalent in the developing world where 1.2 billion live on less than USD 1 per day.

The four gaps – the environmental divide, the policy divide, the vulnerability divide and the lifestyle divide, are a serious threat to sustainable development. This book suggests that one component of a solution should be the redistribution of consumption from the rich to the poorer countries. It argues that it need not exacerbate environmental degradation, appropriately assessed. A complementary policy measure would be the internalisation of environmental externalities – at various levels. Incomplete internalisation – at the local, trans-boundary and international levels – is perhaps the single most important contributor to environmental problems globally. In view of the high costs associated with such lack of internalisation it is pertinent to inquire into the reasons why such internalisation is not forthcoming (Chapter 9).

A summary of conclusions

After emphasising the critical role of global disparities in environmental degradation and attainment in Chapter 1 we examine the extant consumption approaches in Chapter 2. This leads us to reviewing many existing reviews of the literature (Chapters 3 and 4). We discover that our early paper (published in 2000 and reprinted in Chapter 5 of this volume) proposed many of the conceptual planks that have been used by the models in extant literature, for example, the concept of Endogenous Sustainability Hypothesis and the role of a Social Planner (State). This analysis precedes most models relating growth to the environment.

One of the main problems with extant empirical studies that examine the relationship between economic development and the environment and are known as EKCs is that these are based on single pollutants. Clearly, the pollution structure affecting the overall level of pollution cannot be investigated with the help of these models of estimation. Our own methodology overcomes this problem.

The second concern in our methodology is about the global environment. We go on to consider the empirical evidence on these issues, related to the concept of 'EKC'. This evidence indicates that estimated EKC relationships appear to largely hold for local pollution indices, but less so for environmental and resource variables where effects occur on a global scale, such as biodiversity and carbon emissions. Many studies cast a doubt on the empirical results based on panel estimations of an 'inverted- U' relationship between per capita GDP and pollution (Chapter 4). Furthermore, their results challenge 'the existence of an overall EKC for CO_2 emissions'. In our approach this is precisely the question we address. Does a GEKC exist (Chapter 6)?

Extant growth models search for an economic rationale and an appropriate model that explains the inverted U-shaped EKC. Our criticism brings this argument full circle. Insofar as the EKC is an empirical model the prime concern should not be to build up a justification for the purported 'inverted U-shaped EKC' through a well-developed theoretical model but to verify whether the EKC really exists and, if yes, what is its shape, level and downturn, in the global context. Since environmental degradation is a global problem and environmental sustainability needs a global approach. Therefore, there is a need to conceptually define GED (Chapter 4), empirically estimate a GEKC (Chapter 6), verify its shape and finally develop the causal framework for estimating such a construct globally (Chapter 8).

Our notion of environmental sustainability (developed in Chapter 5) has underscored many shortcomings of the extant approach. But it has chosen to concentrate only on the problem of consumption reduction, leaving the spatial dimension and integration for further work. It advocates a complex strategy for attaining the reductions in consumption necessary for attaining sustainability and argues in favour of using group taxes on producers as well as consumers. Further, the tax revenues so collected are to be earmarked for spending for the purpose of the environment. The resulting lowering of the discount rate and behavioural changes would lead to a drop in the rate of increase of prices of natural resources and, therefore, to a postponement of their consumption. All these involve the design of an intermediate run policy that treats environmental goods as *merit goods* as a prelude to their (ultimately) being treated as common resources.

In the long run, it is expected that behavioural changes and well-defined property rights would set-in a social dynamics that would endogenise the process of sustainability (the Endogenous Sustainability Hypothesis). Of course, it may be necessary to introduce and withdraw both the taxes in an iterative manner because social behaviour may not irreversibly change, at one go. A distinct problem relates to the different treatment for renewable and non-renewable resources. This may be looked upon as a problem of the speed of adjustment. In the case of non-renewable resources the speed has to be faster, if such resources are essential to production. In such cases, greater reliance must be placed on exogenous changes in technology and tastes. In the case of renewable resources the expected change is essentially endogenous.

Chapter 5 has argued that current deliberations on sustainability are incomplete. This is because of two principal reasons. First, there is a somewhat narrow interpretation of sustainability in terms of reductions in consumption; the spatial dimension of stability is not considered. Second, even in the context of reductions in consumption, the literature does not make clear the crucial role of behavioural changes and transfer of property rights over natural and environmental resources from the current generations to future generations.

Chapter 6 is a core empirical chapter that has emphasised that the level of environmental degradation in different countries acts as a guide to understanding the links between such degradation and economic development. We argue the case for developing an aggregate index of such degradation and relating it to a better measure (in comparison to PCI) of economic development, namely, the HDIR. We advance a methodology involving PCA to extract information and form an index of GED. This index is then related to HDIR. Thus, the estimated model incorporates the EKC – conceived of an appropriately defined aggregate – on a global scale and relates it to a broader notion of development than per capita consumption. The estimation is done on the basis of data for environmental variables on 174 countries, drawn from *Human Development Report*, UNDP. The model relates a composite index of environmental degraders – the EDI (whose details are given in Chapter 6 along with some other estimation details) that is regressed on another composite index of development (overall – not just economic), that is, on the ranks of the HDI.

A contentious issue is that of the functional form. We have chosen a cubic form since it best fits the data. Hence, the basic model of GEKC can be written as:

$$EDI = F \text{ (HDIRs)}$$

where F is a cubic function. In Chapter 4 we argue that, the EKC is not a quadratic.

There seems to be an inverse link between HDIR ranks and EDI. The US alone has a highly disproportionate (adverse) influence on all the six environmental degradation indicators. In any design of a regulatory mechanism for GEM this factor would have to be recognised explicitly.

In the extant literature, there is no consensus about the empirical basis for the GED. The two contending views only try to verify whether or not an inverted U-shaped EKC exists. Our study argues precisely that an inverted N-shaped GEKC does indeed exist and provides empirical support for this position. We find extreme inequalities in the contribution of low, medium and high HDI country groups to GED with the low country group effectively ameliorating GED and the high-group countries exacerbating it.

Our estimation of GEKC and the related analysis makes other contributions as well. First, it provides a framework for assessing the current state of environmental degradation and its distribution worldwide and could provide inputs to a global agency like a WEO interested in monitoring environmental degradation and its geographical distribution. Second, by relating such degradation to HDI, this relationship highlights the contributions of countries with different levels of human development and assists in assigning liability. The contention that GED is essentially 'caused' by a certain type of development characteristic of high HDI countries is borne out by our results. Any comprehensive international environmental agreement must reckon with this inequality in GED and its intrinsic relationship with inequalities across countries in levels of economic development.

The 2002 ESI is a contending index to our Environmental Degradation Index. The ESI has been developed by collaboration of the World Economic Forum, Geneva, Centre for International Earth Science Information Network, Columbia University, and Yale Center for Environmental Law and Policy, New Haven and is a measure of the overall progress towards environmental sustainability developed for 142 countries. It has aroused considerable controversy. In Chapter 7 we argue that the basic design of the ESI leaves much to be desired. It has conceptual problems in its visualisation of environmental degradation and sustainability. The choice of variables and the statistical methodology of compiling the index are found to be wanting. The chapter proposes an alternative methodology using PCA and argued that this is an improvement upon the ESI methodology. The results of the improved methodology when applied to the same data set as the 2002 ESI, give almost opposite results! Given the likely use of aggregate environmental indices in future environmental management, the critique advanced in this chapter is of considerable significance.

The causal framework of the GEKC is built-up (Chapter 8) and an alternative HDI index based on consumption is used to develop a GEKC based on consumption. The consumption-based HDI only further confirms the fact that rich countries are responsible for GED. A simultaneous equations model explains the causal structure that is responsible for GED. Further, with Canonical Discriminant Analysis it has been shown that GED does not have geophysical basis but an anthropogenic basis. As part of the system of equations a Global Consumption Function has been estimated, which shows the alarming fact that, poor countries have already imbibed the consumption patterns of rich countries. In net, the chapter shows that a certain 'type of development' that characterises high-income countries is primarily responsible for GED.

Trans-boundary and international environmental problems are a pressing concern for the global community and call for innovative institutional design to address them. Whereas the developed countries value the international environment highly, they realise that some of the solutions must originate within the geographic boundaries of developing countries. However, developing countries do not appear to have these problems high on their agendas at least at first glance. More important appear to be economic growth and domestic environmental concerns. However, it is also true that not addressing global environmental problems could hurt, in specific areas, developing country economic growth and their domestic environmental problems. But, the fundamental fact of the indivisibility of the growth and environmental agendas in the developing countries has to be faced.

Since the developed countries seem to consider global environmental problems as an emergent issue and since some developing countries will soon become major contributors to this problem, it would be necessary to have the foresight to conclude a treaty at an early date. This would mean that developing countries would have to be persuaded and provide enough incentives to enter into international environmental negotiations and remain committed to this process.

In this context Chapter 9 has argued that since developing countries have considerable environmental assets, they should probably look for linking slowing-down the depletion of these assets to other areas of linkage to the developed countries. In particular, this would include international trade, transfer of technology and, perhaps, direct transfers. Since this linkage would be very wide ranging, it would be necessary to exploit any positive external effects that might flow from some treaties and avoid duplication and conflicts in others. It makes sense, therefore, to have a WEO to coordinate these efforts.

But what version of a WEO is to be opted for is, at this point in time, an open question. Clearly, a mild version of a WEO that brings all environmental treaties under one umbrella, provides technical know-how and facilitates negotiations would be innocuous enough and, therefore, acceptable. However, such a WEO would also not be very effective in controlling the problem of global externalities, assuming that this problem is of an emergent nature. Stronger versions of a WEO would not be acceptable to many developing countries unless issue linkage of the sort discussed here becomes a reality. Before that is achieved, given the past experience of developing countries with MEA, the WEO would have to build considerable credibility as an organisation that is truly interested in global environmental problems, is sensitive to the needs of developing countries and is not acting as a mechanism for imposing the will of the developed countries on developing countries.

The task of controlling global external effects is complex, not the least because this has to be accomplished by voluntary action of nation states. A properly designed WEO could be a central element of a successful strategy to place the generation of global external effects on a sustainable path. This chapter has espoused the developing country point of view on this and substantiated the window of opportunity that exists at present. It is another matter that this window may start closing sooner rather than later – but that is an issue beyond the scope of this chapter, indeed this book.

A number of aspects of the problem of GED are not highlighted in the developments and proposals outlined in extant literature regarding global governance

(Chapter 10). First and foremost the problem and the conceptualisation of GED is highly empirical by nature. Therefore, the approach towards global environmental governance or mechanism, as may be the case depends on the understanding, conceptualisation and measurement of the problem of GED. Crucial questions exist and have been raised earlier in this book. What is the nature of GED? How is it measured? What is its relationship with local phenomenon? How to form an index of GED? And so on. These questions do not find a place in the extant developments and proposals. Second, our analysis of GED shows that it is a serious problem and needs to be dealt with as such. Third, the source of GED is clearly identified in the 'type of economic development' and 'consumption patterns' that are spreading globally, at the cost of the global environment and more particularly at the cost of poor countries. Fourth, we have shown that the inherent inequity is not just a moral problem but is the source of the GED. Therefore, the policy issue is not one of attaining an efficient growth path, and having the necessary 'efficient mechanism' to do so, but to affect an equitable solution (both spatially and intergenerationally) so that an efficient growth path is reached. In other words, unless global inequalities in development and consumption are removed, or minimised, in the path of global economic development, the 'global social environmental cost' cannot be minimised. We need to arrive at a 'socially efficient path of development' not an 'entrepreneurially efficient path', when the concern is the global environment.

Some remaining issues

Three crucial questions remain:

1   What is the global social cost?
2   What is the solution?
3   How to determine the functions of the GEM?

In essence these three questions have to be resolved by further research. For instance, the global social cost has to be recognised, understood and measured. We have already demonstrated that there are vast disparities between rich and poor countries in terms of developmental variables, consumption variables and environmental variables, and the serious implications these have for GED. Conceptually, this can be treated as an implicit subsidy to the developed countries. Quantifying this subsidy and understanding its incidence are important problems before the global community.

What is the solution – for instance can these externalities be internalised? At the national level, for implementing the concept of internalisation of costs, there are four general questions to be resolved – all of them involving political choices.

1   First, how can environmental and social costs be monetised; that is, how can they be valued in money terms?
2   The second and third questions relate to how the costs, once identified, are to be collected and distributed. Taxes accrue to the government treasury, but the

revenues are rarely if ever reinvested in projects that correct the problem. Gasoline taxes, for example, in theory should be reinvested in public transportation but by the time the tax policy is enacted, the public transportation components tend to be whittled away during the political process.

3   Likewise, if the costs are internalised through prices in the private sector, they may be collected by the firms but rarely if ever are they reinvested in altering production patterns. Unless the price increase is so severe as to alter consumption patterns, little is actually changed. Further the political will to do so is missing.

4   Finally, even if there is sufficient political will, there is a question about the transition process. If implemented so as to truly change producer and consumer behaviour, marginal consumers and marginal producers may drop out of the system.

All of this is problematic enough at the national level. Each of these questions becomes even more complex at the global level. Market shares determine the world price for many traded goods, whether national or corporate. Many commodities are priced by producer cartels via commodity agreements.

Part of the solution may lie in effecting behavioural changes. In Chapter 4 we suggest that behavioural changes can come about collectively. This may lead to environmentally sustainable behaviour through the proposed Endogenous Sustainability Hypothesis. However, this cannot be construed to be an adequate solution – even if it works.

The functions of GEM cannot be predetermined, or assumed away (Chapter 10), by arriving at the mechanism or governance structures before understanding the crucial issues that we have outlined above. Even if a consensus is not arrived at, at least, a common approach needs to be followed for attempting to arrive at this understanding. It is only after a reasonable understanding is reached that the functions can be determined. In our understanding the foremost function of any global mechanism or institution should be to recognise and measure the gross inequalities in GED and their source. The next function should be to look for solutions for a transfer of consumption from rich to poor countries, as a medium-term solution. And, the third most important function should be to evolve behavioural changes.

A final word about the advantages of our approach

Finally, we come back to a central theme that we have laid out in Chapter 4. We had proposed a framework for the assessment of different approaches to environmental sustainability, on a comparative basis. The efficacy of different approaches is sought to be evaluated with the help of the following criteria:

1   ability to explain the 'stylised facts'
2   simplicity
3   consistency with economic theory
4   plausibility

As per our understanding the stylised facts are as follows:

1   The consumption levels are phenomenally higher in developed countries, in absolute and relative terms, as compared to developing countries, as a class.
2   The level of environmental degradation, as measured by a set of environmental degraders, is also much higher, in the case of developed countries, as a class, in absolute and relative terms.
3   There is a high degree of correlation amongst these environmental degraders, in general.
4   There is a convergence of consumptions patterns across the globe, as between developed and developing countries.
5   There is a convergence of the 'type of economic development', with the advent of globalisation, as between developed and developing countries.
6   Finally, all the above 'stylised facts' have a bearing on global environmental sustainability.

While this could be a matter of further study and is open to discussion, in conclusion we can say that, our Consumption Approach to Environmental Sustainability may not be a simpler approach because it takes into account interconnectedness and the composite nature of GED (Chapters 4 and 6). It must, however, be noted that we have shown how GED is by nature a complex problem. Another complexity about our approach is that it establishes the link from consumption to GED through an elaborate framework. Other approaches are simpler because they tend to explain the phenomenon of GED on the basis of single pollutants. We have argued though that, in doing so they essentially miss the point. In contrast, our approach is able to explain the 'stylised facts' better, both in with the help of a better methodology (Chapters 4 and 6) (than other indices like the 2002 ESI which uses a simplistic method (Chapter 7)) and with the help of a sound conceptual and causal framework (Chapters 1–6 and 8). It is also closer to received economic theory because it is the only approach that provides certain mesoeconomic structures (TCC and PCC – Chapter 2) and axiomatic and behavioural analysis (Utility analysis – Chapter 4) that arise out of economic theory. Thus, it scores over extant approaches in terms of explanatory power and consistency. About plausibility it can be said that while other approaches are also plausible, the overwhelming data and empirical evidence (Chapters 1 and 2) shows that consumption is an all-pervasive basis for environmental degradation, which in a sense, subsumes (Chapter 4) all other approaches like the production or technology approach.

Thus, in contrast to the extant literature, the approach taken in this book rests on philosophically more robust ground, has a broader vision of environmental degradation and is better able to relate such degradation to historical and current patterns of economic development. We hope this signals progress in addressing one of the most important questions facing the global community.

Notes

1 Global disparity and environmental sustainability

1 The ecological economics approach is, in general, wary of both these methods.
2 Hoti *et al.* (2004) feel that there should be only one environmental sustainability index because it would create risk and uncertainty if there were many such indices. After quoting our Critique of The Environmental Sustainability Index (Chapter 7 of this book) they ignore and misinterpret all what has been said therein, so as to justify such a conclusion. It is unfortunate that even *Environmental Sustainability Index 2005 Report* (published by World Economic Forum *et al.*) neatly avoids any reference (see Appendix H of ESI Report 2005) to our criticism of their ESI 2002 (which has received wide publicity (see OECD-EC Joint Research Centre: farmweb.jrc.cec.eu.int/ci/CI_Env0001.htm – 10k)).
3 We have mostly used Reports of 1999 and 2000. These were the latest reports available at the time of studying some of our core chapters.
4 Any attempt at using better econometric techniques such as panel regression and GLS estimation would further iron out the differences.
5 The authors were investigators in a joint project supported by MacArthur Foundation (USA), whose intention was to study the possibility of the formation of The World Environment Organization. The authors are thankful to the Foundation for their support but the present work is based on our own views and not that of either the MacArthur Foundation or the erstwhile group that was spread over five countries and various continents, namely, UK, Australia, Argentina, India and USA.
6 Of late, a new type of paper that is made from cotton waste is being manufactured and supplied, by India, to super chain stores in USA. This is, however, handmade paper and is not a substitute for superfine paper.
7 One ton of newspaper is the equivalent of 19 pine trees.
8 See relevant chapters in this book for HDI methodology and Sagar and Najam (1998) for a critique of the Human Development Index.
9 The weight is the actual forest area of each country.
10 The frequent fires in summer in the dry continent of Australia have been partially attributed to the unsuitable vegetation of the forests that have developed there.
11 The data analysis has not been reflected as tables for conserving space but the above data in the description summarises all the trends.

2 Consumption and sustainable development: an overview

1 This section contains the basic principles and background. A more complete analysis appears in Chapter 5.
2 Formally, there exists a distinction between international and global production. While international production refers to production across borders, global production refers to the production of a global product. Global products have standardised features

across the world. Nike shoes, Ray Ban glasses or McDonald hamburgers would be typical examples of global products. In the above analysis this distinction has not been adhered to very strictly.

3   Wal-Mart – the biggest retail chain store uses real-time software (VMI) for maintaining DDSN (Demand Determined Supply Networks).

4   The time is not far when Alvin Toffler's construct – the 'prosumer' (where the consumers virtually dictates to the producer, the design of products and production plans, according to their tastes and preferences), may become a reality.

5   This can easily be identified by advertisement campaigns, like 'Now available in India' or 'You have been waiting for it'.

6   Trade is concerned with profit, trade and economic growth of human beings only and not the entire earth system (the biosphere), including all the species.

7   See Antweiler *et al.* (1998) on free trade and the environment. Also see, Suri and Chapman (1998) on trade pattern and EKC.

8   Some studies attempt to relate the EKC to trade issues (Hettige *et al.* 1992).

9   It is also known as the Second Law of Thermodynamics. Rees (1990) clarifies that 'The Second Law states that in any closed isolated system, available energy and matter are continuously and irrevocably degraded to the unavailable state'.

10 Rothman (1998) also makes out a case for a consumption-based approach to the EKC.

11 In Chapter 5 we discuss a number of definitions of sustainability.

12 Some studies have, however, attempted to highlight the relationship between poverty and the environment (Broad 1994).

13 As indicated above Arrow *et al.* (2004) clearly indicate that their interest is only in the intertemporal aspects of sustainability.

14 World Bank (1992) first used this term.

15 Ekins (1997), de Bruyn (1997a), de Bruyn and Opschoor (1997) – attribute de-linking to at least, de-pollution and dematerialisation.

16 Stern *et al.* (1996) argue that in any attempt to estimate the EKC, corrections for heteroscedasticity need to be made. We address this problem.

3   Methodological issues: a review

1   The initial portion of our review of reviews is mainly based on Bond and Farzin (2004).

2   Since this review chapter overlaps with other chapters there may be some repetition. This became necessary for two reasons; one, certain chapters are already published and hence, could not be edited and two, for the flow of the argument.

3   The simple model which uses the general approach (wherein some pollutant(s) have been studied over time for one country or some countries) has been discussed in Chapter 2. To avoid repetition these are being avoided in this chapter unless some methodological issues are explicitly involved.

4   See for example, Uzawa (1965), Lucas (1988), Rebelo (1991) and Caball'e and Santos (1993). Andreoni and Levinson (2001) and Pfaff *et al.* (2001a,b) develop static models to explain the EKC. Static models tend to simplify the analysis, but may lead to policy recommendations that are not effective in a dynamic set-up, as shown by Stokey (1998) and Chimeli and Braden (2002).

5   Theoretical foundations for the EKC hypothesis have been proposed on the ground of the short-run transitional dynamics generated into neoclassical growth models (Kelly 2003; Tahvonen and Kuuluvainen 1993), as well as in models of endogenous growth where pollution is decoupled from the engine of growth under the premise that not every increase in output due to technological advances will lead to increased pollution (Byrne 1997).

6   Alternative foundations for the EKC hypothesis may be found in Jones and Manuelli (2001). They study a dynamic overlapping generations model. McConnell (1997),

Munasinghe (1999) or Andreoni and Levinson (2001) study this phenomenon in static models.

7 Specific references to models have been avoided in certain cases for reasons of brevity. Interested readers may refer to the concerned works included in the discussion above.

4 Global environmental degradation: concept and methodology of measurement

1 The initial discussion is once again in the nature of a review of reviews, for the reasons quoted in the last chapter. This review is based on recent papers by Dijkgraaf and Vollebergh (2001), Stern (2003), Stavins and Pfaff (1999) Yandle *et al.* (2004), Strand (2002), Borghesi (1999), Dasgupta *et al.* (2002).

2 The techniques of estimation may include non-parametric methods data reduction methods and so on. These are discussed separately.

3 The problems with their work are listed in Chapter 8.

4 de Groot (1999) states, 'No agreement has for example been reached on the usefulness of pooled-cross section estimates (e.g. de Bruyn *et al.* 1998) and the type of conditioning variables one should take into account' (p. 8).

5 Coondoo and Dinda (2002), Day and Grafton (2003), de Bruyn (2000), Stern and Common (2001), Perman and Stern (2003), Friedl and Getzner (2003), Heil and Selden (1999, 2001) are regarded by Stern as good examples of econometrically sound studies.

6 Ekins (1997), Harbaugh *et al.* (2000), Jha and Murthy (2003a), Jha and Whalley (2001) and Perman and Stern (2003).

7 This argument is akin to that of growth models, where K^* (the optimal capital stock) is determined at the point where there is a maximisation of per capita consumption.

8 'Trans-boundary pollution has been over-emphasised in literature, as the cause of GED. So it must be pointed out that it is responsible only for the spread of pollution and would nevertheless remain only one of the factors responsible for GED, not the entire 'cause'.

9 It can be shown that the error of prediction, in general, is orthogonal to the regression line.

5 Sustainability: behaviour, property rights and economic growth

This chapter was first published in *Proceedings of the World Congress on Management and Measuring Sustainable Development*, Toronto 2000. We are grateful to Germain Dufour for permission to reprint this article and to John Whalley for helpful comments.

1 It would be unwise to interpret the notion of sustainability to imply a universal decline in current consumption for at least two reasons: (i) it would be meaningless to ask for cuts in the consumption levels of the vast numbers of the poor spread across different parts of the world, especially Asia and Africa; and (ii) if the EKC has any relevance (see, for example, Grossman and Krueger 1995) growth in per income and consumption of the currently poor countries may ultimately have a beneficial impact on the environment.

2 Suffice it to say here that Jha *et al.* (1999) and Jha and Whalley (1999) have shown that there is considerable room for welfare enhancement through such consumption switching. They have, however, not linked this switch to the notion of sustainability.

3 At the risk of being repetitive, we state that this definition is seen to apply to countries that are seen to be consuming 'excessively' and to not have any spatial dimensions.

4 Our lack of enthusiasm for the Coase process should be tempered with the realisation that there can be a government failure to match the market failure. Apart from the problems of excess burden of taxation (Jha 1998, Chapter 5) there is the notion that the government may not be able to internalise all internal effects effectively, Jha (1998, Chapter 6).

5 An important example of these is multilateral externalities, Jha (1998, Chapter 5). The Coase process implicitly assumes that all externalities are bilateral.
6 These models typically define a Net Welfare Measure (NWM) as dNWM.dt = $r(\mu_1K+\mu_2R)$ where K is the capital stock, R the natural resource, and μ_1 and μ_2 their respective marginal social valuations. Sustainability is attained whenever NWM > 0.
7 Dinwiddy and Teal (1996) have analysed the issue of reduction in the pure rate of time preference in a two-period model. They define:

$$dC_1/dC_0 = -(1+\delta)[1+\beta g] = -(1+i)$$

dC_1/dC_0 = marginal rate of substitution between present and future consumption; δ = rate of pure time preference; β = elasticity of marginal utility of consumption; g = rate of growth of consumption; $-(1+i)$ = slope of intertemporal preference function; and i is the consumption rate of interest. It can be shown that if $i = 0$, consumption is divided equally between two periods. If it is positive there is greater consumption at present and if it is negative consumption it is greater in the future. However, it may not be possible to reverse the rate of time preference so as to treat future consumption as preferable to present. This is because the consumption rate of interest equals the marginal productivity of capital (rk), that determines the transformation rate between present and future output. If the capital market is perfect it would also equal the market rate of interest (rm). That is, i, rk and rm, are all equal in equilibrium. Obviously, there cannot be a negative rk or rm. Hence, i can never be negative. Nevertheless, it could be possible to depress the consumption rate of interest by treating the rate of pure time preference, perhaps to *zero*. *This implies intergenerational equity* (Dinwiddy and Teal 1996, p. 260). The consumption rate of interest would now represent *the social rate of discount since it takes account of the needs of the future generation*. Yet, there would be a positive consumption rate of interest that would still ensure the tangency of the preference function and the 'price line' between present and future consumption. The price of future consumption in terms of the present can be derived from the welfare measure, with present marginal utility of consumption as the numeraire. Of course, certain behavioural questions remain. For instance, will the present generation reduce the consumption rate of interest?
8 In overlapping generation models, Blanchard and Fischer (1989) point out that the preferences of the yet unborn may not be reflected in the present market transactions. They conclude that despite mutual altruism the market solution need not necessarily be dynamically efficient. It cannot generally be said that the market rate of interest would be less than or equal to the social rate of discount. They point out the need for a social planner (a Super Stalin, who would attribute the same weight to all generations and would maximise the social welfare) if the present generation does not care for the next generation. This proposal about social welfare maximisation is not pursued and no framework for property rights is provided. But this approach has the merit of recognising that there is a need for intervention.
9 Institutional change could involve private co-operative arrangements such as car pools, garbage disposal, arrangements for exploitation of natural resources, increasing role of NGOs in decision processes involving environmental matters. These could be backed with changes in tastes, development of backstop technologies (Kolstad and Krautkraemer 1993) and so on.

6 An inverse Global Environmental Kuznets Curve

1 We are grateful to two anonymous referees for their helpful comments, the editors for their extensive comments and encouragement, the John D. and Catherine T. MacArthur Foundation for their financial support and John Whalley and D. Rukmini for their helpful discussions. All remaining errors are ours. (Reprinted from Jha, R. and Murthy, K.V.B. (2003a) 'An Inverse Global Environmental Kuznets Curve', *Journal of Comparative Economics*, 31: 352–68, Copyright (2003), with permission from Elsevier).

2 Kuznets (1955) found a similar inverted U-shaped relationship between inequality and economic growth.

3 Some studies attempt cross-country estimation, for example, Grossman and Krueger (1995), Shafik and Bandyopadhya (1992) and Selden and Song (1994).

4 Jha and Whalley (2001) argue that the notion of the EKC for any given country is tenuous, at best.

5 Two studies consider changes in this level. Lopez (1994) finds that even in the most open economies, the pollution intensity falls with income but the absolute level of pollution rises. Hetttige *et al.* (1998) find that absolute levels of water pollution rise through the middle-income countries and remain stable thereafter. However, both studies focus on pollutants and do not consider the wider phenomenon of GED developed in this chapter.

6 Data limitations require that we define the GED to cover the 174 countries included in the HDI.

7 GED is defined more precisely below. At this point, it is sufficient that GED is a monotonically increasing function of the EDIs.

8 Entropy is the Second Law of Thermodynamics. This implies that, in any closed isolated system, available energy and matter are continuously and irrevocably degraded to the unavailable state. See Daly and Townsend (1993), Georgescu-Roegen (1971) and Ekins (1993).

9 Ekins (1997), de Bruyn (1997b), de Bruyn *et al.* (1998) and de Bruyn and Opschoor (1997) attribute de-linking to de-pollution and dematerialization.

10 Some studies highlight the relationship between poverty and the environment, for example, Broad (1994).

11 We carried out auxiliary regressions with each variable used in the analysis as the dependent variable, in turn, and the remaining ones as independent variables. We found a high degree of multicollinearity among degraders. The results are available from Jha (2003).

12 The error of prediction, in general, is orthogonal to the regression line so that there is no such loss in the PCA methodology used here because the components are orthogonal to each other.

13 Lewis-Beck (1994) provides a full treatment of PCA.

14 Lewis-Beck (1994) argues that care must be taken about the scale and code of variables.

15 The SPSS package provides for substitute means for missing values from neighbouring data points.

16 The interactive model is restricted to the maximum number of countries in the smallest class, that is, LHD.

17 The scree plots are available on request from Jha (on request).

18 The complete results of the rotated component analysis are available from Jha (on request). Three problems occur with unrotated components. First, using unrotated components leads us to retain four variables (PAPCM, $PCCO_2$, CO_2SH and DEFOR) that are not comparable to the four that are retained with rotated components (PCFWW, PAPCM, $PCCO_2$ and CO_2SH). Hence, the indexes formed are not comparable in the two cases. Second, with unrotated weights, the retained variables have less significance than the one that is dropped so that the index formed by unrotated weights has lower overall significance. Third, the variables retained in the rotated variables case represent water degradation, paper consumption and CO_2 emissions and discard the relatively unimportant deforestation variable. Thus, an index based on rotated components is more representative.

19 Hence, the total variation explained was four, one each for each of the retained variables, and $(0.32)^2 + (0.47)^2$ for the discarded variables. The sum is 4.326 so that explained variation is (4.326/6)*100, that is, 72.10 per cent. On the other hand, if only three retained principal components were used, the total variation explained would have been 68.75 per cent.

20 In light of the high correlation between the HDI index and PCI, the informational superiority of HDI is sometimes questioned. There are several reasons for using the

HDI. First, HDI, a priori, has additional information because it is based on social variables. Second, the PCI component of HDI is discounted exponentially (Anand and Sen 1999). Thus, income at the higher level is suppressed. Third, the correlation between PCI and HDI index is not high with R^2 equal to 0.42. However, the rank correlation is high with R^2 equal to 0.86. This contradiction arises because the high-income countries have a compensating variation in social indicators. Fourth, the equation using HDI has a higher adjusted R^2 compared to the one using PCI as the dependent variable.

21 The quadratic relationship is a better fit than the linear one but the adjusted R^2 is only 0.66 whereas it is 0.76 in the cubic form. We test for the significance of the coefficients using t-tests as well as χ-squared tests based on the statistic $\lambda = 2(\log (L_U) - \log (L_R))$, where L_U is the unrestricted likelihood function and L_R is the likelihood with restriction(s). Under the null hypothesis that the relevant r coefficients are zero, λ is distributed as a $\chi2$ with r degrees of freedom. Each of the coefficients is strongly significant according to this test.

22 The use of HDIR rather than HDI is justified on several grounds. First, using ranks ensures that the contribution of each single country is identified. Second, the fit is better with HDIR than with HDI as the adjusted R^2 is 0.76 vs. 0.71. Third, differences between HDI are sometimes very small and of the order of the second decimal place. Heggestad and Rhoades (1976) provide another application using ranks.

23 We are indebted to the editor for suggesting the use of the Lorenz curve. The range of the EDI is different in Figure 6.2 from that in Figure 6.1 because Figure 6.1 graphs predicted EDI whereas Figure 6.2 graphs actual EDI.

7 A critique of the environmental sustainability index

1 The ESI report compares nine indices with the ESI. See table 9, *ESI 2002 Report*, p. 19.
2 In Chapter 8 we report on our analysis of the EKC in a global context.
3 We have tested their raw variables to confirm this (Table 7.2).
4 See Dunteman in Lewis-Beck (1994). We report results on PCA here.

8 A consumption-based human development index and the Global Environmental Kuznets curve

1 The early discussion is based on Rothman (1998).
2 The subsequent volumes of the *Human Development Report* did not contain specific variables that were of interest to us.
3 Lewis-Beck (1994) (an authority on Factor Analysis) argues that care must be taken about the scale and code of variables.
4 SPSS package was used for estimation. It provides for substitute means being used for missing values. Neighbouring data points were used for generating these substitute means. In any case, there were very few missing data points.
5 This discussion is postponed until the analysis of discriminants.
6 Such results have not been reported. Interested readers can obtain these from Jha.

9 Political economy of global environmental governance

1 Some provision is present in Article XX of GATT, now in force through WTO.
2 The Committee on Trade and Environment (CTE) of the WTO has noted that of the 200 MEAs currently in force, only 20 contain trade provisions. In addition, no disputes have thus far come to the WTO regarding a trade provision in an MEA. The CTE at the Singapore Ministerial Conference stated that it fully supported multilateral solutions to global and trans-boundary environmental problems. See WTO (1999).

3 These other concerns include the social clauses on labour standards, use of child labour, protection, health and safety of plant, animal and human life, and so on.

4 Thus, WEO Variant 1 would be a minimal negotiation facilitation arrangement, with no activist attempts to seek out possible agreements, or to actively promote deal-making. WEO Variant 2 would effectively be the WEO-I plus some incremental elaborations such as more aggressive pursuit of environmental deal-making by the WEO Council, explicit binding of minimum standards in existing environmental agreements. This could also provide a framework for exchanges of concessions on standards in the environmental area, beyond the environment deal-making highlighted above. WEO Variant 3 would be the WEO 2 plus further add on elements, for example, an arbitration/mediation facility for possible conflicts over non-environmental arrangements (trade/WTO, for instance) is one possibility.

5 The WTO Director-General while inaugurating the WTO High-Level Symposium on Trade and the Environment on 15 March 1999, called for the creation of a WEO as an institutional and legal counterpart to the WTO. He also emphasised that the WTO is a strong ally of sustainable development and cited a recent ruling by the Appellate Body that the WTO does not stand in the way of environmental protection.

6 Notwithstanding this trade-off, many developing countries are signatories to a large number of MEAs. This might be indicative of three factors: (i) developing countries consider these MEA to be non-intrusive in their development strategies; (ii) the costs of adhering to the terms of the agreements are not unduly high for them; or (iii) as in the case of the Montreal Protocol, a coalition of OECD countries offered enough incentives for joining and enough penalties for not joining that developing countries found it in their best interest to sign on.

7 This is what Whalley and Zissimos (2002a) call WEO I. Stronger versions of the WEO might run the risk of becoming a new pressurising agency.

8 For example, the developed country most interested in reducing the level of deforestation in any given developing country may not be able to offer much inducements in the form of trade concessions since the volume of trade between these two countries may be small. Or, it may be the case that such unilateral trade concessions may not be possible if the developed country has other international trade ties (e.g. it is a member of the EU).

9 The WEO, as an environmental organisation, would have to be seen to be of relevance to the environmental problems of developing countries. By the year 2020, a majority of the developing country population will be in cities. High population density, heavy traffic congestion, and high levels of air pollution and slum proliferation characterise these cities. The traffic-related problems range from inadequate infrastructure, low fuel emission standards leading to excessive lead and CO_2 levels and loss of man-hours in slow-moving traffic. Since the WEO would be dealing with environmental issues, it would need to demonstrate that it would be able to help ameliorate these problems, either directly or indirectly.

10 In a background paper the CTE has itself argued that in well-functioning market-based economies, prices register the relative scarcity of resources and consumer preferences and help allocate resources efficiently. This resource allocation role is undermined if prices do not reflect environmental concerns as they do not in the context of many developing countries. 'Distorted prices obscure the abundance of underutilised environmental resources, contribute to the excessive depletion of exhaustible resources, generate new environmental problems and contribute to the excessive use of environmentally damaging inputs'. See WTO (1999).

11 A number of studies have found that direct and targeted subsidies are better ways of subsidising the poor than tampering with the price mechanism. See, for example, Stuijvenberg (1996).

12 Some examples are the GATT agreement on intellectual property rights, labour standards and the social clause.

13 Having said this, however, it should be recognised that most of the cases that have so far been considered within the ambit of Article XX have involved only developed countries. Three cases have involved developing countries. In the case of the Mexican tuna (1991) and the India–Malaysia–Pakistan–Thailand shrimp case (1997) the WTO appellate ruled in favour of the developing countries and against the developed country (the US in both cases). Only in the case of Thai cigarettes (1990) has the appellate ruled against a developing country. But the developing country harbours the feeling, justified or not, that Article XX has the potential of being used against them. Part of this arises from the US unilaterally taking action in all three cases without going through the WTO.

14 It is interesting to note that the CTE of the WTO has not favoured the participation of NGOs in their deliberations. The main argument in favour of this is the primary responsibility for informing the public and establishing relations with NGOs lies at the national level. In the case of trade agreements, there are well-known pressure groups which would pressurise national governments. In the case of environmental agreements the benefits would be much more diffused. Hence the NGOs could play a more important role in garnering public support and monitoring the progress in policy formulation of national governments.

15 Some tentative estimates exist of the cost to some developing countries of reducing CO_2 emissions. A complete answer would depend upon the policy measures to be adopted in future to switch among alternative sources of energy. For example, coal-based energy sources are more carbon intensive than oil-based source. In the case of India, Parikh *et al.* (1996) find that India's GDP loss would be of the order of 1.3 per cent in the year 2020 if the CO_2 constraint of 20 per cent reduction operates on a *cumulative* basis. On the other hand, if CO_2 constraint of 20 per cent operates on an *annual* basis, GDP loss rises to 3.7 per cent. Moreover, the effects are non-linear: long-term GDP loss turns out to be 0.5, 1.3 and 4.1 per cent and the number of absolute poor rises by 2.1, 5.9 and 17.5 per cent in the year 2020 corresponding to cumulative reduction in CO_2 emissions over the BAU scenario of 10, 20 and 30 per cent, respectively. They then estimate the level of compensation required in the form of additional capital flows to neutralise the loss in welfare due to carbon reduction of 30 per cent. The results indicate that foreign inflows ranging between 0.3 and 0.9 per cent of India's projected GDP could meet CO_2 reduction of 30 per cent without sacrificing welfare (in terms of consumption profile) over the BAU scenario. In absolute terms, this amounts to requiring large additional flows of foreign capital: of the order of US$D 87 to 278 billion over a 35-year period. For China, Zhang (1998) concludes that with business-as-usual CO_2 emissions for China in 2010 would be 2.46 times the level in 1990. If one wants a 20–30 per cent reduction in this level relative to the predicted emission in 2010 the loss would be 1.5–2.8 per cent of the GDP in 2010. The welfare loss in Hicksian terms would be comparable. This loss rises at a rising non-linear rate as emission cuts are increased. Thus, at a conservative level, the extent of compensation (for 20–30 per cent reduction in CO_2) could be expected to vary approximately between 2 and 3 per cent of GDP for the major developing countries of Asia: China and India. This is a huge amount and calling for sacrifices of this magnitude, without compensation, from such poor countries seems not only wrong but also impractical. However, most countries would suffer in the long run to some extent by global warming of GHGs. Thus, there would, in general, be a cost of not joining a coalition aimed at controlling carbon emission. A country would resort to long-term free riding only when the benefit–cost ratio of remaining outside a coalition is higher compared to the ratio for joining it. Xepapadeas and Yiannanka (1997) thus note that even China and India would gain by voluntarily joining a coalition that aims at controlling carbon emission at 1990 level over a 100-year time horizon. For several developing Asian economies, the compensation mechanism we touched upon earlier might be needed for a shorter duration of one generation or so, assuming, of course, that the earth can wait for so long to control CO_2 emissions.

16 Again we refer to a version of the WEO stronger than WEO-I.

17 In a recent paper Abrego *et al.* (1997) use a global numerical simulation model to show that this kind of linkage is inferior, from the point of view of developing countries, to a situation in which bargaining is accompanied by cash side payments. Hence, we need to pursue the possibility of actual trade concessions with side payments.

10 Issues in global environmental management

1 This discussion is based on World Resources Institute's Report with the input and advice of its publication partners (UN Environment Programme, UN Development Programme and World Bank), but final views are those of WRI. We also draw upon Esty and Ivanova (2002), Whalley and Zissimos (2002a), Biermann and Bauer (2005) and Kanie and Haas (2004), amongst others.
2 Jha and Murthy (2003b) provide a complex structure on how various elements, including grassroot workers can be incorporated into an overall governance structure of a proposed WEO and how it can perform various functions, including information warehousing.
3 Esty and Ivanova (2002) alternately use global environmental organisation as 'a new governance approach', 'global-scale environmental architecture' and 'a global environmental mechanism'.
4 Peter J. Newell and David I. Levy (2005) emphasise this aspect of global governance.
5 http://en.wikipedia.org/wiki/Global_governance#endnote_WeissThakur.
6 The involvement of the authors of this book in issues of global governance has come about by virtue of undertaking an international project supported by MacArthur Foundation Project, whose intention was to study the possibility of the formation of the WEO. The offer of the project was consequent to the above involvement of MacArthur Foundation. This is our claim to being part of the debate on global environmental governance.
7 Some of the problems associated with this have been pointed out in Chapter 9.
8 This discussion is based on Porter (1996).

11 Summary and conclusions

1 See *Human Development Report* 1998 and World Development Indicators 2001 for this approach.

References

Abramovitz, J. and A. Martoon (1999) 'Paper cuts: Recovering the paper Landscape', Worldwatch Paper 149, Washington, DC.

Abrego, L. and Whalley, J. (2002) 'Adaptation, Internalization and Environmental Damage', Working Paper, NBER, Cambridge, MA, May.

Abrego, L., Perroni, C., Whalley, J. and Wigle, R. (1997) 'Trade and Environment: Bargaining Outcomes from Linked Negotiations', NBER Working Paper No. 6216.

ADB (Asian Development Bank) (1997) *Emerging Asia: Changes and Challenges*, Manila: Asian Development Bank.

Alewell, C., Manderscheid, B., Meesenburg, H. and Bittersohl, J. (2000) 'Is Acidification Still an Ecological Threat?' *Nature*, 407(6806): 856–58, October.

Amalric, F. (1995) 'Population Growth and the Environmental Crisis: Beyond the Obvious', in *The North, the South and the Environment: Ecological Concerns and the Global Economy*, V. Bhaskar and G. Andrews (eds), Tokyo: United Nations University Press, pp. 85–101.

Anand, S. and Sen, A. (1999) 'Income Components of the Human Development Index – Alternative Formulations', Occasional Papers, United Nations Development Program, Human Development Report Office, New York.

Anderson, D. and Cavendish, W. (2001) 'Dynamic Simulation and Environmental Policy Analysis: Beyond Comparative Statics and the Environmental Kuznets Curve', *Oxford Economic Papers*, 53(4): 721–46.

Andreoni, J. (1989) 'Giving with Impure Altruism: Applications to Charity and Ricardian Equivalence', *Journal of Political Economy*, 97(6): 1447–58.

Andreoni, J. (1990) 'Impure Altruism and Donations to Public Goods: A Theory of Warm-Glow Giving', *Economic Journal*, 100(401): 464–77.

Andreoni, J. and Levinson, A. (2001) 'The Simple Analytics of the Environmental Kuznets Curve', *Journal of Public Economics*, 80: 269–86.

Ansuategi, A. and Escapa, M. (2002) 'Economic Growth and Greenhouse Gas Emissions', *Ecological Economics*, 40: 23–37.

Antweiler, W., Copeland, B.R. and Taylor, M.S. (1998) *Is Free Trade Good for the Environment*, Cambridge, MA, NBER.

Arrow, K., Bolin, B., Costanza, R., Dasgupta, P., Folke, C., Holling, C., Jansson, B.-O. Levin, S., Maler, K.-G., Perrings, C. and Pimente, D. (1995) 'Economic Growth, Carrying Capacity, and the Environment', *Science*, 268: 520–21.

Arrow, K., Dasgupta, D., Goulder, L. Daily, G., Ehrlich, P., Heal, G., Levin, S., Maler, K., Schneider, S., Starrett, D. and Walker, B. (2004) 'Are We Consuming Too Much?', *The Journal of Economic Perspectives*, 18(3): 147–72.

Aznar-Márquez, J. and Ruiz-Tamarit, J.R. (2004) *Demographic Transition, Environmental Concern and the Kuznets Curve*. Universitat de València (Spain) and IRES (Belgium), July.

Barrett, S. (1994) 'Self-Enforcing International Environmental Arrangements', *Oxford Economic Papers*, 46: 878–94.

Bartelle, B. (1994) 'The High Cost of Turning Green', *The Wall Street Journal*, 14: 9, September.

Baumol, W.J. and Oates, W.E. (1988) *The Theory of Environmental Policy*, Cambridge: Cambridge University Press.

Beckerman, W. (1992) 'Economic Growth and the Environment: Whose Growth! Whose Environment?' *World Development*, 20: 481–96.

Beckerman, W. (1993) 'The Environmental Limits to Growth: A Fresh Look', in *Economic Progress and Environmental Concerns*, H. Giersch (ed.), Berlin: Springer.

Bernstam, M. (1991) 'The Wealth of Nations and the Environment', in *Resources, Environment, and Population: Present Knowledge, Future Options*, K. Davis and M.S. Bernstam (eds), New York: Oxford University Press, pp. 333–73.

Bertinelli, Luisito and Eric Strobl (2004) 'The Environmental Kuznets Curve Semi-Parametrically Revisited', CORE Discussion paper 2004/51, Université Catholique de Louvain, Belgium, July.

Bhattarai, M. and Hammig, M. (2001) 'Institutions and the Environmental Kuznets Curve for Deforestation: A Cross-Country Analysis for Latin America, Africa and Asia', *World Development*, 29(6): 995–1010.

Biermann, F. and Bauer, S. (eds) (2005) *A World Environment Organization: Solution or Threat for Effective International Environmental Governance?* Aldershot: Ashgate Publishing Limited.

Bimonte, S. (2002) 'Information Access, Income Distribution, and the Environmental Kuznets Curve', *Ecological Economics*, 41: 145–56.

Birdsall, N. and Wheeler, D. (1991) 'Openness Reduces Industrial Waste in Latin America: The Missing Pollution Haven Effect', *Symposium of International Trade and the Environment*, Washington, DC: World Bank.

Bishop, R.C. (1982) 'Option Value: An Exposition and Extension', *Land Economics*, 58: 1–15.

Blanchard, O.J. and Fischer, S. (1989) *Lectures on Macroeconomics*, Cambridge: MIT Press.

Bohn, H. and Deacon, R.T. (2000) 'Ownership Risk, Investment, and the Use of Natural Resources', *American Economic Review*, 90(3): 526–49, June.

Bond, C.A. and Farzin, Y.H. (2004) 'Freedom from Pollution? The State, the People, and the Environmental Kuznets Curve', Working Paper No. 04-003, Department of Agricultural and Resource Economics, University of California, Davis.

Borghesi, S. (1999) 'The Environmental Kuznets Curve: A Survey of the Literature', FEEM Working Paper No. 85-99, available at http://ssrn.com/abstract=200556. 9 March 2003.

Broad, R. (1994) 'The Poor and the Environment: Friends or Foe?' *World Development*, 22(4): 811–22.

Brundtland Report (1987) *Our Common Future*, World Commission on Environment and Development, Oxford: Oxford University Press.

Byrne, M.M. (1997) 'Is Growth a Dirty Word? Pollution, Abatement and Endogenous Growth', *Journal of Development Economics*, 54: 261–84.

Caball'e, J. and Santos, M.S. (1993) 'On Endogenous Growth with Physical and Human Capital', *Journal of Political Economy*, 101(6): 1042–67, December.

Carraro, C. and Siniscalco, D. (ed.) (1997) *New Directions in the Economic Theory of the Environment*, Cambridge: Cambridge University Press.

Carson, R.T., Jeon, Y. and McCubbin, D.R. (1997) 'The Relationship Between Air Pollution Emissions and Income: US Data', *Environment and Development Economics*, 2: 433–50.

Center for International Earth Science Information Network (CIESIN) (2000) Columbia University; International Food Policy Research Institute (IFPRI); and World Resources Institute (WRI), Gridded *Population of the World (GPW), Version* 2, Palisades, NY: CIESIN, Columbia University, available at http://sedac.ciesin.colum-bia.edu/plue/gpw. 2 June 2003.

Chichilinsky, G. (1994) 'North–South Trade and the Global Environment', *American Economic Review*, 84(4): 851–94, September.

Chichilinsky, G., Heal, G. and Vercelli, A. (eds) (1998) *Sustainability: Dynamics and Uncertainty*, Dordrecht: Kluwer.

Chimeli, A.B. and Braden, J.B. (2002) 'The Environmental Kuznets Curve and Optimal Growth', New York: International Research Institute for Climate Prediction, Columbia University.

Coase, R. (1960) 'The Problem of Social Cost', *Journal of Law and Economics*, 3: 1–44.

Cole, M. (2000) *Trade Liberalization Economic Growth and the Environment*, Cheltenham: Edward Elgar Publishing.

Cole, M.A., Rayner, A.J. and Bates, J.M. (1997) 'The Environmental Kuznets Curve: An Empirical Analysis', *Environment and Development Economics*, 2(4): 401–16.

Commission on Global Governance (1995) *Our Global Neighborhood: Report of the Commission on Global Governance*, New York: Oxford University Press.

Consultative Group on Sustainable Development Indicators, 'Dashboard of Sustainable Development Indicators', dataset dated 9 January 2002.

Coondoo, D. and Dinda, S. (2002) 'Causality Between Income and Emissions: A Country Group-Specific Econometric Analysis', *Ecological Economics*, 40(3): 351–67.

Dahan, M. and Tsiddom, D. (1998) 'Demographic Transition, Income Distribution and Economic Growth', *Journal of Economic Growth*, 3: 29–82.

Daly, H. (1996) 'Consumption: Value Added, Physical Transformation and Welfare', in *Getting Down to Earth: Practical Applications of Ecological Economics*, S. Costanza, O. Segura and J. Martinez-Alier (eds), Washington, DC: Island Press, pp. 49–59.

Daly, H. and Townsend, K. (1993) *Valuing the Earth: Economics, Ecology and Ethics*, Cambridge, MA: MIT Press.

Daly, H.E. (1977) *Steady State Economics: The Economics of Biophysical Equilibrium and Moral Growth*, San Francisco, CA: W.H. Freeman.

Daly, H.E. and Townsend, K.N. (1993) *Valuing the Earth: Economics, Ecology and Ethics*, Cambridge, MA: MIT Press.

Dasgupta, P. (2003) 'The Economics of the World's Poorest Regions', Beijer Institute Working Paper, Stockholm, presented at the World Bank's Annual Conference on Development Economics.

Dasgupta, P. and Heal, G. (1979) *Economic Theory and Exhaustible Resources*, Cambridge: Cambridge University Press.

Dasgupta, P. and Mäler, K.-G. (1995) 'Poverty, Institutions, and the Environmental Resource Base', in *Handbook of Development Economics*, Vol. 3A, J. Behrman and T.N. Srinivaan (eds), Amsterdam: Elsevier Science, Chapter 39.

Dasgupta, S., Laplante, B., Wang, H. and Wheeler, D. (2002) 'Confronting the Environmental Kuznets Curve', *Journal of Economic Perspectives* 16(1): 147–68, Winter.

Day, K.M. and Grafton, R.Q. (2003) 'Growth and the Environment in Canada: An Empirical Analysis', *Canadian Journal of Agricultural Economics*, 51: 197–216.

Dean, J.M. (1996) 'Testing the Impact of Trade Liberalisation of the Environment', Johns Hopkins University, Washington, DC, mimeo.

de Bruyn, S. M. (1997a) 'Economic Growth and Emissions: Reconsidering the Empirical Basis of Environmental Kuznets Curve', *Ecological Economics*, 25(1): 161–75.

de Bruyn, S.M. (1997b) 'Explaining the Environmental Kuznets Curve: Structural Change and International Agreements in Reducing Sulphur Emissions', *Environment and Development Economics*, 2(4): 485–504.

de Bruyn, S.M. (2000) *Economic Growth and the Environment: An Empirical Analysis*, Dordrecht: Kluwer Academic Press.

de Bruyn, S. and Opschoor, J. (1997) 'Developments in the Throughput-Income Relationship: Theoretical and Empirical Observations', *Ecological Economics*, 20(3): 255–68.

de Bruyn, S.M., van den Bergh, J. and Opschoor, J.B. (1998) 'Economic Growth and Emissions: Reconsidering the Empirical Basis of Environmental Kuznets Curve', *Ecological Economics*, 25: 161–75.

de Groot, Henri, L.F. (1999) Structural Change, Economic Growth and the Environmental Kuznets Curve. A Theoretical Perspective', OCFEB Research Memorandum 9911, Erasmus University, Rotterdam.

Deardorff, A.V. and Stern, R.M. (1998) *Measures of Nontariff Barriers*, Ann Arbor, MI: The University of Michigan Press.

Denison, E.F. (1985) 'Trends in American Economic Growth, 1929–1982', Washington, DC: The Brookings Institution.

Dietz, T. and Rosa, E.A. (1994) 'Rethinking the Environmental Impacts of Population, Affluence and Technology', *Human Ecological Review*, 1: 277–300.

Dijkgraaf, E. and Vollebergh, H.R.J. (2001) A Note on Testing for Environmental Kuznets Curves. Research Center for Economic Policy (OCFEB) and Department of Economics and Research Center for Economic Policy (OCFEB) Erasmus University, Rotterdam, May.

Dinwiddy, C. and Teal, F. (1996) *Principles of Cost Benefit Analysis for Developing Countries*, New York: Cambridge University Press.

Divan, I. and Shafik, N. (1992) 'Investment Technology and the Global Environment: Towards International Agreement in a World of Disparities', in *International Trade and the Environment*, P. Low (ed.), Washington, DC: The World Bank, pp. 263–87.

Duchin, F. (1998) *Structural Economics: Measuring Changes in Technology, Lifestyles and the Environment*, Washington, DC: Island Press.

Dunteman, G. (1994) 'Principal Component Analysis (PCA)', in *Factor Analysis and Related Techniques*, M. Lewis-Beck (ed.), New Delhi: Sage Toppan.

Egli, H. and Steger, T.M. (2004) *A Simple Dynamic Model of the Environmental Kuznets Curve*, ETH Zurich, May.

Ehrlich, P.R. and Holdren, J. (1971) 'Impact of Population Growth', *Science*, 171: 1212–17.

Ekins, P. (1997) 'The Kuznets Curve for the Environment and Economic Growth: Examining the Evidence', in *Environment and Planning* A, 29, 805–30.

Ekins, P. and Jacob, M. (1995) 'Environmental Sustainability and the Growth of GDP: Conditions for Compatibility', in *The North, the South and the Environment: Ecological Constraints and the Global Economy*, V. Bhaskar and G. Andrew (eds), Tokyo: United Nations University Press, pp. 9–46.

Eriksson, C. and Persson, J. (2002) *Economic Growth, Inequality, Democratization, and the Environment*, Swedish University of Agricultural Sciences, Department of Economics.

ESI (Environmental Sustainability Index) (2002) *The 2002 Environmental Sustainability Index*, World Economic Forum, Switzerland: Davos.

Esty, Daniel C. and Maria H. Ivanova (2002) 'The Road Ahead: Conclusions and Action Agenda', in *Global Environmental Governance: Options and Opportunities*, D. Esty and M. Ivanova (eds) New Haven: Yale University.

FAOSTAT (2002) 'Statistical Database of the UN Food and Agricultural Organization', available at http://apps.fao.org/. 10 October 2003.

Forster, B.A. (1973a) 'Optimal Capital Accumulation in a Polluted Environment', *Southern Economic Journal*, 39(4): 544–47, April.

Forster, B.A. (1973b) 'Optimal Consumption Planning in a Polluted Environment', *The Economic Record*, 49(128): 534–45, December.

Friedl, B. and Getzner, M. (2003) 'Determinants of CO_2 Emissions in a Small Open Economy', *Ecological Economics*, 45: 133–48.

Gangadharan, L. and Valenzuela, M.R. (2001) 'Interrelationships Between Health, Income and the Environment: Extending the Environmental Kuznets Curve Hypothesis', *Ecological Economics*, 36(3): 513–31.

GATT (General Agreement on Tariffs and Trade) (1992) 'Trade and Environment', *International Trade*, Geneva: GATT.

GATT (1994) *Basic Instruments and Selected Documents*, Geneva: GATT.

GEM PAG (2002) *In Search of Global Fairness: The Promise of a Revitalized Global Environmental Governance System*. Global Environmental Mechanism Policy Action Group (GEM PAG) of the Yale Center for Environmental Law and Policy, Globus Institute for Globalization and Sustainable Development and the Commission on Globalization. New Haven, CT.

Georgescu-Roegen, N. (1971) *The Entropy Law and The Economic Process*, Cambridge, MA: Harvard University Press.

Gjertsen, H. and Barrett, C. (2001) 'Context-Dependant Bio-diversity Conservation Management Regimes', Working Paper Series, Social Science Research Network Library.

Grossman, G.M. (1995) 'Pollution and Growth: What do we know?', in *The Economics of Sustainable Development*, I. Goldin, and L.A.Winters (eds), New York: Cambridge University Press, pp. 19–46.

Grossman, G.M. and Krueger, A.B. (1991 and 1993) 'Environmental Impacts of a North American Free Trade Agreement', NBER Working Paper No. 3914, also in *The US–Mexico Free Trade Agreement*, P. Garber (ed.), Cambridge, MA: MIT Press, pp. 165–77.

Grossman, G.M. and Krueger, A.B. (1994 and 1995) 'Economic Growth and the Environment', NBER Working Paper No. 4634, February; also in *Quarterly Journal of Economics*, 110: 353–77.

Haerdle, W. (1990) *Applied Nonparametric Regression*, Cambridge: Cambridge University Press.

Hall, C.A.S., Cleveland, C.J. and Kauffman, R. (1986) *Energy and Resource Quality: The Ecology of the Economic Process*, New York: John Wiley.

Hamilton, C. and Turton, H. (2002) 'Determinants of Emissions Growth in OECD Countries', *Energy Policy*, 30: 63–71.

Hamilton, K. (1995) 'Sustainable Development, the Hartwick Rule and Optimal Growth', *Environmental and Resource Economics*, 5: 393–411.

Harbaugh, W., Levinson, A. and Wilson, D. (2000) 'Reexamining the Empirical Evidence of the Environmental Kuznets Curve', NBER Working Paper No. 7711, Cambridge, MA: National Bureau of Economic Research, May.

Hawken, P. (1995) *Natural Capitalism: The Next Industrial Revolution*, National Round Table on the Environment and the Economy, Ottawa.

Heerink, N., Mulatu, A. and Bulte, E. (2001) 'Income Inequality and the Environment: Aggregation Bias in Environmental Kuznets Curves', *Ecological Economics* 38(3): 359–67.

Heggestad, A., Rhoades, A. and Stephen, A. (1976) 'Concentration and Firm Stability in Commercial Banking', *Review of Economics and Statistics*, 58(4): 443–52.

Heil, M.T. and Selden, T.M. (1999) 'Panel Stationarity with Structural Breaks: Carbon Emissions and GDP', *Applied Economics Letters*, 6: 223–25.

Heil, M.T. and Selden, T.M. (2001) 'Carbon Emissions and Economic Development: Future Trajectories Based on Historical Experience', *Environment and Development Economics*, 6: 63–83.

Henderson, N. (1993) 'Heritage Landscapes: A New Approach to the Preservation of Semi-natural Landscapes in Canada and the United States', in *Sustainable Environmental Economics and Management, Principles and Practice*, R.K. Turner (ed.), London: Belhaven.

Hettige, H., Lucas, R. and Wheeler, D. (1992) 'The Toxic Intensity of Industrial Pollution: Global Patterns, Trends and Trade Policy', *American Economic Review*, 82(2): 478–81.

Hettige, H., Mani, M. and Wheeler, D. (1998 and 2000) 'Industrial Pollution in Economic Development: The Environmental Kuznets Curve Revisited', Washington, DC: The World Bank, also in *Journal of Development Economics*, 62: 445–76.

Hilton, F., Hank, G. and Levinson, A. (1998) 'Factoring the Environmental Kuznets Curve: Evidence from Automotive Lead Emissions', *Journal of Environmental Economics and Management*, 35: 126–41.

Holtz-Eakin, D. and Selden, T.M. (1992 and 1995) 'Stoking the Fires? CO_2 Emissions and Economic Growth', Cambridge, MA: National Bureau of Economic Research. Also NBER Working Paper No. 4248 and *Journal of Public Economics*, 57: 85–101.

Hoti, S., MacAlee, M. and Pauwels, L.L. (2004) *Modeling Environmental Risk*. HEI, Working Paper 08/2004, Graduate Institute of International Studies, Geneva.

ICC (International Chamber of Commerce) (1990) *Business Charter for Sustainable Development*', Mimeo, London, UK.

IEA (International Energy Agency) (1997) *Energy Statistics of OECD Countries and Energy Statistics and Balances of Non-OECD Countries*, Paris: OECD.

Janicke, M. (1989) 'Economic Structure of Environmental Impacts: East–West Comparisons', *The Environmentalist*, 19(1): 171–82.

Jänicke, M. and Weidner, H. (eds) (1997) *National Environmental Policies: A Comparative Study of Capacity Building*, New York: Springer-Verlag.

Jha, R. (1998) *Modern Public Economics*, London and New York: Routledge.

Jha, R. and Murthy, K.V.B. (2000) 'Sustainability – Property Rights, Behaviour and Economic Growth', *World Congress on Managing and Measuring Sustainability*, Ontario, August (reprinted as Chapter 5 of this volume).

Jha, R. and Murthy, K.V.B. (2003a) 'An Inverse Global Environmental Kuznets Curve', *Journal of Comparative Economics*, 31: 352–68. (Reprinted as Chapter 6 of this volume)

Jha, R. and Murthy, K.V.B. (2003b) 'Some Notes on the Non-Global Role of the WEO', *in Trade and Environment – Recent Controversies*, H. Singer, N. Hatti and R. Tandon (eds), Delhi: Vedam Books.

Jha, R. and Schatan, C. (2001) 'Debt for Nature: A Swap Whose Time has Gone?', United Nations: ECLAC, *Estudios Y Perspectivas* 4, Mexico City.

Jha, R. and Thapa, P. (2003) 'Infrastructure and Electricity Sector Reforms in India', in *Indian Economic Reforms*, R. Jha (ed.), London: Palgrave-Macmillan, pp. 334–54.

Jha, R. and Whalley, J. (1999 and 2001) 'The Environmental Regime in Developing Countries', in *Behavioral and Distributional Effects of Environmental Policy*, C. Carraro and G.E. Metcalf (eds), Chicago, IL and London, UK: University of Chicago Press for NBER, pp. 217–50.

Jha, R., Panda, M.K. and Ranade, A. (1999 and 2002) 'An Asian Perspective on a World Environmental Organization', Discussion Paper No. 1, MacArthur Project on a World Economic Organization, IGIDR, Bombay, and *The World Economy*, 25(5): 643–57.

Johansson, P.-O. (1993) *Cost Benefit Analysis of Environmental Change*, New York: Cambridge University Press.

John, A. and Pecchenino, R. (1994) 'An Overlapping Generations Model of Growth and the Environment', *The Economic Journal*, 104: 1393–410, November.

Jolliffe, T. (1986) *Principal Component Analysis*, New York: Springer-Verlag.

Jones, L.E. and Manuelli, R.E. (2001) 'Endogenous Policy Choice: The Case of Pollution and Growth', *Review of Economic Dynamics*, 4: 369–405.

Jorgenson, D.W. and Wilcoxen, P.J. (1990) 'Environmental Regulation and U.S. Economic Growth', *The RAND Journal of Economics*, 21(2): 314–40, Summer.

Kaiser, H. (1958) 'Varimax Criterion for Analytical Rotation in Factor Analysis', *Psychometrika*, 22: 187–200.

Kanie, N. and Haas, P. (eds) (2004) *Emerging Forces in Environmental Governance*, Tokyo, New York, Paris: United Nations University Press.

Kelly, D.L. (2003) 'On Environmental Kuznets Curves Arising from Stock Externalities', *Journal of Economic Dynamics and Control*, 27: 1367–90.

Khanna, N. and Plassmann, F. (2004) 'The Demand for Environmental Quality and the Environmental Kuznets Curve Hypothesis', *Ecological Economics*, 51(2): 225–26.

Khanna, M. and Zilberman, D. (1999) 'Freer Markets and the Abatement of Carbon Emissions: The Electricity-Generating Sector in India', *Resources and Energy Economics*, 21(2): 125–52, May.

Kolstad, A. and Krautkraemer, V. (1993) 'Natural Resource Use and the Environment', in *Handbook of Natural Resource and Energy Economics*, A.V. Kneese and J.L. Sweeny (eds), Amsterdam: Elsevier.

Kopp, R.J. (1991) 'The Proper Role of Existence Value in Public Decision Making', Discussion Paper: QE91–17, Quality of the Environment Division, Resource for the Future, Washington, DC.

Krajick, K. (2001) 'Long-Term Data Show Lingering Effects of Acid Rain', *Science*, 292(5515): 195–96, April.

Kremer, M. (1993) 'Population Growth and Technological Change: One million B.C. to 1990', *Quarterly Journal of Economics*, 108(3): 681–716.

Kuznets, S. (1955) 'Economic Growth and Income Inequality', *American Economic Review*, 49: 1–28.

Lewis, W.A. (1955) *The Theory of Economic Growth*, London: George Allen & Unwin.

Lewis-Beck, M. (ed.) (1994) *Factor Analysis and Related Techniques*, London, UK: Sage Publications and New Delhi: Sage Toppan.

Likens, G.E., Driscoll, C.T. and Buso, D.C. (1996) 'Long-Term Effects of Acid Rain: Response and Recovery of a Forest Ecosystem', *Science*, 272(5259): 244–46.

López, R. (1994). 'The Environment as a Factor of Production: The Effects of Economic Growth and Trade Liberalization', *Journal of Environmental Economics and Management*, 27(1): 163–84, September.

Lopez, R. and Mitra, S. (2000) 'Corruption, Pollution, and the Kuznets Environmental Curve', *Journal of Environmental Economics and Management*, 40: 137–50.

Lucas, R.E. (1988) 'On the Mechanics of Economic Development', *Journal of Monetary Economics*, 22(1): 3–42, July.

McAbe, G. (1984) 'Principal Variables', *Technometrics*, 26(1): 137–44.

McConnell, K.E. (1997) 'Income and the Demand for Environmental Quality', *Environment and Development Economics*, 2: 383–99.

McMichael, A. (2001) *Human Frontiers, Environments and Disease: Past Patterns, Uncertain Futures*, Cambridge: Cambridge University Press.

McNeill, J. (2000) '*Something New Under the Sun: An Environmental History of the Twentieth Century World*, New York: W.W. Norton.

Magnani, E. (2000) 'The Environmental Kuznets Curve, Environmental Protection Policy and Income Distribution', *Ecological Economics*, 32(3): 431–43.

Maler, K.-G. (1991) 'National Accounts and Environmental Resources', *Environmental and Resource Economics*, 1: 1–15.

Marquez, J. and Tamarit, J. (2004) 'Non-catastrophic Endogenous Growth with Pollution and Abatement', Economic Working papers at Centro de Estudios Andaluces', E2004/80, Centro de Estudios Andaluces.

Metcalf, G.E. (ed.) (2001) *Behavioral and Distributional Effects of Environmental Policy*, Chicago, IL: University of Chicago Press, pp. 217–50.

Michaels, R. (1988) 'Addiction, Compulsion, and the Technology of Consumption', *Economic Inquiry*, 26(1): 75–88.

Millimet, D.L., List, J.A. and Stengos, T. (2003) 'The Environmental Kuznets Curve: Real Progress or Misspecified Models?' *Review of Economics and Statistics*, 85(4): 1038–47.

Mincer, J. (1995) 'Economic Development, Growth of Human Capital and the Dynamics of the Wage Structure', *Journal of Economic Growth*, 1: 29–48.

Moomaw, W. and Unru, G. (1997) 'Are Environmental Kuznets Curves Misleading Us? The Case of CO_2 Emissions', *Environment and Development Economics*, 2(3): 451–70, October.

Munasinghe, M. (1999) 'Is Environmental Degradation an Inevitable Consequence of Economic Growth: Tunneling Through the Environmental Kuznets Curve', *Ecological Economics*, 29: 89–109.

Murray, C. and Lopez, A. (1996) *The Global Burden of Disease*, Cambridge, MA: Harvard University Press.

Myers, N. (1997) 'Consumption: Challenge to Sustainable Development or Distraction', *Science*: 276: 53–57.

Newell, P. and Levy, D. (eds) (2005) *The Business of Global Environmental Governance*, Cambridge, MA: MIT Press.

Newell, P. and Whalley, J. (1998) 'A World Environmental Organization? An Initial Outline', Mimeo, University of Warwick.

Norman, D.A. (1998) *The Invisible Computer: Why Good Products Can Fail, The Personal Computer is So Complex, and Information Appliances are the Solution*, Cambridge, MA: MIT Press.

OECD (1995) 'Pattern and Pervasiveness of Tariff and Nontariff Barriers to Trade in OECD Member Countries', ECO/CPE/WPI/GE(96)3.

OECD-EC Joint Research Centre, available at farmweb.jrc.cec.eu.int/ci/CI_Env0001. htm (10k). 1 May 2002.

Ono, T. and Maeda, Y. (2001) 'Is Aging Harmful to the Environment?' *Environmental and Resource Economics*, 20(2): 113–27.

Panayotou, T. (1997) 'Demystifying the Environmental Kuznets Curve: Turning a black box into a policy tool', *Environment and Development Economics*, 2: 465–84.

Panayotou, T. (2000) 'Economic Growth and the Environment', CID Working Paper No. 56, Harvard University.

Parikh, K.S., Panda, M. and Murthy, N.S. (1995) 'Modelling Framework for Sustainable Development: Integrating Environmental Considerations in Development Strategies', Indira Gandhi Institute of Development Research, Mumbai, India.

Payne, M. (1999) 'Latin America Aims High for the Next Century', *Pulp and Paper International*, 41(8), available at http://www.paperloop.com/db_area/archive/ppi_mag/1999/9908/ppi4.htm. 10 August 2001.

Pearce, D. (1993) *Blueprint Three: Measuring Sustainable Development*, London: Earthscan.

Pearce, D.W. and Warford, J.J. (1993) *World Without End: Economics, Environment and Sustainable Development*, New York: Oxford University Press.

Pearce, D.W., Barbier, E.B. and Markandya, A. (1990) *Sustainable Development: Economics and the Environment in the Third World*, Aldershot: Edward Elgar.

Perman, R. and Stern, D.I. (2003) 'Evidence from Panel Unit Root and Cointegration Tests that the Environmental Kuznets Curve Does not Exist', *Australian Journal of Agricultural and Resource Economics*, 47(3): 325–47, September.

Pezzey, J. (1989) 'Economic Analysis of Sustainable Growth and Sustainable Development', Environment Department Working Paper No. 15, World Bank, Washington, DC.

Pfaff, A.S.P., Chaudhuri, S. and Nye, H.L.M. (2001a) 'Endowments, Preferences, Abatement and Voting: Micro-foundations of Environmental Kuznets Curves', Mimeo, Columbia University.

Pfaff, A.S.P., Chaudhuri, S. and Nye, H.L.M. (2001b) 'Why Might One Expect Environmental Kuznets Curves? Examining the Desirability and Feasibility of Substitution', Mimeo, Columbia University.

Plassmann, F. and Khanna, N. (2003) 'Preferences, Income and the Environment: Understanding the Environmental Kuznets Curve Hypothesis', Department of Economics Working Paper WP0313, Binghamton University.

Ploeg, F. van der and Withagen, C. (1991) 'Pollution Control and the Ramsey Problem', *Environmental and Resource Economics*, 1: 215–36.

Porter, G. (1996) 'Natural Resources, Trade and Environment: The Case of Forests and Fisheries', Centre for International Law, Yale University, available at http://www.ciel.org/Publications/NaturalResourceSubsidies.pdf. 5 June 2001.

Portney, P.E. (ed.) (1990) *Public Policies for Environmental Protection*, Washington, DC: Resources for the Future.

Postel, S., Daily, G. and Ehrlich, P. (1996) 'Human Appropriation of Renewable Fresh Water', *Science*, 271: 785–88, 9, February.

Prasad, P. (2004) 'Environmental Protection: The Role of Liability System in India', *Economic and Political Weekly*, 39(3): 257–69.

Princen, T. (1999) 'Consumption and Environment: Some Conceptual Issues', *Ecological Economics*, 31(3): 347–63.

Quiggin, J. (1989) 'Do Existence Values Exist?' Department of Agriculture and Resource Economics, College Park, MD: University of Maryland.

Radetzki, M. (1992) 'Economic Growth and the Environment', in *International Trade and Environment*, P. Low (ed.), Washington, DC: The World Bank, pp. 121–36.

Raskin, P.D. (1995) 'Methods for Estimating the Population Contribution to Environmental Change', *Ecological Economics*, 15: 225–33.

Rebelo, S. (1991) 'Long-Run Policy Analysis and Long-Run Growth', *Journal of Political Economy*, 99(3): 500–21, June.

Rees, W.E. (1990) 'The Ecology of Sustainable Development', *The Ecologist*, 20(1): 18–23.

Rees, W.E. (1995) 'Reducing the Ecological Footprint of Consumption', the workshop on policy measures for changing consumption patterns, Seoul.

Reisch, L. and Ropke, I. (eds) (2004) *The Ecological Economics of Consumption*, Cheltenham: Edward Elgar Publishing.

Reppelin-Hill, V. (1999) 'Trade and the Environment: An Empirical Analysis of the Technology Effect in the Steel Industry', *Journal of Environmental Economics and Management*, 38(3): 283–301, November.

Rivera-Batiz, F.L. (2002) Democracy, Governance, and Economic Growth: Theory and Evidence, *Review of Development Economics*, 6(2): 225–47.

Roberts, J.T. and Grimes, P.E. (1997) 'Carbon Intensity and Economic Development 1962–91: A Brief Exploration of the Environmental Kuznets Curve', World Development, 25(2): 191–98.

Rosenthal, D.H. and Nelson, R.H. (1991) 'Why Existence Value Should Not be Used in Benefit–Cost Analysis?' *Journal of Policy Analysis and Management*, 11: 116–22.

Rothman, D. (1998) 'Environmental Kuznets Curve: Real Progress or Passing the Buck? A Case for Consumption Based Approaches', *Ecological Economics*, 25(1): 177–94.

Ruttan, V. (1994) 'Constraints on the Design of Sustainable Systems of Agriculture', *Ecological Economics*, 10: 209–19.

Sagar, A.D. and Najam, A. (1998) 'The Human Development Index: A Critical Review', *Ecological Economics*, 25: 249–64.

Schmalensee, R.S., Thomas, M. and Judson, R.A. (1998) 'World Carbon Dioxide Emissions: 1950–2050', *The Review of Economics and Statistics*, 80(1): 15–27, February.

Schrope, M. (2000) 'Success in Fight to Save Ozone Layer Could Close Holes by 2050', *Nature*, 408(6813): 627, December.

Scruggs, L.A. (1998) 'Political and Economic Inequality and the Environment', *Ecological Economics*, 26: 259–75.

Seibert, H. (1998) *Economics of the Environment*, Berlin: Springer-Verlag.

Selden, T.M. and Song, D. (1994) 'Environmental Quality and Development: Is There a Kuznets Curve for Air Pollution Emissions?' *Journal of Environmental Economics and Management*, 27(2): 147–62, September.

Seldon, T. and Song, D. (1995), 'Neoclassical Growth, the J Curve for Abatement, and the Inverted U Curve for Pollution', *Journal of Enviornmental Economics and Management*, 29, 162–168.

Sen, A.K. (1967) 'Isolation Assurance and the Social Rate of Discount', *Quarterly Journal of Economics*, 81: 112–24.

Shafik, N. (1994) 'Economic Development and Environmental Quality: An Econometric Analysis', *Oxford Economic Papers*, 46(3): 757–73.

Shafik, N. and Bandyopadhyay, S. (1992) 'Economic Growth and Environmental Quality: Time Series and Cross-Country Evidence', Background Paper for the *World Development Report, 1992*, Washington, DC: Oxford University Press.

Smith, K., Corvalán, C. and Kjellström, T. (1999) 'How Much Global Ill Health is Attributable to Environmental Factors?' *Journal of Epidemiology*, 10(5): 573–84.

Solow, R. (1974) 'Intergenerational Equity and Exhaustible Resources', *Review of Economic Studies*, Symposium on the Economics of Exhaustible Resources, pp. 29–45.

Spagnolo, G. (1996) 'Issue Linkage, Delegation and International Policy Cooperation', Discussion Paper No. 49.96, Stockholm School of Economics, Stockholm.

Stagl, S. (1999) 'De-linking Economic Growth from Environmental Degradation: A Literature Survey on the Environmental Kuznets Curve Hypothesis', Working paper series of the research focus, 'Growth and Employment in Europe: Sustainability and Competitiveness'. Working Paper No. 6, Vienna: University of Vienna, May.

Stagl, S. (2003) 'Multi-Criteria Evaluation and Public Participation: In Search of Theoretical Foundations', Frontiers 2 Conference, European Ecological Economics Society, Spain.

Stavins, R.N. and Pfaff, A.S.P. (1999) 'Readings in the Field of Natural Resource & Environmental Economics', KSG Working Paper, available at http://ssrn.com/abstract=168969. 3 September 2000.

Stern, D.I. (2003) The Rise and fall of the Environmental Kuznets Curve Rensselaer Polytechnic Institute, Number 0302, October.

Stern, D. and Chapman, D. (1998) 'Is There an Environmental Kuznets Curve for Sulfur? An Analysis of Bias in Environmental Kuznets Curve Estimation'. World Congress on Environmental Economics, Venezia, p. 27, May, unpublished manuscript.

Stern, D.I. and Common, M.S. (2001) 'Is there an Environmental Kuznets Curve for Sulfur?' *Journal of Environmental Economics and Management*, 41(2): 162–78.

Stern, D.I., Common, M.S. and Barbier, E.B. (1994) 'Economic Growth and Environmental Degradation: A Critique of the Environmental Kuznets Curve', Discussion Paper in Environmental Economics and Environmental Management, No. 9409, University of York.

Stern, D., Common, M. and Barbier, E. (1996) 'Economic Growth and Environmental Degradation: The Environmental Kuznets Curve and Sustainable Development', *World Development*, 24(7): 1151–60, July.

Stokey, N.L. (1998) 'Are There Limits to Growth?', *International Economic Review*, 39: 1–31.

Strand, J. (2002) 'Environmental Kuznets Curves: Empirical Relationships Between Environmental Quality and Economic Development', Department of Economics, University of Oslo, March.

Stuijvenberg, P. (1996) 'Structural Adjustment in India – What About Poverty Alleviation?' in *Economic Reforms and Poverty Alleviation in India*, C. Rao and H. Linnemann (eds), New Delhi, Thousand Oaks, CA and London: Sage Publications, pp. 31–89.

Suri, V. and Chapman, D. (1998) 'Economic Growth Trade and Energy: Implications for the Environmental Kuznets Curve', *Ecological Economics*, 25: 147–60.

Tabata, K. (2003) 'Inverted U-shaped Fertility Dynamics, The Poverty Trap and Growth', *Economics Letters*, 81: 241–48.

Tahvonen, O. (1991) 'On the Dynamics of Renewable Resource Harvesting and Pollution Control', *Environment and Resource Economics*, 1: 97–117.

Tahvonen, O. and Kuuluvainen, J. (1993) 'Economic Growth, Pollution and Renewable Resources', *Journal of Environmental Economics and Management*, 24: 101–18.

Torras, M. and Boyce, J.K. (1998) 'Income, Inequality, and Pollution: A Reassessment of the Environmental Kuznets Curve', *Ecological Economics*, 25(2): 147–60.

UNCTAD (1994): *Trade and Development Report.*

UNDP (United Nations Development Program) (1998) *Human Development Report 1998*, Oxford and New York: Oxford University Press.

UNDP (1999 and 2000) *Human Development Report*, New York: Oxford University Press for UNDP.

UNEP (United Nations Environment Program) (2001) *Improving International Environmental Governance Among Multilateral Environmental Agreements: Negotiable Terms*, Nairobi, Kenya.

UNEP (2003) *Global Environmental Outlook*, New York.

UNEP (2004) *Understanding Environment, Conflict and Cooperation*, Nairobi, Kenya.

United Nations, Economic and Social Council (2001) 'Implementing Agenda 21: Report of the Secretary General', E/CN.17/2002/PC.2/7, 20, December.

Uzawa, H. (1965) 'Optimal Technical Change in an Aggregative Model of Economic Growth', *International Economic Review*, 6(1): 18–31, January.

van den Bergh, J., Ferrer-i-Carbonell, A. and Munda, G. (1998 and 2000) 'Models of Individual Behaviour and the Implications for Environmental Policy', *World Congress of Environmental and Resource Economics*, Venice, Italy: Fondazione Eni Enrico Mattei Note di Lavoro, 77/98, p. 28, November and *Ecological Economics*, 32(1): 43–61.

van den Hove, S. (2000) 'Participatory Approaches to Environmental Policy-Making: The European Commission Climate Policy Process as a Case Study', *Ecological Economics*, 33: 457–72.

Vincent, J. (1997) 'Resource Depletion and Economic Sustainability in Malaysia', *Environment and Development Economics*, 2(1): 19–38.

Vincent, J., Panayotou, T. and Hartwick, J. (1997) 'Resource Depletion and Sustainability in Small Open Economies', *Journal of Environmental Economics and Management*, 33(3): 274–86, July.

Vitousek, P., Ehrlch, P., Ehrlich, A. and Matson, P. (1986) 'Human Appropriation of the Product of Photosynthesis', *Bioscience*, 36: 368–73.

Vitousek, P., Mooney, H., Lubchenco, J. and Melillo, J. (1997) 'Human Domination of Earth's Ecosystem', *Science*, 277: 494–99, July.

Wackernagel, M. (2000) 'The Footprints of Nations Study', available at http://www.prorgress.org/resources/nip/ef/ef_nations.html

Weisbrod, B.A. (1964) 'Collective Consumption of Services of Individual Consumption Goods', *Quarterly Journal of Economics*, 78: 471–77.

Whalley, J. and Zissimos, B. (2002a) 'An Internalisation Based World Environmental Organization?', *The World Economy*, 25(5): 619–42.

Whalley, J. and Zissimos, B. (2002b) 'Making Environmental Deals: The Economic Case for a World Environmental Organization' in D. Esty and M. Ivanova (ed.) *Global Environmental Governance: Options and Opportunities*, New Haven, CT: Yale University.

WHO (1997) *Health and the Environment: Five Years After the Earth Summit*, Geneva: World Health Organization.

WHO (2002) 'Environmental hazard Kill At Least 3 Million Children Aged Under 5 Every Year, available at http://www.who.int/inf/en/pr-2002-12.html. 1 July 2004.

World Bank (1992) *World Development Report: Development and the Environment*, Oxford: Oxford University Press.

World Bank (2003) *World Development Indicators*, World Bank, Washington, DC.

World Commission on Environment and Development (Brundtland Report) (1987) *Our Common Future*, New York: Oxford University Press.

World Economic Forum (WEF) (2002) *The 2002 Environmental Sustainability Index*, Switzerland: Davos.

World Economic Forum (2005) 'Appendix H – Critiques and Responses', *2005 Environmental Sustainability Index – Benchmarking National Environmental Stewardship*.

World Resources (2002–2004) *Decisions for the Earth: Balance, Voice, and Power*, United Nations Environment Programme, World Bank, World Resources Institute.

WRI (2004) *World Resources*, 2002–2004, Washington.

WTO (1999) *High Level Symposium on Trade and Environment, Background Document*, Trade and Environment Division, WTO.

Xepapadeas, A. (1996) *Economic Policy for the Environment and Natural Resources*, Brookfield, WI: Edward Elgar.

Xepapadeas, A. (2004) 'Economic Growth and the Environment', University of Crete; prepared for the *Handbook of Environmental Economics*, K.-G. Maler and J. Vincent (eds), Amsterdam: Elsevier Publishers.

Xepapadeas, A. and Yiannaka, A. (1997) 'Measuring Benefits and Damages from Carbon Dioxide Emissions and International Agreements to Slow Down Greenhouse Warming', in *International Environmental Negotiations: Strategic Policy Issues*, C. Carraro (ed.), Cheltenham: Edward Elgar Publishing.

Yandle, B., Bhattarai, M. and Vijayaraghavan, M. (2004) *The Environmental Kuznets Curve, A Primer*, PERC, available at http://www.perc.org/publications/research/kuznets2.php#authors. 3 February 2005.

Zhang, Z.X. (1998) 'Macroeconomic Effects of CO_2 Emission Limits: A Computable General Equilibrium Analysis for China', *Journal of Policy Modeling*, 20(2): 213–50.

Index